Fashioning the Eighteenth Century

Sharon Diane Nell, *Series Editor*

Fashioning the Eighteenth Century embraces works focusing on the
century's social history, material culture, and literature, toward
the end of illuminating the cultural fabric itself.

ALSO IN THE SERIES

Napoleon and the Woman Question, by June K. Burton

Louder than Words

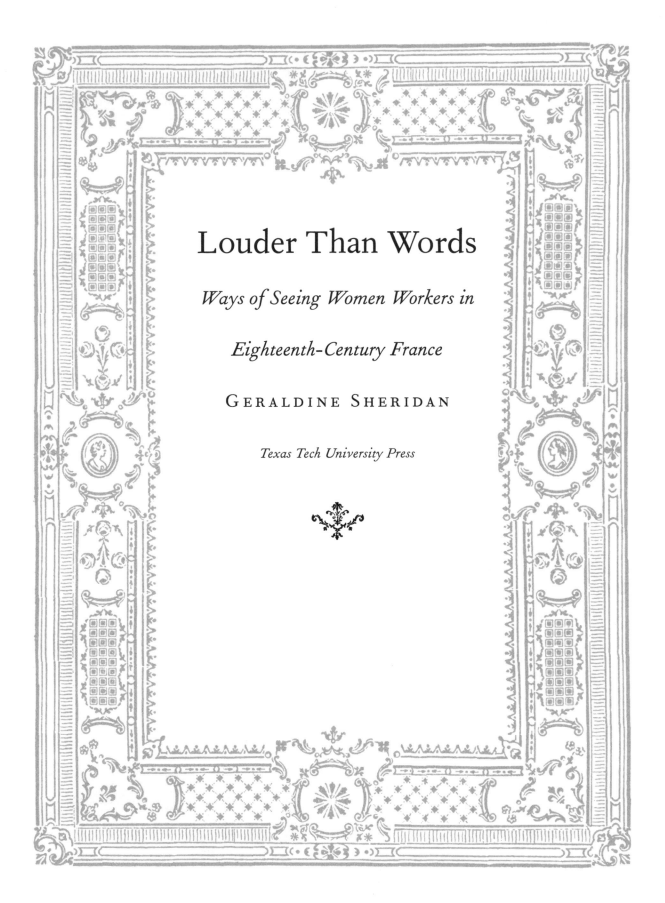

Louder Than Words

Ways of Seeing Women Workers in

Eighteenth-Century France

Geraldine Sheridan

Texas Tech University Press

This book is typeset in Monotype Fournier. The paper used in this book meets the
minimum requirements of ANSI/NISO Z39.48-1992 (R1997). ∞

Designed by Barbara Werden

LIBRARY OF CONGRESS CATALOGING-IN-PUBLICATION DATA

Sheridan, Geraldine.
Louder than words : ways of seeing women workers in eighteenth-century
France / Geraldine Sheridan.
p.   cm.—(Fashioning the eighteenth century)
Includes bibliographical references and index.
Summary: "Because eighteenth-century French trade law and corporate archives
rarely mention women workers, Sheridan analyzes nearly two hundred period
engravings to interpret women's roles in pre-industrial France. Images primarily
from Diderot's Encyclopédie and Panckouke's 1777 supplementary volume
document women as workers, finishers, and managers in manufacturing,
commerce, and the crafts"—Provided by publisher.
ISBN-13: 978-0-89672-622-2 (hardcover : alk. paper)
ISBN-10: 0-89672-622-3 (hardcover : alk. paper)   1. Women—
Employment—France—History—18th century. 2. Working class women—
France—History—18th century. I. Title.
HD6145.S44 2008
331.40944'09033—dc22
2008011041

Printed in the United States of America

09   10   11   12   13   14   15   16   17 / 9   8   7   6   5   4   3   2   1

Texas Tech University Press : Box 41037 : Lubbock, Texas 79409-1037 USA
800.832.4042 : ttup@ttu.edu : www.ttup.ttu.edu

For Jim Pidgeon,
with love and thanks

Contents

Acknowledgments xi
List of Plates xiii

Introduction   3

1 :: The Traditional Economy   21

Agriculture   29
Mining   35
Fishing   42

2 :: Artisanal Trades   75

Ornamental and Luxury Products   83
Essential Goods   124

3 :: Textiles   141

4 :: Manufactories   183

5 :: Commercial Activity   203

Conclusion   217

Notes   231
Manuscript Sources   237
Works Cited   239
Index   247

Acknowledgments

I WOULD LIKE TO THANK a number of people who have assisted and supported me in the completion of this book. I began the research while I was a Fulbright Fellow at Boston College, and I would like to thank my hosts in the Department of Romance Languages for their interest and encouragement, especially Professor Ourida Mostefai. The Department of Languages and Cultural Studies, the College of Humanities, and the Dean of Research of the University of Limerick have supported the research financially, and my colleagues have advised and encouraged me in many other ways. The task of locating and arranging for the copying of the images was greatly facilitated by the very helpful staff of several libraries and archival collections, particularly the Archives de l'Académie des Sciences; the Bibliothèque de l'Institut de France; the Houghton Library, Harvard University; and the Old Library of Trinity College Dublin. I would also like to thank Eoin Stephenson of the Department of Audiovisual Services at the University of Limerick for his advice and assistance, as well as the photographic services of the libraries who supplied the images. For their help in the completion or correction of the manuscript I am very grateful to Rebecca Breen, Dr. Catherine Lawless, Dr. Cormac Ó Cuilleanáin, Ruairí Pidgeon, and Darach Sanfey. The staff at Texas Tech University Press have shown extraordinary professionalism and patience in the preparation of this book, and I would like to thank them all most sincerely; I have to mention especially Judith Keeling, editor-in-chief, for her help and advice throughout the project and Barbara Werden, design and production manager, for her beautiful artwork and layouts. Jim Pidgeon, to whom this book is dedicated, has helped in more ways than I could possibly say.

::

The images reproduced in this book are drawn from a number of sources and copies. The *Ency-clopédie* images are mostly copied from the original (Paris) edition, with some from the Geneva (counterfeit) edition, both of which are described in detail by Schwab (1984). A small number can be shown to belong to a third group that does not correspond exactly with Schwab's criteria. The caption to each image from the *Encyclopédie* includes the volume number and the relevant identifying number in Schwab's *Inventory* where full information, including the name of the designer (a term used here in prefer-ence to *artist*) or engraver is given: readers interested in the complex bibliographical history of the plates can check the origin of each of my copies through the reference to the library of origin. The differences between the versions are minute, and are not of relevance to the subject of this study. The plates from the *Descriptions* are drawn likewise from a number of copies, together with unpublished images from the manuscript collections of the Archives de l'Académie des Sciences; the Bibliothèque Nationale de France; the Houghton Library, Harvard University; and the Institut de France. Two prints from Panckouke's *Encyclopédie méthodique* are reproduced from the copy in the Bibliothèque Sainte Geneviève in Paris. In the captions to the plates from the *Descriptions,* I have included the name of the designer and engraver for each image, as they are not otherwise available, but I have noted the date only in cases where it does not correspond to the date of the volume in which it was published (listed in the works cited).

List of Plates

I AM VERY GRATEFUL to the following libraries and archives who granted permission to reproduce these images: Archives de l'Académie des Sciences de l'Institut de France, Paris (AASP); Bibliothèque de l'Institut de France, Paris © Photos RMN Gérard Blot (BIFP); La Bibliothèque Nationale de France, Paris (BNFP); Bibliothèque Sainte Geneviève, Paris, Photos N. Boutros (BSGP); Board of Trinity College, Dublin (BTCD); Houghton Library, Harvard University (HLHU).

PART 1: THE TRADITIONAL ECONOMY

1.1. Plowing and sowing (BTCD) 30

1.2. Haymaking and harvesting (AASP) 32

1.3. Dairymaid churning (BTCD) 32

1.4. Hemp preparation (BTCD) 33

1.5. Cotton industry, West Indian colonies (BTCD) 34

1.6. Turf-cutting (BSGP) 35

1.7 and detail. Windlass women (BTCD) 36

1.8. Sleds for transporting coal (AASP) 37

1.9. Barrow-woman (AASP) 37

1.10 and detail. Hod carriers: *botteresses* (HLHU) 38

1.11. Hod carriers: *botteresses* (HLHU) 39

1.12. Sorting coal (HLHU) 40

1.13. Making briquettes (HLHU) 41

1.14. Making and repairing nets (BTCD) 42

1.15. Attaching floats to nets (BTCD) 43

1.16 (a). Treating nets at the tanner's yard; (b) and detail. Carrying and drying fishing nets (BTCD) 43–44

1.17. Shore fishing: hauling nets (BTCD) 44

1.18. Hauling nets with a pulley (BTCD) 45

1.19. Repairing lines and baiting hooks (BTCD) 46

1.20. Preparing fishing lines (BTCD) 46

1.21. Gathering bait on the strand (BTCD) 47

1.22. Raking the sand for bait (BTCD) 48

1.23. Shallow-water lance fishing (BTCD) 49

1.24. Transporting bait (BTCD) 50

1.25. Gathering and raking kelp (BNFP) 50

1.26. Shrimp fishing at low tide (BTCD) 51

1.27 and detail. Shrimp fishing in shallow and deep water (BTCD) 52

1.28 (a). Night fishing: *la montée* (BTCD); (b) Catching shellfish using traps (BTCD) 54

1.29. Catching shellfish using large nets (BTCD) 55

1.30 and detail. Shore fishing with the *grand haveneau* (BTCD) 56

1.31. In-shore fishing with small boats and nets (BTCD) 56

1.32. In-shore fishing with small boats and harpoons (BTCD) 57

1.33. Shore fishing with harpoons (BTCD) 57

1.34. Shore fishing with traps (BTCD) 58

1.35 (a). Shore fishing with traps (AASP); (b) Shore fishing with traps (BTCD) 59

1.36. Finnish peasant woman with oar (AASP) 60

1.37. Greenlanders harpoon fishing (AASP) 60

1.38. Hod-porters (BTCD) 61

1.39. Methods of transporting fish (AASP) 61

1.40. Transporting herring (AASP) 62

1.41. Transporting herring with vehicles (AASP) 62

1.42. Transporting sturgeon (AASP) 63

1.43 (a-c). Salting and pressing sardines (AASP) 64

1.44 (a and b). Preparing and pressing herring (AASP) 65

1.45. Gutting herring, detail: *caqueuse* (AASP) 66

1.46. Washing and gutting herring: *caqueuses* (AASP) 67

1.47. Washing and salting cod (AASP) 68

1.48. Drying cod or stockfish, northern Europe (AASP) 68

1.49. Washing and packing in the carrier's yard (BTCD) 69

1.50. Packing, baskets: detail (AASP) 69

1.51. Preparing herring for transport (AASP) 70

1.52 and details. Smoking herring (AASP) 71

1.53. Smoking sardines (AASP) 72

1.54. Trading herrings and anchovies (AASP) 73

1.55. The marketplace (BTCD) 73

PART 2: ARTISANAL TRADES

2.1. Making toys and knickknacks (BIFP) 84

2.2. Fan making (BIFP) 85

2.3. Steps of manufacture in fan making (BTCD) 85

2.4. Painting of fans (BTCD) 88

2.5. Assembling of fans (BTCD) 89

2.6. Feather dresser (BTCD) 90

2.7. and details. Decorating gold and silver snuffboxes (BTCD) 91

2.8. Making artificial pearls (BTCD) 92

2.9 and details. Filling and finishing artificial pearls (BTCD) 93

2.10. Enamelling workshop: filling and finishing artificial pearls (BIFP) 94

2.11 and detail. Making and stringing artificial pearls (BIFP) 95

2.12 and detail. Artificial flower fabrication (BTCD) 96

2.13 and detail. Damascening with gold and silver (HLHU) 97

2.14. Silver plating (BTCD) 98

2.15. Mirror making (BIFP) 99

2.16. Gold beating (BTCD) 100

2.17. Gold beating (BIFP) 100

2.18. Frame gilding (BTCD) 101

2.19. Bookbinding (BTCD) 102

2.20. Bookbinding: gilding (BTCD) 102

2.21. Bookbinding: gilding (BTCD) 103

2.22. Pinking and perforating (BTCD) 104

2.23. Embroidery (AASP) 106

2.24 and detail. Embroidering heavy fabrics (AASP) 108

2.25. Tailoring (AASP) 109

2.26. Seamstress's workshop (BSGP) 110

2.27. Fashion shop: "Marchande de mode" (AASP) 111

2.28. Making bobbin lace (BTCD) 113

2.29. Making cord and decorating buttons (AASP) 114

2.30. Making cord and decorating buttons (HLHU) 115

2.31 and detail. Upholstery workshop (BTCD) 116

2.32. Wig making (BTCD) 117

2.33. Wig making (BTCD) 118

2.34. (a) Hatmaking: stripping fur (BTCD); (b) Stripping fur: hands of *la coupeuse* (BTCD) 120

2.35 and detail. Saddle and carriage making (BTCD) 121

2.36 and detail. Making playing cards (AASP) 122

2.37. Making playing cards (AASP) 123

2.38 and detail. Manufacture of objects from horn and bone (AASP) 123

2.39. Pottery: finishing tasks (AASP) 124

2.40. Making pewter cutlery (AASP) 125

2.41. Making vermicelli (BTCD) 126

2.42. Making vermicelli: shaping noodles (BTCD) 126

2.43. Wax making: blanching works (BTCD) 127

2.44. Sealing-wax manufacture (BTCD) 128

2.45. Sealing-wax manufacture (BTCD) 128

2.46. Candle making (BTCD) 130

2.47. Cutler's workshop (AASP) 130

2.48 and detail. Pin making (HLHU) 000

2.49. (a) Making small nails (HLHU);
(b) Making small nails (BTCD)
133

2.50 and details. Needle making
(BTCD)   134

2.51. Making shot (BTCD)   135

2.52 and detail. Typecasting:
smoothing new type (AASP)
136

2.53 and detail. Typecasting: setting
up new type (AASP)   137

2.54 and detail. Making button molds
(HLHU)   138

2.55 and detail. Making catgut
(AASP)   139

2.56. Edge-tool making (BIFP)   140

PART 3: TEXTILES

3.1. (a) "Small wheel" spinning
technique (AASP); (b) Reeling
warp (AASP)   147

3.2. Spinning techniques (BTCD)
149

3.3. Preparation of yarn for weaving
(BTCD)   149

3.4. French and Dutch spinning
wheels (BTCD)   151

3.5. Winding thread for broadcloth
(BTCD)   151

3.6. Preparing the warp (HLHU)
152

3.7 and detail. Winding the warp
(BTCD)   153

3.8. Fingers of the warper (AASP)
153

3.9. Square mill for twisting yarn
(HLHU)   154

3.10. Mill for reeling wool thread
(AASP)   155

3.11. Unwinding cocoons (BTCD)
156

3.12. Reeling the thread (HLHU)
157

3.13. Reeling the thread: escouladou
(HLHU)   157

3.14 and detail. Reeling the thread
(BTCD)   158

3.15. Reeling the thread: escouladou
(AASP)   159

3.16. Four-wheel reeling machine
(HLHU)   160

3.17. (a) Stocking making (AASP);
(b) Stocking making (AASP)
161

3.18. Stretching the warp (HLHU)
162

3.19. Removing the warp (HLHU)
162

3.20. Warping with a circular frame
(HLHU)   163

3.21. Unwinding the finished warp
(HLHU)   163

3.22. Lyon-style creel with circular
warper (HLHU)   164

3.23. Setting up bobbins: removing
the warp (HLHU)   164

3.24. (a) Woman warper's hands,
detail (AASP); (b) Woman
warper's hands, detail (AASP)
165

3.25. Warping with a large spool
(BTCD)   166

3.26. Reeling silk onto a spinning
wheel (AASP)   167

3.27. Loading silk onto quills from a
doubling frame (AASP)   167

3.28. (a) Guiding the silk onto a quill
(AASP); (b) Rejoining broken
thread and returning to quill
(AASP)   168

3.29. (a) Making heddles on
horizontal frame (AASP); (b)
Making heddles on horizontal
frame (AASP)   169

3.30. Making heddles on horizontal
frame (BTCD)   170

3.31. Ribbon-maker's loom: drawing
cords (HLHU)   171

3.32. Weaving at a small loom for
making braid (HLHU)   172

3.33. Ribbon making: finishing
techniques (HLHU)   173

3.34. Ribbon making: nonpareil
(HLHU)   174

3.35 and detail. Passementerie:
making braid and cartisane
decorations (HLHU)   175

3.36 and detail. Making upholstery
fringes (HLHU)   176

3.37. Passementerie: making reeds
(BTCD)   177

3.38. Warping frames (BTCD)   178

3.39. Finishing laces with brass tips
(BTCD)   178

3.40 and detail. Drawing, reeling,
and laminating gold wire (BIFP)
179

3.41. Covering thread with gold or
silver (BIFP)   180

3.42. Covering thread with gold or
silver (BIFP)   181

3.43. Making gold wire (BIFP)   181

PART 4: MANUFACTORIES

4.1. Papermaking: rag shredding
(BTCD)   188

4.2 and detail. Papermaking: drying
room (BTCD)   189

4.3. Papermaking: drying room
(BTCD)   190

4.4. Papermaking: glazing, sorting,
counting sheets (BTCD)   191

4.5 and detail. Woman porter in
shipbuilder's yard (AASP)
191

4.6. Papermaking: little girl folding
sheets (BTCD)   192

4.7 (a, and detail). Soap factory
(HLHU); (b) Soap factory
(HLHU)   193

4.8 and detail. Les Gobelins:
unwinding skeins of yarn
(BTCD)   194

4.9. La Savonnerie: unwinding skein
of wool (BTCD)   195

4.10. Making Turkish carpets (BTCD)
197

4.11. Sandstone preparation (BIFP)
198

4.12. Breaking crucibles (AASP)
198

4.13. Sorting broken glass (BTCD)
199

4.14. Glass collector (BTCD)   200

4.15 and details. Tin making:
scouring surfaces (BTCD)   201

PART 5: COMMERCIAL
ACTIVITY

5.1 and detail. Goldsmith-jeweller's
shop (BTCD) 207

5.2. Furrier's shop (BTCD) 208

5.3 and detail. Hatter's shop (BTCD)
209

5.4. Belt-maker's shop (AASP) 210

5.5 and detail. *Marchande de mode*
(AASP) 211

5.6. Linen-draper's shop (AASP)
212

5.7 and details. Cutler's shop (HLHU)
213

5.8. Baker's shop (BTCD) 214

5.9 and detail. Pastry shop (BTCD)
215

5.10. Cork maker's shop (BTCD)
215

5.11. Tinsmith's shop (BTCD) 216

Louder than Words

Introduction

THIS BOOK takes as its subject a corpus of visual representations of women workers in eighteenth-century France; it features a wide range of activities, from women's secular roles in the traditional economy to the many tasks they performed in the worlds of craft, manufacture, and commerce. The images studied and reproduced here are all related to two major collections of engravings: the first, and better known, consists of the plates of Diderot's *Encyclopédie,* published in Paris between 1762 and 1772, with a supplementary volume added by Panckouke in 1777.[1] The second collection is the *Descriptions des arts et métiers* by the Académie Royale des Sciences, published between 1761 and 1788, but incorporating some plates engraved as early as the 1690s;[2] this work is far less widely available and has been relatively ignored by scholars, other than those studying specific technologies or trades. Many plates (certainly more than a hundred) prepared for this collection, but never actually published, now lie in far-flung manuscript repositories.[3] The plates in both of these collections were retouched, reworked, and added to in subsequent (often counterfeit) editions and new enterprises based on them; the history of these changes and adaptations is enormously complex, and beyond the scope of this study, which confines itself to the original state of the images.[4]

It is well known that there is a dearth of source documents relating to working women's lives, in part because they were so often excluded from the statutory provisions regulating trade and manufacture.[5] The vast majority of trade guilds in France, which witnessed a growing professionalization of occupations in the seventeenth and eighteenth centuries, excluded women as members in their own right, recognizing their existence only as widows of masters carrying on the family business (Wiesner, 2000; Truant 1988). There were a few exceptions, and we will consider them later. But the body of law regulating the trades, and the archives of the corporations, rarely referred to women as workers; as Michael Sonenscher has remarked in *Work and Wages,* his study of work in France, "where the words of the law did not supply a name that could be challenged, little trace of the things that women said and did could survive" (1989, 66; see also Collins 1989, 443). Yet Daryl Hafter, among other historians of women's economic activity, has underlined how women worked in all sorts of roles across the economy, often in contravention of the regulations:

> Guild families used a variety of strategies to apply women's work to current needs. By alternately revealing and concealing women's activities, depending on how the political climate shaped guild regulations, guild families took advantage of women's work capacity without necessarily crediting them with the skills so automatically pressed into service. Because contemporaries in the crafts were perfectly conversant with this shadow economy, these practices were not necessarily recorded. (1995, 45; see also Hafter 2001, 13; Hudson and Lee 1990, 2)

Studies of wealth and occupations in French towns have demonstrated that the number of women workers and business owners actually increased from the mid-seventeenth century onward, in spite of the rules (Musgrave 1997; Collins 1989); and in Lyon, for example, women in some areas of underground enterprise (silk making, hatmaking, and button making) managed to thrive by securing control of raw materials, labor, and distribution (see Hafter 2001).

Clearly, then, any alternative sources in this field are valuable and desirable: my own research on women in the book trades, based on records from the shadow side of the law—police interrogations of women taken to the Bastille for a variety of transgressions—has shown that women were indeed active in many aspects of publishing, despite the official discourse to the contrary (Sheridan 1992). When I looked for visual material where such activities might have been recorded, however, I found that the images devoted to the book trades in Diderot's *Encyclopédie*—the obvious first port of call—showed no female presence at all, their absence in itself serving to strengthen aspects of my argument. But I began to note the copperplate engravings in that collection depicting work situations in which women *did* actually appear, sometimes unexpectedly, and it became evident that the artists—or designers, a more general term I will use in preference, following Schwab (1984, 30), to cover the variety of people who prepared these images—had registered many elements of the contemporary cultural and social context within which these women operated, and that were not recorded elsewhere. In this work I shall point to numerous instances in which the images record the continuing presence of women in trades where they had formerly held guild rights that were gradually eroded by regulation. This visual material provides a source of information distinct from, as well as additional to, the written texts; as Roland Barthes remarks in his study of journalistic photographs, "It is impossible for the word to mirror the image: for in the passage from one structure to the other secondary signifiers inevitably come into play" (1993, 1: 945). As primary material rather than as secondary "illustrations" subordinate to the written word, these images can provide historical, cultural, and anthropological evidence, thus adding to our understanding of the circumstances in which working women lived and died under the *ancien régime*.

::

THE CORPUS

The *Descriptions des arts* and the *Encyclopédie* were the two most extensive and coherent attempts in eighteenth-century Europe to record and codify traditional work practices across the economy, with particular emphasis on artisanal crafts and manufacture. Although the plates featuring women represent a small minority of the overall number of images in both works—many of which are devoid of any human figures at all—together they offer a significant and varied corpus of some two hundred images: this includes over thirty images prepared for the *Descriptions* but never actually published.[6] A brief summary of the genesis of these collections will serve to situate them in their historical and intellectual contexts, and explicate the nature of the relationship between them.

The initiative for this kind of project dates back to Colbert's injunction to the Académie Royale des Sciences in 1675 to undertake a description of the trades and crafts; an earlier, similar project had actually been discussed from 1660 onward in the Royal Society in London, but though some promising studies were presented to the society, the interest in the applied study of the trades fizzled out, with the "purer" sciences of mathematics and physics finding greater favor (Cole and Watts 1952, 5 and 14; Jammes 1961, 5). When little progress had been achieved over the following two decades, the highly placed abbé Bignon (1662–1743), Chancellor

Pontchartrain's nephew, made a deliberate decision to bypass the Académie of which he had become president in 1691 and chose instead to bring together a small group of talented people in his own Parisian townhouse toward the end of 1692 to revive the project.[7] René-Antoine Ferchault de Réaumur himself, who later became responsible for the project, recognized that this group was entirely independent of the Académie des Sciences, a factor that had the potential to revolutionize the way in which the scientific establishment regarded the "baser" activities of craftwork and manufacture.[8] The three key members of Bignon's group were Gilles Filleau Des Billettes (1634–1720), Jacques Jaugeon (1646–1724), and Fr. Sebastien Truchet (1657–1729), all of whom had a background in mathematics or natural science and a strong interest in the "mechanical arts." They quickly established that the purpose of their project was to serve the national interest by enabling "technological" progress (a term only slightly anachronistic in this context); they would do this by describing and promoting best practices, and by facilitating comparison with relevant trades in other countries to the mutual benefit of the inhabitants.[9]

The methodology developed by this group was deeply innova-

tive. First, background research on a particular trade or manufacture was carried out by a scholarly scientist, who then drafted questions that were to form the basis of field investigations.[10] These investigations (tantamount to "experimentation") were carried out in an actual manufactory or workshop by a reliable and knowledgeable person: this included the visual recording of processes and tools in sketches, often by a designer accompanying the researcher.[11] These drawings were central to the project; once they were carefully reviewed and corrected by the authors of the eventual treatise, they were prepared for engraving, with numbers or letters inserted into the images for the purpose of cross-referencing with the descriptive text. The typical layout of many, though not all, of the finished plates—a vignette in the top section of the folio page and the illustration of machinery and tools in the lower section—was already fully evolved in 1695 and was later used in a considerable portion of the Académie's illustrations. The detailed development of this model has been studied elsewhere (Salamon-Bayet 1970 and Sheridan 2008); its most influential precursor, in terms of the illustration of technical processes, is undoubtedly Agricola's *De re metallica* (1556), in which the woodcuts offer full-page views of various operations in the mining and treatment of metals, including machines, tools, and human agents at work. Agricola succeeded in tying together text and image so that they were mutually illuminating, and he used a system of cross-referencing in a manner that differentiates his work from the contemporary sixteenth-century genre of *Théâtres des machines,* impressive collections of technical drawings whose illustrations were often close in subject and technique to those of Agricola, but in which textual explanation was of minimal importance (Endrei 1995, 179–81). The model developed by Bignon's group later became the classic pattern for the *Encyclopédie.*

Archival documents attest to the advanced state of planning for a coherent publication of the *Descriptions* under Des Billettes' direction; he adopted a classificatory approach which, as Salomon-Bayet has commented, would have resembled more closely that of Panckouke's *Encyclopédie méthodique* (1782–91) than the eventual publication of unconnected single volumes by the Académie, or the alphabetical arrangement of Diderot's *Encyclopédie* (1970, 250n1). But the efforts of the group began to dissolve in the very different environment of the Académie des Sciences, into which the three key members were inducted in 1699.[12] In what was perhaps an attempt to refocus the work, Bignon's trusted young friend Réaumur, aged twenty-six, and on the first rung of the academic ladder, was appointed to direct the project around 1709. With the support of the Regent, he himself prepared a substantial number of documents, particularly in the first decade, and ordered the engraving of 260 plates (Jaoul and Pinault 1982, 338). Yet none of this material came into the public domain at the time, and not a single volume of the projected mammoth work was published by Réaumur, despite the fact that the treatise on papermaking by Jaugeon was ready for press.[13] Jacques Proust has suggested some reasons why the work of the *Descriptions* became bogged down, stressing in particular the accelerated rate of change in the processes of production in the first half of the eighteenth century, with which the lengthy and weighty treatises the Academicians were drafting could not keep pace (1962, 186). Though such factors might have increasingly come into play by the mid century, they do not explain the earlier failures, or why the project, moribund for almost forty years, was resumed immediately after Réaumur's death in 1757. The work was then revitalized under the direction of the Academician Henry-Louis Duhamel du Monceau (1700–1782) and with the very active assistance of his nephew Auguste-Denis Fougeroux de Bondaroy (1732–89).[14] Under pressure from the rival *Encyclopédie,* some of the *Descriptions* were finally published between 1761 and 1788, incorporating a number of the plates engraved as early as the 1690s.

The Académie's focused studies of particular trades were comprehensive and specialized and remain one of the most valuable European sources of information on the operation of eighteenth-century workshop enterprise. In comparing the two collections, it should be noted that the prints in the *Descriptions* are somewhat more likely to reflect personal experience, whether that of the author (scientifically trained expert or highly experienced practitioner), designer, or engraver, and in these circumstances, we can ascribe a higher level of authority to what might be called their "witness" quality. But even trade practitioners undoubtedly had their blind spots, formed partly by their experiences and expectations in relation to trade regulations, and cannot provide unmediated access to a transparent reality. It is often, paradoxically, in the incidental details (as in realist art) that women's work becomes visible. That said, the proportion of plates in which women's work is illustrated is higher in the *Descriptions des arts et métiers*: eighty-nine, or 4.8 percent of the total, as opposed to the *Encyclopédie* with seventy-six, or 2.7 percent. There are many reasons for this, but it should be noted in particular that the Académie collection featured lengthy studies of aspects of the traditional economy, where women were widely represented (for example, the treatise on fishing: Duhamel 1769), and the strongly female-associated textile trades, particularly silk making (Paulet 1773; Duhamel 1765). Where the images in both collections were significantly alike, I have generally chosen to publish the *Descriptions* versions in preference to those of the *Encyclopédie*, since the *Descriptions* is the earlier source and is less widely known.

It should be noted that the people who created and published the Académie's images did not intend to give a "realistic" representation of any individual workshop in any particular location. Rather, they aimed to give an analytical, and to some extent ideal, version of best practice in a specific trade, drawing on research they themselves carried out from a variety of sources and in a variety of locations, and these not just French (see Sheridan 2008). The treatise on mining, for example, refers to visits undertaken by the author, Morand, to a number of locations in England (1768–79, Introduction). The aim was to incorporate the most relevant information on manufacturing processes and work practices, and so the scholars from the Académie looked to Lyon, Nîmes, and even Bologna for silk manufacture; to the Auvergne for paper making; and to Aubusson for carpet making. The series of plates on any one trade could incorporate images based on research in several different geographic areas. Where a specific location for the research was mentioned in the text, or where sketches taken of a specific workshop could be identified, I have noted this information as it is clearly of relevance to the contextualization of the images. At the same time, it is important to remember that the images were intended to have a universal application and that the recording of the local details was not of concern to the originators. The approach and perspective that was adopted disregarded to a large extent the political and economic dominance of guild structures, with their local and sectional interests, and concentrated instead on a national conception of the economy and a supranational ideal of technological development. This was, of course, an unavowed challenge to the guild system itself and its culture of secrecy (see Sheridan 2008). Given the approach of their creators, reading and decoding these images requires us to constantly vary our perspective from the particular to the general, from the urban to the rural, from the regional to the European context. I have endeavored to flag these shifts as appropriate in the descriptions of individual trades.

The genesis of the *Encyclopédie* and its plates has been documented by Jacques Proust (1962, 189–95; 1957) and Madeleine Pinault (1988). From the *Prospectus* of 1750 through the early volumes of text, Diderot spelled out his conception of and program for a "Description des arts": his work would be more comprehensive than any of its predecessors; it would involve a wider group of experts and be free of government control; and it would be more up-to-date, being produced within a reasonable space of time, than the interminable efforts of the Academicians.[15] Diderot had a more specific political and social agenda than the latter, and a utopian zeal for a world in which guild allegiances and traditional practices would be superseded by the rationalized laws of technological advance and increased production (see Proust 1985; Sheridan 2007). In fact, however, Diderot worked in an eclectic manner in preparing the *Encyclopédie*, gathering and editing information from a wide variety of secondary sources, with only a small percentage of his texts actually drafted or edited by persons with firsthand knowledge of the field (Proust 1957; 1962, 191–92). We know that he plagiarized many of his images from plates that the Académie, and in particular Réaumur, had had engraved: he effectively bribed the Académie's engravers to release these prints to him, and he used them as a basis for his own.[16] It is clear that Diderot grossly overstated the degree to which the Académie's prints were outdated, as his images mirrored them very closely: I will highlight many such examples from the corpus in what follows. He was disingenuous in declaring in the article "Encyclopédie" (in an oblique, but obvious reference to the earlier plates) that there was "scarcely a figure which did not need to be redrawn." In some cases, however, Diderot was forced, when the charge of plagiarism was made against him, to revise and improve his images; as Seguin remarked in 1964, "Diderot showed proof of intelligence and good taste in taking

[the Académie plates] as a model, because they are generally excellent from the technical point of view," and where he chose—or was obliged—to adapt an Académie engraving, the outcome was invariably an improved version (1964, 31–32). For certain of the plates, his designers did visit workshops to produce original sketches, or correct existing drawings, as the Academicians had done from the start. Diderot refers to Goussier's drawings on glassmaking, sketched on a visit to a manufactory (*Ency. Planches*, vol. 4: 9; Schwab 1984, 31): "We can count on their accuracy," he remarks, and this series is indeed among the best in the collection.

On the negative side, the illustrations in the *Encyclopédie* were never closely integrated with the studies, unlike the rival *Descriptions*: for the most part they were produced after, and often long after, the descriptive texts. They were published separately from the relevant discursive articles and were always intended to be so: this was the single greatest weakness in the conception of the *Encyclopédie*.[17] The brief explanations provided as legends in the actual volumes of plates, and intended to compensate for this latter weakness, were often inadequate.[18]

Despite these distinctions, and whatever the relative merits

of the two works, it is clear that the two enterprises were related on a variety of levels that set them apart from preceding or contemporary sources. They shared a set of goals and a number of assumptions about the best way to achieve those goals: in particular, the engraved images would capture aspects of contemporary reality that language alone could not render effectively, and they would enhance the didactic effect. As Diderot remarked, "To amuse and to please is to fail in one's purpose, when one can instruct and impress" (*Ency.* article "Encyclopédie"). The focus of the plates in both collections being on the processes of production, they included the human agents, the "common people" who were the producers and traders of goods. This gave these works an ethnographic dimension of which the creators were to some extent conscious; Réaumur, in his unpublished notes, gestures toward the need to record information normally excluded from the dominant categories of knowledge:

> We frequently study the history of the Greeks and Romans, while knowing nothing of the history of France; and a scholar familiar with French history is sometimes unaware of the history of his

own family, or of what goes on in his household [. . .] We are pleased to know about the practices, the skills, the ways of working of the Indians, yet we do not know how the things we use most commonly are made. The more available the opportunity to learn about things, the more likely we are to remain forever ignorant about them.[19]

Madeleine Pinault has further highlighted the personal and intellectual links between the two parallel groups of scholars and designers through the 1750s to the 1770s, with significant crossover between the two teams (Pinault 1988, 361). They can be seen as being, in many respects, complementary, despite their overt rivalry.[20] The first volume of the Académie's collection was distributed late in 1760; the first volume of the *Encyclopédie*'s engravings appeared in 1762.[21] From then on, Proust emphasizes, "the two publications pursue their parallel courses, each one observing the flaws of the other in order to improve itself" (1962, 56; see commentary on plate 3.25). Jaoul and Pinault have highlighted the interest that Fougeroux de Bondaroy himself took in the *Encyclopédie* plates (1986, 24–26).

It is important to remember, however, that even taking the two collections cumulatively, we do not find comprehensive coverage of women's many work activities across contemporary society. In general, the attention devoted to any one area of the economy reflects primarily the particular agenda of the editors and cannot be supposed to correspond to the importance of that area in terms of the number of people employed or the value of goods produced. Women who worked in cities in the casual sector, inferior in status and pay, and who accounted for a substantial portion of the working population, do not feature here: domestic servants (other than those effectively recruited to work in the family trade), laundresses and washerwomen, women who mended linen and clothes, women who cared for the sick, secondhand clothes traders, and street sellers of all types are absent (Milliot 1995, 35–38; Hufton 1993); these women workers are featured more strongly in other genres of engravings, such as the *Cris de Paris* (discussed later). They clearly did not count as part of the "productive" economy as defined by our editors. And, for similar reasons, although higher on the social scale, the few Parisian trade guilds specifically reserved to women are also poorly represented in the corpus of images: I will offer many examples in this book of writers (in both collections) overlooking even highly skilled and lucrative activities where they were solely the province of women.[22] In an unknown number of cases, and for reasons that remain impenetrable to us, the authors and designers failed to show women in other sectors where we know them to have been active: engraving is a case in point, ironically, as a considerable number of the plates discussed in this study were engraved by women.

The corpus I have collected is nonetheless of major significance. When William Hamilton Sewell examined the large collections of the Cabinet des Estampes of the Bibliothèque Nationale for visual material representing workers and work practices from the sixteenth to the nineteenth centuries, he concluded that this category of print showed male workers almost exclusively, or presented women as sexualized objects, and he remarked that, for the producers of such images, "whatever the reality of the situation, work was seen as essentially a male activity" (1986, 259–60). While acknowledging the peculiarity that women were known to have worked in the trades where only men were illustrated, Sewell decided to confine his otherwise very perceptive article to images of men's work.[23]

The present study, while recognizing that women are indeed featured in only a minority of contemporary prints, nonetheless redresses the balance in terms of retrieving these valuable sources, and points to the ways in which they illuminate the role of the woman worker in this period.

The decision to exclude other possible visual materials related to this topic was based on the advantages to be gained by retaining the integrity of the two collections. While consistently foregrounding the images—reversing the usual hierarchy of text over image—the continual cross-referencing from the text of one collection to the other has enabled me to explicate many problematic pictures: for example, one image in the *Encyclopédie*, supposedly of women in the nude setting up nets in the sea, could be shown, through a study of the more exact *Description*, to have been interpreted erroneously. The common source of origin specified that these were men, and it was accordingly eliminated from the corpus.[24] Even where the image alone bore witness to the work women actually did—a dilemma not confined to the previously unpublished images from manuscript collections for which no written text was discovered—such images could be read, their signification sought in relation to the codes dominant in

the collections as a whole. I have, however, included two images from the later *Encyclopédie méthodique*, published by Panckouke in the 1780s. For his treatment of the arts and crafts, Panckouke in the main drew directly from the plates of the original *Encyclopédie* and the Académie's *Descriptions des arts et métiers*, but in the case of a plate on the extraction of turf for fuel (*Tourbier*) and a plate illustrating a seamstress's workshop (*Couturière*, conspicuously absent from the earlier works), the images and explanatory texts added new areas of women's activity to the corpus and are reproduced here. The inclusion of images from other, disparate sources would have risked turning this book into an eclectic album rather than a focused study.[25]

::

STYLISTIC CONTEXT

Related to these questions concerning which subjects are addressed in these images and texts, and in what manner, is the major issue of the relationship of these prints to earlier and contemporary art practice. Whereas I have indicated that the primary function of the plates was didactic and have contextualized them in the history of technology, it is clear that their distinctive modes of representation and the idioms

they draw on share common ground with other types of artistic endeavor. The visual representation of women workers is in itself a vast subject, and here I can make only a few brief remarks situating this corpus of prints within the wider parameters of visual culture.

From medieval times, people at work appear mainly in scenes of rural life associated with the rhythms of nature and the seasons, such as those featured in the Books of Hours or in the earliest examples of the "monumental" genre, the large fifteenth-century tapestries depicting peasant life (*Paysages* 1994, 43, 101; Barnes 1995, 3). But in the traditions of "high" art, there was generally limited scope for the representation of "low" elements in society going about their daily tasks. The Renaissance, with its renewed emphasis on earthly affairs and human agency, and subsequently the Reformation, which ascribed greater dignity to labor, gave new impetus for depictions of daily life, the works of Albrecht Dürer (1471–1528) and Pieter Brueghel (c. 1525–69) being particularly notable. Wherever the market for religious iconography was drying up, works that represented everyday activities and people of lower social origin began to flourish; this was especially the case in the Netherlands in the seventeenth century (Barnes 1995, 3; 1988, 5–7). In the latter part of that century, and the beginning of the next, large paintings of peasants or urban workers depicted in life size found favor: Jan Siberechts (1627–1703) in the Netherlands, Giacomo Ceruti (1698–1767) in Italy, and the Le Nain brothers (first half of the seventeenth century) in France are cases in point. Their work shows young peasant women transporting food, looking after livestock, and performing tasks around the farm: these images often accentuate the women's strong physique, fecundity, and a kind of rural eroticism. Similarly, in the same period, servants and peasants selling their produce at markets are often represented in their relationship to the animal and vegetable world, the sensual contact of those who sell or prepare food being frequently a metaphor of sexuality (*Paysages* 1994, 129).

However, the main function of such works was not to offer the viewer a glimpse of the reality of peasant life but rather to offer a satisfying contrast with the world of the aristocratic clientele for such pictures. Nature was purified in accordance with the dictates of the prevailing neoclassicism (*Paysages* 1994, 145). The preem-inent aesthetic critic of the early eighteenth century, the abbé Du Bos, reflected on the wide gap between the representation of country folk and shepherds in contemporary pastoral literature and art and the realities of rural life in France as he saw them, where the peasants were weighed down by heavy labor and poverty and brutalized by the harsh climate (1733, 175). Such creatures could not be considered models for Jean-Antoine Watteau (1684–1721) or François Boucher (1703–70), in whose work "low" subjects were idealized under the influence of contemporary literary and theatrical categories. It was only in the middle years of the eighteenth century that attention to the technological and economic imperatives of agriculture by writers such as Duhamel du Monceau (1753; 1762b)—one of the principal Academicians associated with the collections studied here— began to be reflected in painting with a new sense of the status of rural endeavor. Agriculture is seen by the physiocratic movement as the source of renewable wealth for the nation, and the rehabilitation of the peasant-worker as a model of "natural" man by the *philosophes* is mirrored in the glorification of agricultural labor by painters such as Jean-Baptiste Greuze (1725–1805). The countryside was now to be painted "after nature," in preference to the Arcadian idylls of Watteau, and to evoke daily life. Fragonard's peasants are poorer than those of Boucher, but they are not ridiculous or grotesque (*Paysages* 1994, 145–52); nonetheless, in comparison with Brueghel's rough peasants, as Vardi has noted, these rural workers "have been civilized and domesticated to fit the elite's desire to fit them within an Enlightenment vision of progress and happiness" (Vardi 1996, 1394). In the latter part of the century, from 1760 to 1790, more and more details drawn from peasant life were introduced into paintings: Nicolas-Bernard Lépicié's (1735–84) representation of a large farmyard moves away from the dominant picturesque images of cottages and features several women, carefully depicted in their local costume, engaged in work activities (*Paysages* 1994, 176).

Linda Nochlin has highlighted how women in relation to work has been a notable theme in types of painting and drawing to which the epithet *realist* has been variously attributed (1971; 1999). Whereas in art history the term is mainly used to refer to a specific period in the nineteenth century, aspects of "realism" are also evoked in relation to Dutch genre paintings of the seventeenth century (Demetz 1963), and to the works of the eighteenth-century French painter who most closely relates to its themes, Jean-Baptiste-Siméon Chardin (1699–1779). Such paintings, which favored the particular over the general and the "natural" over the ideal, and which concentrated on banal objects and scenes from everyday life (with attention to detail and to what was seemingly irrelevant), offer the best possibilities for finding reflections of women at work (see Solomon-Godeau 2001, 71–73). Roland Barthes called the Dutch genre paintings to mind—what he refers to as an "iconographie 'progressiste'" (1964, 12)—in relation to the way in which objects are tamed by the human presence in the *Encyclopédie*. The analogy is equally relevant to the way the objects themselves are represented: their materiality is highlighted by a close attention to form, qualities also found in Chardin. It has been suggested that aspects of Chardin's work reflect an artistic reaction to empiricism and the progress of science, and this contextualization of high art in the scientific concerns of the period evokes interesting resonances with the print traditions of which the collections studied here are the most outstanding exemplar.[26] It prefigures the nexus identified between the natural sci-

ences and painting in nineteenth-century realism (Nochlin 1971, 40–45).

Of central interest to the present work in such genre paintings is the parallel in subject matter: women of humble origins involved in work activity, such as Vermeer's *Lacemaker* and *Milkmaid*, or Chardin's *Ecureuse* scrubbing in the scullery and his *Pourvoyeuse* bringing provisions back from market. Without supposing transparency in such pictures, or mistaking the apparently random arrangement of people and objects for a "true" reflection of life in the period, the quiet attention to the contextual details of the featured women's lives has resonances with the images in our collections. Diderot himself, in his "Salon" of 1761, qualified Chardin's subjects as "lowly, commonplace and homely" (1875, 10: 129), and therefore, by implication, strange subjects for art, but he admired him as a painter, and in his *Essai sur la peinture* defended both Chardin and Greuze, and their representations of "common and domestic life," as true imitations of the "nature of things."[27] It should be noted, however, that nowhere in the traditions of painting just mentioned do we see reflected the suffering and deformities imposed on the human body by work, a

topic I will later raise in relation to the plates in this study. The worker's experiences as such were never of primary interest or concern before the mid-nineteenth century and the Revolution of 1848. Courbet is perhaps the first painter to abandon the demands of the academic style and the picturesque in his representation of the working body, reproducing the stiffness and awkwardness associated with heavy labor (in *The Stone Breakers*, 1849, to which I will refer later), followed by Millet's well-known *L'Homme à la Houe* (1860–62), which emphasises the brutalization and exhaustion of the peasant laborer (see Nochlin 1971, 112–20).

There is clearly a distinction—which would have been made by Diderot as editor of the *Encyclopédie*—between the major art of painting and the minor art of the print. The print-buying public was much more diverse than those who could acquire original paintings. Individual prints could be bought cheaply from shops and chapmen by those of the most modest means, or in book form: such volumes were acquired by middle-income families (Barnes 1988, 5–7, 9n7, 9n8; also Milliot 1995, 98–111). The subject matter of prints reflected this wider audience, and favorite topics were those familiar presences of every urban landscape: the artisans, shopkeepers, and street sellers. The most interesting genre from the point of view of this study is the cycle of craft pictures, often accompanied by a didactic or moralizing text. The most influential model of this genre was the *Ständebuch* (originally titled *Eygentliche Beschreibung aller Ständ auf Erden*): published in Frankfurt in 1568, it incorporated woodcuts (by Jost Amman) with text in verse form (by Hans Sachs) and became the model on which many later print series (and some paintings) were based (Stone-Ferrier 1988, 14). Rifkin, in his introduction to his edition of the *Ständebuch*, associates the interest in "low" working people, and the moral values reflected in this genre, with Protestant ideology (1973, xxi; xxxix). He summarizes the moral purpose, as directed at trade and craft workers by Sach's verses, as follows: "They should refrain from idleness; give true work and measure, and avoid all vices; praise and love the God who feeds us all; and know that whoever runs an evil business, no matter what the temporal rewards, loses all in the end" (xx). Though the collections from which the images in this text are drawn reflect a different—desacralized and scientific—set of concerns, they do

share the sense of the seriousness of work, and the vital importance of its being performed with care and attention to ensure a positive outcome in production.

The majority of the 114 images in the *Ständebuch* focus on craftspeople in their workshops, with precise attention to the detail of the working processes and the illustration of tools and equipment. Rifkin concludes that Amman, in comparison with his contemporaries, "maintains a high standard of verisimilitude in all of his pictures, generally reflecting and furthering the increasingly strict criteria for scientific illustrations emerging in his generation" (xxix). Only a very few images feature women workers: one is pictured alongside a nailer, sharpening the points, and another is handing the yarn to the male weaver, tasks that were strongly female-identified across the ages. In the image of a bakery, a woman in the background carries a large platter of loaves on her head, the same task of transporting that will be reflected in our corpus (see plates 4.4, 4.5, and 4.7a, for example). None of the images feature a woman as the main protagonist. The doggerel verses Sachs composed do not add anything to an understanding of the processes but list the products of a trade and thus do represent

an early, rudimentary effort at recording a trade vocabulary.

The *Ständebuch* woodcuts, often reprinted and augmented (as in a Latin edition in 1568), were hugely influential in northern Europe. In the Netherlands, a series of eighteen etchings produced by Joris van Vliet (c.1635) confines itself to a narrower group of tradesmen but shows the influence of Amman's images (Barnes 1995, 4). The plates, with no accompanying text, are detailed accounts of the specific work activities: the stress of physical effort is indicated in the bodies and postures of the working men, clothed in the garb typical of their trade. No women are featured in these prints. In 1694 van Vliet's fellow countryman Jan Luycken, a poet, painter, and engraver, produced a series of one hundred prints, *Het Menselyk Bedryf*.[28] Looking back to both his predecessors, he adds new trades that reflect economic developments in the intervening period; his accompanying verses, however, are religious in tone and refer to passages from the Bible, and appear curiously outmoded. They were replaced by the verses of a Dutch poet, Antoni Jansen, when the plates were re-engraved in Amsterdam by Reiner and Joshua Ottens (c. 1725). Five of these prints show women workers—sewing, folding sheets of paper, carrying fish to market, and helping with the harvest.

It has been suggested by Donna Barnes (1988, 7) and Benjamin Rifkin (in his introduction to Amman and Sachs 1973, xxxix–xl), among others, that the subject matter of genre painting in the Netherlands was strongly influenced by this tradition of prints. The latter can also clearly be seen as a precursor to the works studied in this text, with the privileging of the subject matter of creation and production, its contextualization in workshops, which helps to confer dignity and status on the worker, and its concern to show the detail of tools and machines. There are also significant differences in that in the *Ständebuch* tradition, each trade is represented by single images that tend to represent the unity of that trade; in our corpus, the stages in production are analyzed and broken down into discrete though related steps in a series of images, with the depiction of tools and machinery separated and developed as a new style of technical representation. There is more movement and life in many of the former prints than in our more schematic representations. Unity of a trade as a theme and lively imagery are also features noted by Sewell in his study of the many prints depicting the trades and

sold singly: he highlights the influential work of Jan van der Straet (1523–1605), who worked in Antwerp, Lyon, and Italy, and Abraham Bosse (1602–76), who worked in Paris, both of whom produced series of prints with an explicitly didactic intent. Sewell suggests that these images "mirrored the ideological continuity between ideas about labor and reigning conceptions of the cosmos and social order" (1986, 263–68); the prints in our corpus break significantly with these ideological assumptions.

Lastly, I will mention the genre of print in which women were most widely represented, the "Street Cries." Originating in France and Italy in the sixteenth century, these prints represented street traders in what is often a highly romanticized or, alternatively, caricatural mode destined primarily for ornamentation. Vincent Milliot's masterly analysis of the French collections of *Les Cris de Paris* from the sixteenth to the eighteenth centuries highlights many aspects that serve to contrast these prints with those of our corpus. The *Cris* represent those involved in the itinerant selling of food and drink (mainly women), or services, such as the chimney sweep, the rat-catcher, or the shoe-mender (mainly men). Placed low on the scale of skill, the subjects of these images are al-

most never associated with productive activity or shown with any tools or other distinctive signs of their trade; the mode of representation tends to obscure or obliterate the realities of work (see Milliot 1994, 14–25). The poverty, misery, and physical abasement connected with many street trades, involving the portering of heavy materials on the seller's back, are almost never indicated (Milliot 1995, 208); the aesthetic conventions of the day, coupled with the moralizing or comic intentions of the legends commonly attached to these images, all serve to act as a barrier between the viewer and the supposed subject of representation. In the case of the many images of women, these legends most frequently serve to sexualize the image, whether a pretty oyster seller suggestively offering her wares or a buxom milkmaid: as in high art, women's sexuality is overtly—and in this case crudely—identified with natural products, animal and vegetable (Milliot 1994, 14). Alternatively, the tone is moralizing, warning against vices such as alcoholism, of which Bouchardon's *Vendeuse d'eau de vie,* for example, stands accused;[29] in either case, there is never any technical vocabulary associated with these workers in the legends (Milliot 1994, 12). As has already been noted, the female occupations located at the bottom of the social and economic scale, and omitted in the two collections considered here, are precisely those privileged by the *Cris*. Both subject matter and treatment in our corpus are distinctly different: technical vocabulary, both textual and iconographic, is of primary importance; the worker is, in almost all cases, situated in relation to an identifiable environment, often a workshop, with its particular tools or machinery; and the women are in no sense presented as sexual objects.

Turning to the corpus considered in this work, then, the first thing to note is that it is not homogeneous; even within the small subset I have extracted from the two large collections, there are many different types of images, with different conventions of presentation, scale, and layout. There are some large foldout images of good artistic quality and rich in detail: typically, they represent retail establishments, such as the image of the cutler's shop from the *Descriptions* (by Goussier and Bénard, plate 5.7), or the upholsterer's establishment from the *Encyclopédie* (by Radel and Bénard, plate 2.31). In size and quality, these images are closer to the "high" end of the print market and could be—and no doubt were—extracted for use as decorative prints. Second, there

are smaller images featuring the human agents in specific work contexts, arranged horizontally, two to a folio page, as in the early engravings for the series on papermaking in the *Descriptions,* or three to a page, as for many of the images on fishing in both collections (see plate 1.21 for example). The particular layout in this last example reflects the arrangement of the original drawings, which were a common source for both the *Encyclopédie* and the *Descriptions,* as will be discussed later. In general, images such as these in part 1 of this work ("The Traditional Economy") can be located closest to other artistic genres: for example, many of the seaside images are reminiscent of marine scenes in Dutch drawing and painting of the preceding century, such as the work of Willem van de Velde, the Younger (1633–1701; see Barnes 1988, 35). Third, individual details of human figures performing specific tasks have been grouped together in large plates (see, for example, the woman making vermicelli in plate 2.42).

But the majority of plates in our corpus correspond to the typical layout described previously, which became synonymous with the *Encyclopédie* (see plate 2.54, the button-mold maker, as an example): the workers bend to their tasks in the vignette across the

top, with the objects "naturalized" in a human world, while underneath, tools, machines, and materials are presented in what Barthes qualifies as a didactic paradigm (Barthes 1964, 13). The full-page plates can be read in a circular fashion, bottom to top as well as top to bottom, but for the purposes of this book I have concentrated in the main on the vignette section (frequently omitting the lower section in reproduction). These images—where each scene, dense with signification, tells a story—clearly have much in common with realist modes of representation. They feature relatively humble human subjects, as in Dutch genre painting, but they represent them resolutely, without caricature, sexual objectification, or Christian moralizing. Linda Stone-Ferrier highlights how female tasks such as spinning, lace making, or embroidery could create either positive or negative connotations concerning the female worker's character—whether lascivious or chaste—in Dutch paintings and prints (1988, 14). Such is not the case in the corpus I consider here, where the worker is always justified, even dignified by the work itself: see, for example, the plates on embroidery (plates 2.23 and 2.24), or lace making (plate 2.28). The images reproduced here also pay close attention to things, to the raw materials, the products, tools, and machines of workshop life, as in the *Ständebuch* prints; they depict, with seriousness of intent, actions that would not have been considered fit subjects of art, at least not before the nineteenth century: the washing of gut strings (plate 2.55) and the crushing of stone for glassmaking by female counterparts to Courbet's *Stone Breakers* (plate 4.11) are good examples. They reject an "academic" style, with rare exceptions that stand out from the rest of the corpus, as, for example, the elegant figure of a woman carrying paper in a mill, who is represented with the bearing of a dancer (plate 4.4), or the two plates on women in mining-related activities, which are clearly copied from earlier paintings (plates 1.12 and 1.13).

The plates are, in the main, executed by relatively unknown artists whose practice veers toward technical drawing rather than the aesthetics of high art. Engraving as a practice had remained closer to the traditional craft model of apprenticeship and training than painting, where the influence of the Académie Royale de Peinture et de Sculpture had created a more elitist and intellectualized tradition of learning.[30] In the work of the designers and engravers considered in this study, we witness the development of a style based, in large part, on the attempt to apply scientific principles to the analysis of work activities; it originated with Des Billettes' group, as has been shown previously, and was developed through close cooperation between the researchers and writers, on the one hand, and those actually producing the plates on the other, working as a team. Jaoul and Pinault, in their study of the drawings in the Houghton Library, Harvard University, have emphasized how the drive toward "objectivity," using the analogy of the natural sciences—the dominance of geometric perspectives against a neutral background being one example—informed the methodology of Réaumur's designers (1982, 353–55). Pinault has remarked that Louis-Jacques Goussier and J. R. Lucotte, designers who worked for both collections, were also authors of texts for the *Encyclopédie*, "a fact which implies they had a good knowledge of scientific and technical problems," and suggests that they can be seen as moving toward the status of "technical draughtsman" eventually established in the revolutionary period (2002, 167). Proust likewise notes, of the *Encyclopédie*'s group of designers, that the greater part of their overall output was devoted to technical material in the service of the artisanal trades and industry (1962, 31), giving them a distinct profile within the main body of contemporary artist/engravers. However, Proust also draws attention to the individual differences that can be noted, even between the work of these latter two designers, with Lucotte's work tending more toward ornamentation and the picturesque (1973, 71; see, for example, plates 5.1 and 5.2). The *Encyclopédie*, nonetheless, is more consistent in approach, which is not surprising given that the majority of the plates were drawn by a relatively small number of designers and craftsmen under the direction of one chief editor.[31] The *Descriptions*, whose preparation stretched over more than half a century, clearly involved a larger, more disparate group. Their images are occasionally crude or poorly engraved (see plates 2.2, 2.13, and 3.6, for example.)

Some distinctive aspects of the dominant style should be noted, as in these respects the images cannot be expected to faithfully reproduce the conditions of the contemporary workshop and its occupants. Most of the workshops portrayed are highly stylized: huge (dwarfing the human figures), bare, clean, and well lit by large windows, with no evidence of the confusion of materials, food, and drink that would have cluttered real work spaces.[32]

The analysis of the steps in production, and the consequent choice of a series of images to reflect this, increased didactic clarity but reduced any sense of the collaborative nature of much workshop activity: there is a curious lack of communication among the workers, each bent to their individual tasks, which contrasts strongly with earlier genres (Sewell 1986, 270). The workers are only rarely differentiated in appearance or physiognomy: they are mainly young and able-bodied, with singularly little individualization in terms of facial expression. The women's clothes can sometimes help to situate them socially, as in many of the plates on the traditional economy, or images such as that of the *marchande de modes* (plate 2.27), but in the majority of workshop images, the young women wear a standard costume: they are neatly and cleanly dressed in a shift, skirt and bodice, apron, and neck scarf, sometimes with a cross around their neck, or a simple necklace. Instead of the distinctive guild workers, guardians of the skills of their trade, who dominated in other genres of print, these workers have been reduced to minor agents in a cycle of production, elements of "an anonymous and publicly available science" (Sewell 1986, 276). In Koepp's view, the "*Encyclopédie* was an ef-fort to take the knowledge and language of work out of the workers' hands, to decode it, to distill its fundamental principles, to devise a new language of mechanical arts available to the whole society," and this agenda was in many respects repressive (1986, 36 and introduction). As I have already indicated, many aspects of this agenda were already present in the work of the Académie, particularly the imperative to take control of the "secrets" of trade skills away from the artisans themselves.[33] Robert Darnton rightly challenged Roland Barthes' view (in 1964, 11) that the *Encyclopédie* images represent a golden age of artisanal activity: he suggests that, on the contrary, "in stripping artisanal work down to its technological base [. . .] the *Encyclopédie* eliminated a fundamental aspect of its culture" (1979, 242).[34] Thus, Sewell argues, "The plates of the *Encyclopédie* argue for a cultural construction of the capitalist mode of production well in advance of its practical realization" (1986, 279).

Despite these caveats, and accepting that many aspects of a specifically artisanal culture are absent from both sets of plates, the images are still rich enough to provide glimpses of how lives were actually lived.[35] Take the plate depicting a *bouchonnier*'s shop to which Jacques Proust drew attention (1985, 35: plate 5–10): into the empty street the designer has sketched what, for him, must have been a familiar scene: a faceless man and woman dragging their cart and its load through the streets. It can speak volumes to us about the way in which a couple such as this (market workers? street sweepers?) toiled together as a unit to keep a family afloat, too poor to afford an animal to pull their cart. As we study the detail of plate after plate, an accumulation of information comes to the fore despite the limitations of the genre. It is precisely their refusal to be contained by the authority of the written texts or the didactic intentions of their creators (what Barthes called their "resistance to meaning" [1964, 13]) that allows these pictures to communicate a message, with freshness and vivacity, to a modern audience.[36] For example, the several images of women workers with their young children (see plates 1.2, 1.43a, 4.2, 4.8) prefigure, without the sentimentality or the moralizing, the later painting *The Laundress* by Daumier (1863), which has been foregrounded by feminist art historians (see Nochlin 1971, 57). These images speak volumes about the difficult conditions in which women worked and raised children to work alongside them, issues that rarely attracted much comment from the learned authors of the accompanying texts who took child labor for granted.

::

S O M E justification is called for regarding the categories I have chosen for the presentation of this material, and their relative importance within this book. The images grouped under the heading "The Traditional Economy" form a distinct group: in subject matter as well as stylistically (as has already been indicated), they differ from the patterns common to the other sections. The workshop environment is clearly not relevant to these images from the sectors of agriculture, fishing, and mining, where outdoor scenes dominate. All of the other headings in this study group together work activities classed as craft and trade—"Arts et métiers"—under the Old Regime. In the section "Artisanal Trades" I have included a wide range of activities carried out in both the cottage and the workshop environment. The images are presented in two subsets, reflecting the special status attaching to the luxury trades, which were centered in the largest cities, as opposed to the basic trades, which were practiced throughout the country. Under the heading "Manufactories" I

have grouped images reflecting the large, centralized, and often prestigious institutions where significant numbers of workers were brought together, often in rural locations. "Textiles" are given a separate heading; the activities reflected in this section could clearly have been grouped with other artisanal trades, but given the importance of this activity within the contemporary economy, the fact that it was the single biggest area of employment for women, and the large number of images reflecting textile trades in the collections I drew from, it made more sense in terms of balance and coherence to devote a separate heading to this sector. I have provided a list of the plates that will facilitate cross-referencing between sections.

One aim of this book is, clearly, to make the corpus I have established available to a wider audience than heretofore. More important, however, I have tried to decode the images, highlighting the interest they can hold for readers across a range of disciplines. The pictures featuring women generally represent only a small proportion of the plates devoted to any one trade in the original treatises; I have tried to suggest ways in which each image can be interpreted with regard to its immediate pictorial, textual, and historical contexts. I aimed—

in the commentary, analysis, and introduction to each section—to relate each subject to specific issues highlighted in the scholarly literature on women, work, the traditional economy, trades, craft, and manufacture under the *ancien régime,* and I have endeavored to evaluate the ways in which the images complement, contradict, or add to our knowledge of women workers' occupations, roles, and lives in France throughout the lengthy period reflected in this corpus. On the one hand, it is important not to downplay the complexity of the social and cultural contexts of work in France in the period. Sonenscher has underlined how work was a continuous process of negotiation:

> Relationships between master artisans, between masters and journeymen, between men and women, adults and children were grounded upon subtle and complex reciprocities, differences, inequalities and affinities whose existence was both the outcome and the basis of endlessly changing configurations of identity and power. Some rights and obligations were formal; others were not. The division between the two was never absolute and never stable. (1989, 47)

I will have frequent opportunities

to allude to the ambiguities of work situations where specific (local) regulations conflicted with practices reflected in the images. On the other hand, for reasons indicated before, the roles reflected in the plates are often emblematic of the condition of the woman worker across cultures, and, indeed, across time: the role of women as load-bearers in early modern Europe represented in these images (see, for example, plates 4.4, 4.5, and 4.7a) clearly evokes the role of women in parts of the developing world today (see Bradley 1989, 36). Hudson and Lee underline how, despite differences in regional and national social contexts and labor policies, "the urban working experiences of women throughout Europe seem to have had remarkable similarities both in nature and in the impact of long- and short-term variations emanating from changing institutional structures, production methods, domestic ideologies and labor supply conditions" (1990, 10). In the analysis of specific images, I have therefore frequently referred to similar conditions and practices in other European societies, and highlighted issues—such as the shifting parameters of skilled and unskilled work, for example— that have been foregrounded in the research on women and work over the last twenty years, and that have multiple resonances beyond the specific context of France in this period.

The images reproduced here retain their freshness, the power to inform and to mystify, to enthrall and to frustrate. As Barthes noticed, they can bridge time, spilling beyond the cultural, even epistemological, context in which they were created.[37] In so doing, these plates afford us a unique opportunity to encounter the irrepressible women workers of the eighteenth century.

The Traditional Economy

T HAS LONG BEEN recognized that women played a significant role in many aspects of the traditional economy in *ancien régime* France. Evidence of this participation in the three main areas of agriculture, fishing, and mining is offered by the plates in both collections. Agriculture was covered to a certain extent by the *Encyclopédie,* though Diderot and his associates clearly privileged the urban crafts and trades over the agricultural economy. The *Descriptions* did not deal with agriculture, perhaps, in part, because Henri-Louis Duhamel du Monceau, director of the *Descriptions* at a crucial period, was publishing his research in this area separately (1753–61; 1762b). Fishing was covered by both collections, but far more extensively by the Académie than the *Encyclopédie* (Duhamel du Monceau 1769–[1782]), while coal mining was not covered at all in the *Ency-*

clopédie but was treated in great detail in the *Descriptions* (Morand 1768–79). It is important to remember that the relatively minor place of agrarian occupations in these collections does not reflect their importance in the economy and society of the Old Regime: according to Pierre Goubert, 85 percent of the population of France lived and worked in the countryside in the late seventeenth and early eighteenth centuries (Goubert 1973, 53; also Sewell 1980, 16) and depended mainly on such activities. The workers reflected in the images in this section fall more under the social category of *gens de bras,* their activities being regarded as base manual labor, than *gens de métier,* the tradespeople reflected elsewhere in this book whose manual labor "was raised by the application of intelligence to the level of art" (Sewell 1980, 21–23). They did whatever work they could to get by: the same family members could be involved, at the same time, or at different times of the year, in different types of activity, such as agriculture and mining.

The plates on agriculture (dating from the late 1750s or early 1760s), though few in number, evoke the age-old occupations of women across many European societies. Women's roles in the traditional economy of pre-revolutionary France, as elsewhere, were far removed from those deemed appropriate in developed western societies today. The ideological construction of women as weak, inferior in physical strength, and more vulnerable than men developed over the course of the eighteenth century, influenced by Jean-Jacques Rousseau among others (see Coffin 1996, 39–40). The often-quoted comment by Arthur Pringle in 1794, on a visit to Westmoreland in England, on the incongruity of seeing a girl with "elegant features and nicely-proportioned limbs" sweating as she shovels dung (qtd. Hill 1984, 186) indicates a shift in gender ideology on the part of this privileged observer; but there is much evidence that such ideas did not significantly affect the rural laboring masses until a later period (see Bradley 1989, 79–83). In fact,

many activities in the traditional rural economy were interchangeable between men and women; it was taken for granted throughout the agricultural areas of Europe that women's contribution to the domestic economy would include physically demanding work in the fields, especially at peak periods of activity, such as sowing and harvesting. Women only rarely got to work with horses, which were strongly identified with men (81): as Segalen has shown, horses were an important sign of relative social and economic status, distinguishing the farmer, for example, from the sharecropper or day laborer (1983, 95). But women worked *like* horses, especially in poorer households with few beasts, often doing the fetching and carrying of farm work, bringing water to the fields, carrying heavy milk pails, or bringing produce to market (see Clark 1992, 62; Hill 1984, 194–95). The need for physical strength as the primary quality in a peasant wife is reflected in many French proverbs, such as "*Le corps vaut plus que le dot*" ("The body's worth more than the dowry"), from Gascony (Segalen 1983, 108), and such strength was likewise highly esteemed in mining women, as will be shown later in this chapter.

Moreover, the sexual division

of labor rarely relied purely on physical capacity, but customary practices and ideas about gender and appropriate roles were instrumental in delineating tasks as male work and female work, high and low status (Simonton 1998, 30–36; Wiesner 2000, 103–6; Segalen 1983, 96–111). Although practices varied greatly from region to region, there were nonetheless trends common to much of Europe, such as the identification of men with the scythe and women with the sickle (see plate 1.2; see Wiesner, 86). Hudson and Lee have underlined how low-status fieldwork seems to have been predominantly in female hands over many centuries, despite changes in the structure of the economy and the market environment, and they highlight the fact that "this cannot be conveniently explained by the need for women's work to be fitted in around household and maternal responsibilities or by being physically undemanding" (1990, 5).

Olwen Hufton has shown how in France in this period, "the natural economy of the working classes was a family economy dependent upon the efforts of each individual member and one in which the role of both partners was equally crucial" (1975, 1). The women involved in the many activities associated with the production of food, glimpsed only briefly in these plates, belonged to several categories. Wives of small landholders would have been routinely responsible for hoeing and weeding, the gathering of grass and weeds for animal fodder, dairying, carrying produce to and from the market, and ferrying water to high terraces, as well as caring for children, doing the laundry, and providing household meals (generally—and necessarily—simple affairs). At harvest time, they would be called on to labor in the fields, as well as to carry refreshment to those working out on the land (see plate 1.2). Vardi has indicated that in large areas of France, gleaning by harvester families (wives and children) for wages in kind formed part of the laborer's contract (1993a, 1441). Unmarried daughters or sisters would have been assigned similar tasks in the dairy, the yard, or the field.

Larger establishments employed farm servants to undertake the most taxing work, and many of the women in our pictures might have fallen into this category: young country girls knew they would require a dowry to found a family of their own, the best option in life available to them. They typically left home at twelve years of age (two years younger than their brothers) and

were fortunate if they gained employment as a *servante* on a farm in their own area, the alternative being work in a more alien town. A girl needed to work for at least twelve years to build a dowry sufficient to provide the most basic essentials of furniture for a marital home. She was literally "*bonne à tout faire,*" a maid of all work, with the distinction blurred between the roles of domestic servant and servant in husbandry (see Hill 1984, 178–79 and 229 regarding similar patterns in Great Britain); and where the household was involved in cottage industry, she would also be required to turn her hand to this work. Frequently, the *servantes* were employed only on a year-to-year basis and would not be paid until they left the placement (see Hufton 1975, 3–4; and 1993, 16–17). The wives of farm laborers were also hired for heavy work but were paid far less than the men; and where the day's food was part of the wage bargain, as was often the case, this further disadvantaged women, as they were deemed to need less food than men, especially protein foods. The result was that these women, doing physical labor, were chronically undernourished and debilitated (Wiesner 2000, 108–9; Clark 1992, 67–73). As will be seen later on, the assump-

tion that women needed less nourishment carried over into the world of manufacture. The poorest women *journalières,* who hired out their labor on a daily basis whenever they could, were reduced to begging for part of the year when no employment was available (Collins 1989, 450).

The French dairymaid illustrated in plate 1.3 would undoubtedly have been such a hired servant (albeit in an exceptionally fine placement); the dairymaid would normally have been expected to rise at 3 A.M. or 4 A.M. to go to the pastures and milk the cows and to carry heavy milk pails back to the dairy before the actual making of butter or cheese began. Having churned until midafternoon, she would have to repeat the whole process again, working well into the evening (see Pinchbeck 1969, 10–16). In the early nineteenth century, reports on women in agriculture in England noted that dairy women suffered the most from overexertion and the consequences of lifting heavy objects; one observer in Cheshire in 1808 reported that "the labor of turning and cleaning cheese is performed almost universally by women; and that in large dairies, where the cheeses are upwards of 140 pounds each upon an average" (Holland 1808, 282, qtd. Pinchbeck 1969, 14).

The dairymaid was not just expected to be physically robust, however: hers was one of the most skilled occupations on the farm, as is indicated in the text originally accompanying our image (see commentary on plate 1.3). Thus, experienced and reliable dairymaids were in demand where the wife could not oversee all operations herself, and they commanded the highest wages for rural women (see Simonton 1998, 122–23). Shahar underlines how, in the medieval period, manuals on estate management listed the traits required of a dairy overseer as "cleanliness, responsibility, honesty, scrupulous care of the instruments"; yet the records of English manor estates show that the wage of the female dairy overseer corresponded to the lowest wage paid to men, that of swineherds or oxherds (Shahar 1983, 242).

Martine Segalen, whose research emphasizes the interchangeability of tasks and cooperation between peasant men and women in France, has raised the question as to why observers so often overlooked the participation of women in agricultural work, artists such as Jean-François Millet being the notable exceptions. She concludes that outsiders tended to concentrate exclusively on the technology of agricultural operations and neglected to ask who did what. Moreover, Segalen continues, "Female participation in work in the fields was so much taken for granted in the rural environment that it was hardly mentioned; it was engraved upon the peasant mentality, which ceased to be aware of it: women no more mentioned their occasional help in tilling or sowing than they did the care they devoted to their children" (1983, 99). The majority of images from the *Encyclopédie* relating to this sector do indeed concentrate on agricultural technologies, with just a small minority of the images, all of which are reproduced here, allowing a glimpse of the women's world. In some, women feature only incidentally: in the image on wheat harvesting (plate 1.2), for example, we see, as part of the composition, a woman who is slaking her thirst, having presumably carried the heavy containers of food and drink (lying on the ground) to the other workers. She is accompanied by her child and no doubt also contributes to the harvesting activities. Such women's tasks go unremarked in the text.

Another traditional sector in which many women worked across Europe, right into the nineteenth century, was mining; this work could fall within the domestic economy, with the women of the family working in a family-owned concern. Alternatively, women worked as a hired team with their husbands (Vanja 1993, 102). In her study of mining, Vanja finds no evidence of women working in this sector in France (with the exception of Alsace), and the specific evidence of our images relates rather to the independent principality of Liège. The writer of the *Art d'exploiter les mines de charbon de terre* (1768–79), Jean-François Morand, a member of the Académie and a professor of anatomy at the Collège de France, had observed workers in research visits he made to the coal mines of Liège, Newcastle, and Manchester. He took care to locate the illustrations precisely by including geographic reference points in the district of Liège and by describing the specialist vocabulary used within the area to refer to tools, functions, and the people who performed them. This knowledgeable researcher, however, failed to indicate in his commentary whether the situation in the smaller mines in France (mainly in the area of the Massif Central) differed in any considerable way from the practices he described for Liège; though his descriptions were intended to have a general application within the French economy, the extent and nature of women's participation in mining remains an open question, needing further research.

Though women, as part of a household enterprise, would seem to have participated equally in mining tasks in medieval Europe (Pinchbeck 1969, 240; Vanja 1993, 101–3), by the eighteenth century, women in some countries were confined to the surface work, where they did much of the heavy drawing and carrying. Great Britain, where women are known to have worked down in the pits, was an exception (Bradley 1989, 105–8; Pinchbeck 1969, 240–43). That women were doing the surface work is borne out in the main by our images, though there is some suggestion in Morand's text that women also drew the carts from belowground (see my commentary on plate 1.8). Although Morand clearly states that women were banned from working underground in contemporary Liège, other evidence shows that women were doing this work in the mines of Liège in the nineteenth century— over four thousand of them at the time of the Belgian coal strike of 1886—and continued to do so until their exclusion in 1911 (John 1984, 224). John notes that sketches by Constantin Meunier in the 1880s showed the pit-women dressed in mid-calf-length

trousers (143), while women doing the surface work were shown by Van Gogh wearing long blue skirts (183). Were Morand's observations colored by what he knew of the regulations, and did he fail to see a different reality? Humphries (1984) has argued that the employment of women belowground in mines was a late development, even in England, and was a product of the onset of capitalism, but concrete evidence is lacking for both countries, and more research is required on these practices. The family-based nature of work organization in the mines, persisting into the late nineteenth century, is widely recognized, even by Humphries (6 passim); by its nature, it was difficult for an outsider to document and observe. For this reason, the 1842 Children's Employment Commission Reports on Mines for Great Britain (Parliamentary Papers) are an exceptional source of information; they contain the comments of the workers themselves (see John 1984; Humphries 1984) and can add to our understanding of the practices seen in our plates.

The most striking feature of much of the surface work undertaken by the women is its physically demanding nature, requiring great strength and stamina (see Bradley 1989, 106–7). The work

of the windlass women, shown in plate 1.7 (detail), involved bringing both baskets of coal and the workers themselves to the surface. Though the text of the *Descriptions* does not speak much about the volume of work that the windlass-women handled, evidence from Wales in the Commission Report of 1842 described one woman who wound four hundred loads of between one and a half and four hundredweight daily; another sixteen-year-old windlass woman is quoted in the same report explaining that men did not like winding, as it was "too hard work for them."[38] There is little to suggest that this work was any less onerous in the previous century.

Two images illustrate the technique used by women of carrying great hods on their shoulders, which originates from a much earlier period and was common throughout Europe. The 1842 commission reported that women in Scotland, aged from six to sixty, were carrying up to two, two and a half, or even three hundredweight of coal on their backs, the commissioner remarking, "Such is the weight carried that it frequently takes two men to lift the burden upon their backs" (qtd. Pinchbeck 1969, 252). The Scottish mining women carried these loads from belowground, up ladders and steep inclines, as shown in an illustration that accompanied the 1842 commission report (reproduced in Burton 1976, 22). Such practices also operated in the previous century, as one remark from the pen of Archibald Cochrane, ninth Earl of Dundonald, published in 1793, bears witness. Exceptionally for the times, Dundonald was concerned about working conditions in the coal mines on his Perthshire estate at Culross Abbey, where he sought to banish "the *barbarous*, and *ultimately expensive method* of converting the Colliers wives and daughters into *beasts of burthen*, and causing them to carry Coals to the pit bottom or to bank *on their backs*" [italics in original]; aware of the efficiencies gained from the innovations of the Birmingham industrialist Matthew Boulton (the partner of James Watt), he advocated "the adoption of water and Steam Engines to wind up the Coal from the pits" (1793, 55). This coal-bearing can be compared to the transporting of large hods of fish, as we shall see (plates 1.39, 1.44b), but the weights carried in the mines were even greater. Vanja quotes evidence from Hallstatt in Germany of women carrying rock salt on their backs in the same type of baskets, weighing about eighty pounds, right up to the end of the

nineteenth century when young men began to move it on sleds (1993, 111n31). With reference to the colliery women of Liège, Morand tells us, "They are famous in all the surrounding area for their occupation, which involves bearing the most enormous burdens, and withstanding the greatest exhaustion" (*L'Art d'exploiter les mines*, 2nde partie, 212); to further illustrate this, he quotes a Latin poem he found on a (then) old map of Liège:

Carbones trudit vel portat bajula qualo,
Gratus & est illi nocte dieque labor.
Fæmina majori non stringitur ulla labore,
Quam quæ Legiacis bajula nata locis.[39]

The reference to working "day and night" is consistent with what we know of the long workdays—often more than fourteen hours—that were the norm in both rural and urban environments.[40] We cannot know how these women negotiated such conditions within the overall context of their lives, but we can counterpoint this praise with the complaint of one Scottish woman coal-bearer to a commissioner at the later period: "It is only horse work and ruins the women; it crushes their haunches, bends their ankles and

makes them old women at forty. Women so soon get weak that they are forced to take the little ones down to relieve them" (qtd. Bradley 1989, 108; see also Pinchbeck 1969, 261). Given that many women continued this work right through pregnancy, it is little wonder that they complained of a high rate of miscarriage and stillbirth. Carrying heavy loads was known to be a cause, and at times a means of abortion, from Roman times through the Middle Ages (in translations of the Islamic medical texts of Avicenna, for example: Shahar 1983, 123), but such medical knowledge would have had little relevance to, or impact on, the lives of ordinary mining women.

The women pictured in our plates may belong to the same family as the men digging belowground, in which case they were unlikely to be remunerated separately but would simply have shared the husband's wage (Vanja 1993, 103; Pinchbeck 1969, 257–58); in cases where the women were separate wage laborers, research suggests they probably earned little more than half the man's wage for the day's work, and, as in agriculture, where the day's food was part of the wage bargain, the women were badly served (see Vanja, 113; Pinchbeck, 251; Wiesner 2000, 108–9;

Clark 1992, 60–68). A woman bearer in Scotland was paid only 8d. for a ten-hour day as late as 1842, scarcely enough to feed even herself, though the same work was somewhat better paid in other parts of Britain, and it must be remembered that other occupations for women received even less remuneration (Pinchbeck, 253–57). These women's earnings were vital to the survival of their families.

For that reason, the Mines Act, which banned women from underground work in Britain in 1842, was a double-edged sword: if it gave them some protection, it also seriously reduced their earning opportunities. Though the work (especially belowground) was grueling and the conditions arguably unfit for any workers, Humphries suggests that it was not so much the hard and burdensome nature of the work that motivated the Commission of 1842 and subsequent debates but its "immoral" and "unfeminine" aspects (1984, 24–26). The reports had shown that the women underground sometimes worked almost naked, or bare-breasted, "feminine" clothing being a handicap to their movement: alternatively, they wore trousers, which made them indistinguishable from men (Bradley 1989, 110–12). This closely echoes our evidence of

fishing women wearing breeches a century earlier (see plates 1.29 and 1.53). It may well be that in reality, working women donned a "male" style of clothing appropriate to certain types of work on a more widespread basis than we know of, because artists balked at illustrating such occurrences (see pp. 222–23).

In any event, we have seen that the other types of employment left open to the women, for example in surface mine work, were not necessarily less physically exhausting; and it was not consideration for the women's health that eventually led to the disappearance of these roles. The gradual exclusion of women from surface work resulted from the opposition of male craft organizations anxious to exclude cheap labor, together with the evolving campaign for the "family wage" and the development of labor-saving technologies such as railway tracks to carry the coal from the pits (Vanja 1993, 101 and 117; Bradley 1989, 111–13). Crucially, however, the case of mining paved the way for other redefinitions of what was "fit" work for women.

The plates concerning fishing—not as a sport, but as a livelihood—are of particular interest. Most of our sample is drawn from the Académie collection; a num-

ber of these pictures are almost identical to the better-known plates in the *Encyclopédie;* this is indicated in the individual commentaries. Madeleine Pinault (1987) has studied the genesis of these images, which in this case is less a matter of plagiarism from one collection to the other than one of a shared origin. Le Masson du Parc, Commissaire de la Marine, carried out detailed inspections of the fisheries along the coast of France from 1723 to 1737, recording his findings meticulously in a series of reports (published by Dardel, 1941a and b). In addition to these reports, and *Mémoires,* which he drafted for an unfinished *Histoire des pêches,* Le Masson had detailed drawings made and bound into albums. Most of these drawings are now missing or in private hands, but one miscellaneous volume, preserved in the Bibliothèque Nationale, Paris (Dépt. des Estampes, ms. Ke 82), allows us to see the close relationship between the original drawings, and the plates published more than thirty years later[41]: for example, plate 1.18 in this volume, from the *Encyclopédie,* is a direct copy of one of these drawings. I have included one drawing from the Bibliothèque Nationale album that does not feature in either of the collections, and that shows women forking kelp into heaps (plate 1.25). Diderot apparently had access to these manuscripts—he declared in a letter that he had kept his designer, Goussier, working at his home for three months on "*les ms du Roi sur les pêches,*" among other materials[42]—and they formed the basis for the plates and the alphabetical articles relating to fishing. Henri-Louis Duhamel du Monceau, the esteemed academician and author of the Académie's *Traité général des pesches* (1769–82) for the collection of *Descriptions,* clearly had access to the same material; not only the texts, but also the images in the two collections are very close. Pinault has suggested that the views reproduced are more picturesque than real, owing to the fact that they were probably executed by the designer on the basis of Le Masson's reports rather than sketched from life (1987, 349); as I have commented previously, many of these images are strongly reminiscent of the marine scenes in Dutch drawing and painting of the seventeenth century, and this stylistic influence must clearly have had an impact on the manner in which the subject matter was recorded. Nonetheless, the detail offered by the images suggests an originator familiar with the workings of coastal communities, and it is quite possible that rough

sketches were furnished to the designer by one of the members of Le Masson's team. The certainty that the information on which these plates were based was recorded on field trips to very specific locations, by eyewitnesses, undoubtedly underpins their value as historical and anthropological documents; images such as that of the women fishing from platforms constructed above the sea, supported on stilts (plate 1.27), might appear fanciful were it not for this assurance that they are based on firsthand and reliable evidence. The pictures presented in this volume offer a comprehensive view of women's contribution to fishing in French coastal communities, a contribution very likely replicated along other European coasts. It should be remembered that many of the fishing families were also involved in other activities, such as agriculture and mining, and could not survive on fishing alone, a fact to which Le Masson's reports bear witness.

As was the case in agriculture and mining, the work women undertook in fishing required great physical strength and stamina: carrying massive weights on their heads or backs, as women still do today in the developing world; digging and scraping in the sand for bait; fishing under rocks with

heavy, handheld nets for shrimp and other crustaceans, the water up to their waists. They were also skilled in baiting and preparing longlines, in mending nets, and in salting and smoking the catch. A study of fishing communities in Great Britain in the twentieth century shows the remarkable persistence of gender roles, and the specific activities of women in fishing, right up to the modern period: the major division between women working on the shore and men working in boats was largely consistent across most European countries, and across the centuries (Thompson, Wailey, and Lummis 1983, 173). Thompson, Wailey, and Lummis remark that "men [. . .] have normally relied on women both in preparing for the fishery and still more for disposing of the catch afterwards" (167); while we will see that this was true of France in the eighteenth century, it will also be shown that women were involved in many types of shore fishing, and sometimes even went out in small boats. Thompson, Wailey, and Lummis reproduce some photographs from the late nineteenth century that show a striking similarity to the plates in this collection: in one, a woman from Whitby, in a ragged apron, carries the fishing lines on her head from the shore to her home, where she will mend and bait them (174: photo 1). In others, we see women baiting lines inside or outside their cottages (175: photo 6); or Scottish herring girls, who performed the work of gutting, salting, smoking, or packing, very much like their counterparts in the eighteenth century (174: 25, 26).

Lespinasse, in his codification of trade guilds, points out that a community of fish merchants and sellers existed in the medieval period, and women were included among its officers. From 1543, however, royal offices were created that superseded the community ones, and these offices appear to have been open only to men (1886, 1: 408). Despite the fact that they were excluded from the exercise of hierarchical power and the control of major capital, women continued to play multiple roles in the portering and selling of fish, and our images bear witness to the extent and nature of this work.

In general, the texts of the Académie on fishing are more detailed, and more precise concerning location, than those of the *Encyclopédie*; they frequently mention the contribution of women and children in specific types of activity, sometimes offering unique anthropological information concerning, for example, the manner of their dress. Whereas the plates in the *Ency-*

clopédie do show women and children at work, the texts often fail to mention them[43], and in at least one instance, Goussier—no doubt working under time pressure—misinterpreted an original drawing, correctly transposed and described in the Académie version (see Sheridan 2003b, 173). This confusing intertextuality underscores how careful we must be in evaluating these images, and the greater reliability of the work of the Academicians over that of Diderot's team, which was more market-driven and pressured for time.

This set of plates on fishing diverges strikingly from that of the majority of the plates in both collections on other areas of the economy, where no overt poverty is illustrated: in the fishing images, however, the women are frequently shown with ragged skirts, working barefoot. As previously mentioned, we also find women represented as adopting a male style of dress to facilitate their work: they are wearing breeches or have tucked up their skirts between their legs. These images seem to bring us closer to the realities of life in this period than other visual genres or written texts.

The combined effect of these plates detailing the demanding and physically arduous work of women across many areas of the

traditional economy throughout the eighteenth century strongly counteracts the notion that female roles were determined by either biological character or maternal function (see Hudson and Lee 1990, 9). As has already been noted, the woman depicted working with a sickle in the fields might well be the same woman who, at another time of the year, rakes kelp along the shore, carries coal from the pit, spins wool or flax for her family's clothes, or undertakes some other type of domestic production (poultry, garden crops, butter) for cash sale (Collins 1989, 441). Women were purveyors of multiple services within what Hufton has described as "an economy of expedients" (1984, 363). And we should remember that, as Collins showed for the seventeenth century, despite severe institutional restrictions, some 10 to 20 percent of all French enterprises, including farms, were run by women, with wives increasingly cosigning leases after 1650 (Collins 1989, 439).

:: AGRICULTURE

Plate 1.1 shows the work of plowing and sowing, with a woman (*la semeuse*; at the lower right in the plate)—most probably the wife of the man who handles the plow (lower left), with whom she forms a team—pushing the seeding ma-

Pl. 1.1. Plowing and sowing. *Ency. Planches,* vol. 1. "Agriculture, Labourage; Pl. I." S27.

chine along the furrow where he has just passed with his team of two horses. As he plows the next furrow (along the dotted line illustrated), the "ears" of the plow will throw the soil sideways to cover the seeds she has sown with accuracy. The type of plow illustrated here was invented by the English reformer Jethro Tull and was not common in France, where oxen would have been the more likely draft beasts: the efforts of this couple reflect the aspirations of the Encyclopedists to show technological progress in agriculture rather than the common practice of the French peasantry. The seeding machine in plate 1.1 was invented in France by the abbé Soumille; the physically demanding task of pushing it through the furrows is unintentionally highlighted by the article

"Semoir," which describes (and illustrates in three further plates) not the machine this woman is using but one approved by the Académie des Sciences, ascribed to Tull and Duhamel, and pulled by a horse (*Ency. Planches,* vol. 1: "Agriculture, Semoirs"). Even though all four plates were probably from the hand of the same engraver (Defehrt), the incongruity between the images—horse-drawn seeder versus woman-propelled seeder—stood without comment by the editor. Working with horses, like plowing, was gender-identified with men across much of Europe.

In the first of two rather romanticized images (plate 1.2) that devote as much space to dramatic clouds as to the illustration of the work, we see (on the left) men using the scythe to cut hay, which women then rake into small stacks. In the illustration of harvesting (on the right) women are working with the sickle, with which there was a strong female gender identification: the textual article of that name (*Ency.:* "Faucille") refers exclusively to reapers in the feminine ("*moissonneuses*"); other women bind the wheat into sheaves ready for transporting. We see one woman slaking her thirst, her child beside her:[44] women combined working in the fields at peak periods with responsibility for the care of the

children, and the supply of basic provisions such as the bread and wine (or water?) illustrated in both images. The scythe, identified with men, came into use for mowing the primary grains, wheat and rye, during the early eighteenth century and increasingly took over from the sickle (Roberts 1979, 20; Simonton 1998, 33–35; Snell 1985, 61–62); nonetheless, Vardi emphasizes that well into the nineteenth century, many farmers continued to prefer the sickle for the wheat harvest because it caused less damage and loss to the crop (1993a, 1429). A photograph from the first half of the twentieth century, reproduced by Martine Segalen, shows men in the Beauce region harvesting grain with the scythe while women collect the sheaves with the sickle, underlining how long-lived the gender identification with tool and task remained (Segalen 1983, 101). The raking of the hay or the cutting and binding of sheaves shown in these images could objectively be read as equally demanding of strength as cutting with the scythe, but the status of the scytheman came to be construed as superior partly on the basis of an argument that it required greater upper body strength than the sickle (Wiesner 2000, 106). Such status was, of course, associated with higher

pay, as women were pushed into less well-paid jobs as followers and rakers (Roberts 1979, 17; Vardi 1993a, 1430).

The *Encyclopédie* plate on butter-making (plate 1.3) shows, rather bizarrely, the dairy of one of the great royal houses, which, as the editor tacitly admits, is scarcely typical of farm practices throughout France. In the middle of the large, imposing, splendidly equipped, and utterly sterile room sits a lone dairymaid churning, reminding us that this area of the agricultural economy was reserved to women: there was a strong nexus of associations, both mythological and ideological, connecting women to the production of milk, butter, and cheese (Simonton 1998, 31). The dairymaid in this image is shown using a conventional churn, although the author considers the Flemish butter churn (shown in front of the window on the right) to be superior. There is no sign in this image of the products that might have been stored on shelves, although in front of the window on the left is a "cage" on which the fresh cheeses are placed to let them drain into the sink. The lonely little dairymaid is dwarfed within these surroundings, and robbed of life: the static image gives no sense of the physical effort involved in churning (in contrast to Millet's painting, done a

Pl. 1.2. Haymaking and harvesting. *Ency. Planches,* vol. 1. "Agriculture, façon des foins, et moisson." S35.

Pl. 1.3. Dairymaid churning. *Ency. Planches,* vol. 1. "OEconomie rustique: Laiterie." S106.

Pl. 1.4. Hemp preparation. *Ency. Planches,* vol. 1. "OEconomie rustique, culture et travail du chanvre; Pl. I." S58.

century later, of a peasant woman churning: *La Baratteuse,* reproduced in *Paysages* 1994, 213). However, the relative size of the receptacles on the benches (although the perspective is rather dubious) gives us some indication of the kind of weights this young woman would be required to lift. The brief comment devoted to this relatively skilled and demanding activity in the *Encyclopédie* article "Laiterie" concentrates on hygiene: the dairy must be kept scrupulously clean and therefore should be in the charge of "a female servant who is intelligent and loves cleanliness." So this young woman is intended to be a model worker, not just strong but clever and clean as well, mis-

tress of a rationalized, sterilized, "enlightened" dairy.

Hemp was prepared in rural workshops where, typically, the whole family could be involved. The legend to image 1.4 asks the viewer to suppose that "the back wall has been knocked" away to allow us a view of earlier stages in the preparation. A young girl at the right corner is stripping the bark from the stem; the text remarks that in large families, the children could keep up with this task when not busy with other occupations, or while tending animals. Smaller families relied on an alternative method of drying the hemp in an oven and then crushing the plants to remove the bark, which is being performed by the

man at the table in the center of the plate. The "tanning" oven had to be separate from the main dwelling because of the highly combustible nature of the material, and might be of very crude construction, or simply a natural rock outcrop. The oven in the background on the left was tended by "an attentive woman" whose job was to feed all areas of the fire regularly with just enough waste hemp stalks (*chènevottes*) to dry the material without setting it on fire; she also had to turn the hemp to dry it evenly, removing and replacing it when ready. These ovens were open to the elements, and the preparation of the hemp was generally undertaken when the weather was frosty and the

Pl. 1.5. Cotton industry, West Indian colonies. *Ency. Planches,* vol. 1. "OEconomie rustique, culture et arsonnage du coton." S60.

farmer could not work the land; but working in these conditions was perhaps preferable to being in the workshop, where, as the text underlines, the workers' lungs were damaged by the hemp dust (*Ency.:* "Chanvre").

Plate 1.5 is one of several images purporting to illustrate life in France's West Indian colonies: Guadeloupe and Santo Domingo supplied the cotton industry of Rouen and Troyes, and cotton was grown here on shrublike perennial plants. This romanticized image owes as much to the art and literature of the period as to the more hard-nosed economic concerns of some of the *Encyclopédie* texts: there, slavery is

presented as "*indispensable*" for the continued development of commerce in cotton, sugar, and other colonial products, and the hardships imposed on slaves are described in an unapologetic manner: "Slaves are chattel" ("Esclave"); "their [owners] punish them when they are found wanting, and these grown men submit to their own kind with great resignation" ("Negres").[45] Here the "*négresse*" is milling the cotton bolls—gathered and picked over by her male companions—to remove the seeds from them; slave women also milled the sugar cane ("Negres"). She is thoughtfully shaded from the sun by the overhang and the exotic

coconut palms. Her costume is of an unlikely design from a realistic point of view, and it might be ascribed alternatively to the exoticist fantasies of the illustrator (it was unusual for a woman's exposed leg to be shown in this genre of print), or to the opposite impulse of modesty, and even some element of utopianism, given that the conditions of slavery were well known in France. Almost two decades later, in a rapidly changing intellectual climate, Diderot would follow the lead of Helvétius, Voltaire, and Bernardin de Saint Pierre in denouncing slavery.[46] In his revisions of the abbé Raynal's influential *Histoire des deux Indes* (1781),

Pl. 1.6. Turf-cutting. *Encyclopédie méthodique. Recueil de planches; 2ème division des arts et métiers,* vol. 4. "Tourbier." ©
Bibliothèque Sainte Geneviève, Paris. Photo N. Boutros.

he laments: "Even imaginary mis-
fortunes draw tears from us in the
silence of our libraries, and especially in the theatre. Only the
deadly destiny of the misfortunate
negroes fails to interest us. They
are tyrannized, mutilated, burnt,
stabbed, and we hear about this
coolly, with no emotion. The tor-
ments of a people to whom we
owe our delights never touch our
hearts." (Raynal 1781, 3: 177;
qtd. Benot 1981, 209).

The final image (plate 1.6) in
this section is closely linked to
those in the next section on mining, as it describes the activity of
turf cutting in a bog in northern
France. Turf was used both as a
fuel for domestic heating and in

ironworks and the mining industry. Two images newly commissioned for the *Encyclopédie
méthodique* show how the turf was
produced by hand cutting and
through the use of a mechanical
scoop. Areas of bog were drained
by a pumping system based on the
Archimedean screw. In this activity, as in mining, women were involved in transporting and stacking the turf as it dried. They used
a special type of barrow, one
closely related to that used for the
transport of coal in mining areas
(see plate 1.9). In the traditional
economy, whole families participated in such seasonal activity.

::

MINING

Plate 1.7 shows a mine near the
city of Liège; it was intended to illustrate the nature of the soil, but
it incidentally gives a good representation of the most common
form of gender relationships in
mining. The man works down the
shaft digging the coal; two
women (called *trairesses*) turn a
windlass to let down the bucket
and raise the coal—a physically
demanding task that was gradually taken over by the horse
whims. Christina Vanja, in her research on mining women in Europe (1993, 109), found little evidence of women performing this

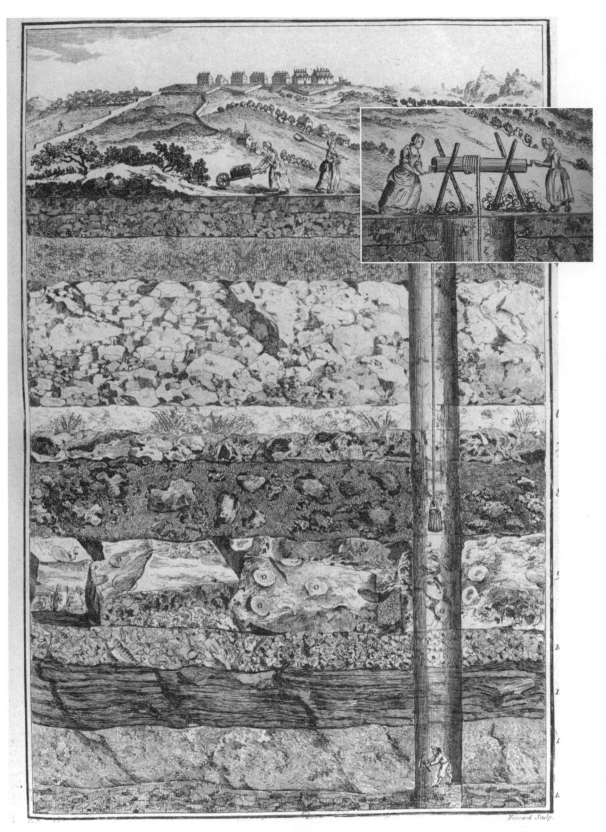

Pl. 1.7 and detail. Windlass women. Morand, *L'Art d'exploiter les mines, 1ère partie*, Pl. II. Designed by Carême, engraved by Fessard.

Pl. 1.8. Sleds for transporting coal. Morand, *L'Art d'exploiter les mines*, 2nde partie, Pl. VIII. Des. Galhausen, eng. Fessard.

Pl. 1.9. Barrow-woman. Morand, *L'Art d'exploiter les mines*, 2nde partie, Pl. XV. Des. Galhausen, eng. Fessard.

role but speculated that it might well have been common in small operations like the one illustrated in plate 1.7; however, the 1842 commission report on Wales showed that "windlass-women" were common there (Bradley 1989, 106–7). John records that in Pembrokeshire in 1842 men refused to do the windlass work as they found it too hard, and left it to young girls (1984, 40). Children as young as nine pulled sleds (known as *slypes* in Scotland: John 1984, 40) through the underground galleries (Morand 1768, 209–11), and with some types of shaft, the women used a hooked implement (*rayetray*), illustrated in plate 1.8, to drag the laden wooden-framed sleds up onto the ground (228). The image of the woman with a large shovel on her shoulder, and another with a full barrow, indicate how the coal is transferred to the barrows and then transported to depots. In a manner unusual for these images, the angle of the windlass-women's bodies indicates the physical effort involved in the work.

The author underlines how

this surface transporting of coal was reserved to women in Liège, as they were forbidden to work belowground. The women given these jobs, variously called *rakoyeux* (perhaps from the verb *recueillir,* meaning to collect), *berwettresses, monresses,* or *meneuses,* had mothers or fathers who had also been employed in mine work (Morand, 212). The women pushed the heavy barrows, of varying designs, along tracks laid from the pithead to the store (as illustrated in plate 1.9), but also across uneven ground, often for distances of up to two kilometers (212). Woodcuts dating from the sixteenth century similarly show women transporting ore at a stamping works in Alsace and highlight how this type of work has been done by women since the middle ages (see Vanja 1993, 105).

Plate 1.10 illustrates how small mines were integrated with

Pl. 1.10 and detail. Hod carriers: *botteresses.* Morand, *L'Art d'exploiter les mines,* 2nde partie, Pl. XVII. Des. Galhausen, eng. Fessard. A10.10.15F (v. 7), Houghton Library, Harvard College Library.

Pl. 1.11. Hod carriers: *botteresses.* Morand, *L'Art d'exploiter les mines,* 2nde partie, Pl. LVI, no. 2. Eng. Fessard. A10.10.15F (v. 15), Houghton Library, Harvard College Library.

the rural economy, mining being carried on side by side with farming activities. This image shows the work of the women called *botteresses,* who used a very ancient method of carrying coal in baskets or hods on their backs; these baskets (*bots*), very similar to those used for carrying fish, could contain a vast weight, and we can see how women were competing with the horse in this kind of heavy carrying. Indeed Vanja mentions the case of a miner in Germany in 1870 who complained that, with the death of his wife, who transported ore to the city, he lost his horse (1993, 103). Our image shows how the women used a walking stick to help propel themselves forward against the weight of the pack, which can be seen in greater detail in plate 1.11. Their strength is evoked in the text, with the author extolling their abilities (see p. 26).

Plates 1.12 and 1.13 are engravings of exceptionally good artistic quality in comparison with the rest of this collection;

they are almost certainly copies of preexisting paintings (see Vanja 1993, 105) and illustrate the preparation of the poorer-quality coal and dust for heating purposes, work again reserved for women. In plate 1.12, with the Château de Warsutée featured in the background, we see the women shovelling the coal to separate it according to quality and to remove any stones or other imperfections; the women with the barrows remove the larger coal for sale or delivery to merchants. The separation is also accomplished by mashing or stamping the coal by foot, as we see in the foreground. This image is unusual in the overall corpus for its emphasis on movement and a sense of community and cooperation between the women, who are represented almost as dancers: it contrasts starkly with the vignettes in the *Encyclopédie,* where the workers are most often represented as engrossed in their individual tasks. Plate 1.13 is notable for the way

in which it indicates the physical effort being expended in the preparation of round briquettes made from the coal slack and dust, separated out and mixed with loam. As early as the 1550s, Agricola, in his *De re metallica* (367–68), described this process as work for women. The workers in the upper part of the image use molds, which they wet in the vat of water, to form the round briquettes, while the women in the lower part of the picture are shaping their briquettes by hand, a method the author regards as inferior (Morand 1768–79, 1345). Of note is the cooperative effort demonstrated as one woman loads up the basket for another who is seated and will presumably have to be hauled to her feet to carry the load. The ragged ends of the skirts and bodices differentiate this image— like those on fishing, to appear later in this chapter—from the majority of the plates in our corpus, from which overt poverty has been banished.

Pl. 1.12. Sorting coal. Morand, *L'Art d'exploiter les mines*, 2nde partie, Pl. LVI, no. 1. Eng. Fessard. A10.10.15F (v. 15), Houghton Library, Harvard College Library.

Pl. 1.13. Making briquettes. Morand, *L'Art d'exploiter les mines*, 2nde partie, Pl. LVI, no. 2. Eng. Fessard. A10.10.15F (v. 15), Houghton Library, Harvard College Library.

FISHING

Making and mending nets and preparing other kinds of equipment for fishing were essential and time-consuming tasks for all fishing communities, and it is not surprising that the women of the household played a pivotal role in this work. Nets demanded a major investment of scarce resources and were carefully maintained against tearing and rot. Plate 1.14 (top image) shows a woman inside the house spinning the hemp or flax to make fishing nets: spinning has always been strongly gender-identified with women, as we shall see in part 3, on textiles. Outside (see the lower panel in the image below) a "little girl" assists in the repair of nets, using a special type of netting needle. In plate 1.15, a young woman attaches floats to a net. Plate 1.16a represents a tanner's yard, where the nets and ropes are brought to be treated: the women play a full role in this work, carrying the heavy ropes and nets on their backs, as we see illustrated in the right foreground of plate 1.16b. The tanned nets, carried back wet from the yard, are being laid out to dry on the sand or on a special rack. The plate legend and text make no mention of the women, using the non-gender-specific *gens* to describe the workers: as often occurs in this group of plates, only the image stands as witness to the women's contribution (Duhamel 1769: part 1, vol. 1, sect. 2: 24 and 185).

Women also helped to draw in the nets for various types of onshore fishing: plate 1.17 illustrates

Pl. 1.14. Making and repairing nets. Duhamel, *Traité des pesches*, 1ère partie, [T. I], 2nde section, Pl. V.

Pl. 1.15. Attaching floats to nets. *Ency. Planches*, vol. 7. "Pesches de mer; Pl. I." S143.

Pl. 1.16a. Treating nets at the tanner's yard. Duhamel, *Traité des pesches*, 1ère partie, [T. I], 2nde section, Pl. VI. Eng. Angelique Moitte.

Pl. 1.16b and detail. Carrying and drying fishing nets. Duhamel, *Traité des pesches*, 1ère partie, [T. I], 2nde section, Pl. VI. Eng. Elisabeth Haussard.

Pl. 1.17. Shore fishing: hauling nets. Duhamel, *Traité des pesches*, 1ère partie, [T. I], 2nde section, Pl. XLIII.

a type of net called the *aissauge*, used on the Mediterranean coast, which is pulled out by a small boat and hauled in by two groups on the beach: the text tells us that "men, women and old people" are used, without distinction, for this work and are rewarded for their efforts with a few fish. Thirty to thirty-five people might be required to pull in one net. The *Encyclopédie* illustrates (plate 1.18) a woman helping to pull in a smaller net of a type used in the areas of Bayeux and Quimper: this turned on a pulley placed in the sand at low tide and was aptly called a *"vas-tu-viens-tu."* This is a good example of how both picture and text were closely copied from the manuscript album commis-

Pl. 1.18. Hauling nets with a pulley. *Ency. Planches*, vol. 8. "Pesches de mer; Pl. XVII." S159.

sioned by Le Masson du Parc and preserved in the Bibliothèque Nationale, Paris (Ms. Ke 82, fol. H481 and 482).

In areas where the men fished with various types of line and hook, we are told that the responsibility for the washing and drying of the longlines, and the provision of some of the baits, kept the women constantly busy during spells of good weather when the men could fish. Their work is "almost as tough as the men's. [. . .] As each fisherman must furnish his own longlines well baited, those who have a large family have a big advantage over others" (Duhamel 1769: part 1, vol. 1, sect. 1: 44–45 and 83). In plate 1.19, beautifully drawn by

Angelique Moitte, women referred to as *aqueresses* (probably from the French *acquérir*, meaning "to get") repair the lines and bait the hooks; in the background they can be seen stringing out the lines. Plate 1.20 depicts a type of shore fishing in which the women and children prepare and bait fishing lines of different types (lower section) for the family to carry to the shore at low tide. "The old, weak women" (as shown in the center foreground of the plate) then attach stones to the lines, while the men and "robust women" dig holes in the sand with a spade in which to bury each stone (Duhamel, 64 and 84). The aim is to catch fish as the tide rises again: the image gives a highly opti-

mistic projection of the catch left on the sand as the tide recedes.

It was generally up to the women in fishing communities to find the bait for the men going to sea, to fish for shrimp, and dig for worms and insects. Plate 1.21 (top image) shows a group of men and women using various instruments—a hook with a long handle, a knife with a serrated edge called an *étiquette*, and an old sickle (which we have seen was strongly gender-identified with women)—to detach mussels from the rocks and to extract worms and small fish from the sand. The text for the center image tells us that "men and women" dig in the sand with various types of old spades and forks for worms and

Pl. 1.19. Repairing lines and baiting hooks. Duhamel, *Traité des pesches*, 1ère partie, [T. I], 1ère section, Pl. XIV. Eng. Angelique Moitte.

Pl. 1.20. Preparing fishing lines. Duhamel, *Traité des pesches*, 1ère partie, [T. I], 1ère section, Pl. XVII. Eng. Berthault.

Pl. 1.21. Gathering bait on the strand. Duhamel, *Traité des pesches*, 1ère partie, [T. I], 3ème section, Pl. II.
Eng. Elisabeth Haussard.

Pl. 1.22. Raking the sand for bait. Duhamel, *Traité des pesches,* 1ère partie, [T. I], 3ème section, Pl. III. Eng. Catherine Haussard.

flat fish, which might lie a foot or more below the surface—though in this instance, the designer seems to have illustrated only male figures, judging by the headgear. The text underlines the exhausting nature of this occupation but emphasizes that between February and Easter, it can make an important contribution to a family's subsistence. The bottom image shows a similar type of ac-

tivity undertaken at night, by lamplight, in the region near Etreham (Normandy): one person digs and turns over the rocks while the other collects whatever is hiding underneath (Duhamel 1769: part 1, vol. 1, sect. 3: 4–5 and 53).

Plate 1.22 (the top image) illustrates how, at low tide in the warmer months, women and men raked over the sand for worms,

shellfish, and flatfish; sometimes sole, turbot, or eels could be found hiding in the sand. This was hard work, and those who were fortunate enough to have an ox to harness up to a harrow used it for the same purpose (bottom image): the man leads the beast, we are told, with "children or women" following behind to collect the spoils, obviously backbreaking work. Both

Pl. 1.23. Shallow-water lance fishing. Duhamel, *Traité des pesches*, 1ère partie, [T. I], 3ème section, Pl. IV.

of these types of fishing are condemned by the author because of the damage they cause to the small fry (Duhamel, 6 and 53). We see another example of a woman raking in plate 1.23, which also illustrates an alternative technique used for catching flatfish, such as plaice and flounder, in many areas of France: the mouth of the Loire, the rivers of Picardy, the Ile de Ré, and the admiralty of La Rochelle are specifically mentioned. The women and men carry a long cane with a sharp metal point or nails attached to the tip: they walk in the shallow water barefoot, and when they feel the fish move in the sand under their feet, they try to pierce them with their lance. Clearly this was a difficult and time-consuming activity, and the ingenuity and tenacity of these fishing communities in seeking food is noteworthy. We see here an interesting example of a woman with her skirts tucked up to her knees.

Plate 1.24 illustrates a woman hurrying to deliver lugworms to the fishermen while they are still alive: they will be used to bait hooks. Again, the unusual drawing of a woman's bare leg showing through her ragged dress signifies poverty, but also the extent to which she relies on the strength and movement of her legs for her livelihood.

Plate 1.25 is a drawing from Le Masson's album; it was not engraved for either of our collections but is included here as an example of the style and quality of the drawings on which this series of prints was based, as well as for the interest of its subject. It illustrates another shoreline activity in which the women of the community were involved with the men: the raking and collection of kelp from the beaches. We see a pulley system, powered by a horse, being used to raise the seaweed from the shore to the top of the cliff, where it is forked into piles by other women, shown working barefoot with ragged skirts. The kelp might have been used as fertilizer on the land, or, more likely, burned for the production of soda, an important element in the

THE TRADITIONAL ECONOMY :: 49

Pl. 1.24. Transporting bait. Duhamel, *Traité des pesches*, 1ère partie, [T. I], 3ème section, Pl. IX. Eng. Marie-Jeanne Ozanne, femme le Gouaz.

Pl. 1.25. Gathering and raking kelp. Ms. Ke 82 f. 493. Cliché Bibliothèque Nationale de France.

Pl. 1.26. Shrimp fishing at low tide. Duhamel, *Traité des pesches,* 1ère partie, [T. I], 2nde section, Pl. XIII. Eng. Catherine Haussard.

making of glass. Auguste-Denis Fougeroux de Bondaroy was later (1771) to publish a study on the pernicious effects of the smoke from this practice in the Caux region of Normandy, probably based, in part, on Le Masson's research (see Pinault 1987, 348).

It is clear from many images that women played a major role in the infinitely varied types of hand-net fishing practiced along the coast of France. Plate 1.26 illustrates "women and girls" fishing for large shrimp on the Ile de Ré (Duhamel 1769: part 1, vol. 1, sect. 2: 33 and 186). They used flat-headed wooden push-nets, the name for which varied from region to region, to fish under

rocks and seaweed at low tide; the illustrator, Catherine Haussard, has depicted the women with skirts tucked up above their knees and the most simple of head-coverings, a more realistic portrayal than is offered in other plates. More commonly, the nets for shrimping were circular in shape (see those used in the top section of plate 1.27). The other style of net illustrated in this plate, where the hoop is suspended by three cords, is used for fishing on the sea bottom and is called a *caudrette* (on the right in the lower left panel): this is the net used in the strange image of shrimp fishing at the lower right, another version of which can be

found in the *Encyclopédie* (*Ency. Planches,* vol. 8: "Pesches de mer," plate 2). This offers evidence that certain gender-specific roles assigned to women in fishing were challenging and hazardous. The text describes this type of fishing, specific to the little port of Saint-Palais on the west coast of France, where the sea does not uncover the rocks sufficiently to allow shrimp fishing with hand nets. To facilitate access to the shrimp, platforms were built on pine poles over twenty feet high, jutting twenty yards into the sea. Women and girls—to whom this type of fishing is almost exclusive—dropped the nets, armed with bait, over the side of the

Pl. 1.27. Shrimp fishing in shallow and deep water. Duhamel, *Traité des pesches,* 1ère partie, [T. I], 2nde section, Pl. IX. Detail: *Ency. Planches*, vol. 8. "Pesches de mer; Pl. II. S144.

cage—they might have up to four or five nets each—and pulled them up again by a long cord to retrieve the shellfish (Duhamel, 35–36). The text of the article "Salicots" in the *Encyclopédie* is almost identical to that in the *Descriptions*; both emphasize the fragility of these structures, which had to be substantially rebuilt every year, and add that "Despite these precautions, accidents frequently occur, either because the wind blows the women into the sea while they are walking out to their cages, or because the poles break while they are fishing" (*Ency.*: "Salicots"). It is highly unlikely that these women would have been able to swim, and they would have drowned if they fell, fully clothed, into more than fifteen feet of water. These careful and detailed descriptions were based on Le Masson's research.

Plate 1.28a depicts an extraordinary night scene, with women in two long, neat rows fishing with small nets or "sieves" made of horsehair for tiny fish called *la montée,* the name of which derives from the fact that they are caught when the tide is rising, and only in the period of the full moon in March. This female-only activity is identified with the banks of the river Orne, near Caen, and the text tells us it is a type of fishing done by the common people of the town, rather than the professional fisher folk. We might suspect Angelique Moitte, the engraver, of a romantic flight of fantasy here, but the text does state that the number of people who turned out for this fishing was very large, and the spectacle created by the lanterns on a dark night was rather pleasing to the eye. This information was furnished to Duhamel, the author of the treatise, by a local marine administrator, M. Viger, Lieutenant General of the Admiralty of Caen, a knowledgeable firsthand witness (Duhamel, 34 and 185).

Plate 1.28b describes a method of fishing using a basket or pot made of wicker that could either be left between the rocks at low tide with some bait inside or placed in the sea by a small boat. It was mainly used to catch crabs or lobster but sometimes also eels. Called a *bouraque,* it was commonly used, in varying sizes, along the Normandy coast: the women, who rarely went out in boats, would presumably have been confined to the version used on the shore. No mention is made of them in the text, but again, the woman in the ragged skirt towards the left of the picture bears witness to their activity.

The nets used in shoreline fishing could be very large and grew quite heavy when wet; it required great strength to use them. We might also note that along parts of the Atlantic coast, where this type of fishing was carried out—Brittany, for example—the average temperature of the water would scarcely rise above 16°C (61°F) even in summer. Plate 1.29 (bottom section) shows the size of a net called the *grenadière* in relation to the woman holding it: it is mainly used for shrimp fishing and takes its name from the term for shrimp used in Flanders (*grenades*). The text remarks: "One can imagine that it is extremely exhausting to run in water that rises above your waistline, pushing what is often a fairly large net in front of you. Nonetheless, this type of fishing is practiced by women and children equally with men, but each person takes a net whose size is in proportion to their strength." This text is exceptional in that it addresses the obvious difficulty for women in undertaking such activities while wearing skirts: "Ordinarily the women abandon their skirts to don a kind of breeches with canions" (*"culottes à grands canons"*; Duhamel, 37). But, as has been remarked, it was very unusual for women to be depicted in male dress in the period, and the designer has chosen to show the woman in the lower half of the

Pl. 1.28a. Night fishing: *la montée*. Duhamel, *Traité des pesches*, 1ère partie, [T. I], 2nde section, Pl. X. Eng. Catherine Haussard.

Pl. 1.28b. Catching shellfish using traps. Duhamel, *Traité des pesches*, 1ère partie, [T. I], 2nde section, Pl. X. Eng. Catherine Haussard.

Pl. 1.29. Catching shellfish using large nets. Duhamel, *Traité des pesches,* 1ère partie, [T. I], 2nde section, Pl. XI. Eng. Angelique Moitte.

THE TRADITIONAL ECONOMY :: 55

Pl. 1.30 and detail. Shore fishing with the *grand haveneau*. Duhamel, *Traité des pesches*, 1ère partie, [T. I], 2nde section, Pl. XII. Eng. Elisabeth Haussard.

Pl. 1.31. In-shore fishing with small boats and nets. Duhamel, *Traité des pesches*, 1ère partie, [T. I], 2ème section, Pl. XXX.

plate in what appears to be the more traditional short shift or petticoat with a skirt tied up at the front. Thus, the lower part of her legs are exposed, allowing more freedom of movement; we will find similar strategies adopted in a number of images of working women, but without contravening gendered codes of dress. Plate 1.30, however, shows two women fishing with another type of large net, the *grand haveneau* (a term still current today), and apparently clad in a type of pantaloon or breeches like the men alongside them: the very basic figures in this image do not suggest any addi-

Pl. 1.32. In-shore fishing with small boats and harpoons. Duhamel, *Traité des pesches,* 1ère partie, [T. I], 3ème section, Pl. VI.

Pl. 1.33. Shore fishing with harpoons. Duhamel, *Traité des pesches,* 1ère partie, [T. I], 3ème section, Pl. V.

tional flounce or "canion" adding length to the women's trousers. The men further out from shore use long poles to chase the fish in toward the line of net-holders.

It was unusual in the French context, as we have noted, for women to go out in fishing boats, but there are two examples in these plates of women fishing from small boats near the shoreline. Plate 1.31 shows a type of fishing referred to as "*au Loup,*" common in the region of Nantes, where a net attached to poles is placed near the shore after the tide has turned; a small boat is used to retrieve the fish caught in the net.

Pl. 1.34. Shore fishing with traps. Duhamel, *Traité des pesches*, 2nde section. "Des filets," Chap. 5, Pl. XXVIII.

We are told that "this type of fishing is commonly done by a man and two women," as we see in the illustration (Duhamel, 77–78). In plate 1.32 a woman and man prepare to go out in a small boat, from which they will try to catch flatfish or eels in the sand near the shore by spearing them with various harpoons, some shaped like a rake and others like a trident (cf. plate 1.23). This type of fishing is undertaken in the Admiralty of Abbeville, as well as in the Veys and at Isigny in Normandy (Duhamel 1769: part 1, vol. 1, sect. 3: 9). A similar technique is also used in the Languedoc—St. Tropez is specifically mentioned—even at night by torchlight: plate 1.33 shows a little girl holding the basket for the catch while the males of her family try to spear the fish.

Many different types of *parcs* or *tentes*, elaborate constructions using wattles, nets, and grills, were installed on tidal beaches to catch fish as the sea receded. We see three examples of such constructions (1.34, 1.35a, and 135b), where women and men came to search for fish or shellfish with spears, nets, or baskets.

Duhamel du Monceau describes how practices in other countries differ from those of France: women are "just as involved as men" in sturgeon fish-

Pl. 1.35a. Shore fishing with traps. Duhamel, *Traité des pesches,* 2nde section. "Des filets," Chap. 4, Pl. XXI. Eng. Angelique Moitte.

Pl. 1.35b. Shore fishing with traps. Duhamel, *Traité des pesches,* 2nde section. "Des filets," Chap. 5, Pl. XXIX. Eng. Catherine Haussard.

ing in the Caspian Sea, where they "row boats and drag the nets just like the men." He remarks that he came across good illustrations of these peasants, which he subsequently had engraved (Duhamel 1769–82, part 2, vol. 3, sect. 8: 228–29). These illustrations are, not surprisingly, much more highly stylized than the images relating to France, being distinct both in form and function. Plate 1.36 represents a "Finnish peasant woman" carrying an oar, presumably used to row in the Baltic. Her ethnic dress and jewellery seem very elaborate and unlikely as a working costume to

be worn in a boat. Somewhat more convincing is the illustration of a fishing woman from Greenland and her child (plate 1.37) carrying different types of harpoons. As the origin of images such as these remains, for the most part, unspecified, they cannot carry the degree of authority we can ascribe to the plates based on Le Masson's albums; nonetheless, it is clear that Le Masson, as well as Duhamel and Fougeroux de Bondaroy, had a network of correspondents on whom they could rely for information on foreign fisheries (see Pinault 1987, 346).

Everywhere in the illustrations of fishing communities we see women transporting great loads of fish: the work of fetching and carrying and the transporting of very heavy burdens was strongly associated with women throughout the traditional economy. Plate 1.38 shows women and men waiting on the shore with their baskets as the fish is unloaded; mostly, this work was reserved for professional porters with the priority right to transport fish, but when a great abundance of fish was landed, other men, women, and children from the towns were also allowed to porter,

Pl. 1.36. Finnish peasant woman with oar. Duhamel, *Traité des pesches*, Suite de la 2nde partie, T. III, 8ème section, Pl. IV. Eng. Milsan.

Pl. 1.37. Greenlanders harpoon fishing. Duhamel, *Traité des pesches*, Suite de la 2nde partie, T. IV, 10ème section, Pl. XV. Eng. Milsan.

Pl. 1.38. Fish porters. Duhamel, *Traité des pesches*, 1ère partie, [T. I], 3ème section, Pl. IX. Eng. Angelique Moitte.

Pl. 1.39. Methods of transporting fish. Duhamel, *Traité des pesches*, 2nde partie, [T. II], 3ème section,
Pl. XI. Eng. Elisabeth Haussard.

and were known as *petits hotterons* (Duhamel 1769: part 2, vol. 2, sect. 3: 371). Plate 1.39 illustrates the varied types of basket used: the woman in the foreground is portering the *hotte de quai* (hod), which is used for transporting the larger, tough fish, like ray or monkfish, and for carrying various types of fish over long distances. We can see from the illustration the huge size of this receptacle, which held a great weight; a pole attached to the hod could be rested on the ground and helped the bearer to relieve her or his back a little (see plate 1.49, where a woman uses this *hotte*,

Pl. 1.40. Transporting
herring. Duhamel, *Traité des
pesches*, 2nde partie, [T. II],
3ème section, Pl. XIV. Eng.
N. Ransonette.

Pl. 1.41. Transporting herring with vehicles. Duhamel, *Traité des pesches*, 2nde partie, [T. II], 3ème section,
Pl. XI. Eng. Elisabeth Haussard.

her back bent under the weight).
The large, good specimens of
more refined species had to be
transported in the *manne,* or creel,
carried here by two women (on
the right), while two others use a
stretcher to transport their basket
(on the left). Alternatively, these

large fish might be carried by one
woman in a smaller basket on her
shoulder or arm, or in single units
by hand to avoid damage (like the
woman on the left in plate 1.39;
Duhamel, 370). The smaller fish
like herring or mackerel could be
carried in all sorts of vessels: plate

1.40 shows a woman transporting
a load of prepared herring on her
shoulders. The text tells us that
the basket could contain two hundred herring, about twenty kgs. or
fifty lbs. (Duhamel, 414).

In plate 1.41 we see women
helping to push heavy transport

Pl. 1.42. Transporting sturgeon. Duhamel, *Traité des pesches*, Suite de la 2nde partie, T. III, 8ème section, Pl. III. Des. Elisabeth Haussard.

vehicles carrying barrels of herring already salted at sea. No comment is made on their contribution in the text, but the image gives a good sense of the effort involved: each barrel could weigh over three hundred *livres* when full (Duhamel, 434). This picture, like many in this series, was drawn and engraved by a woman, Elisabeth Haussard; in plate 1.42 she has also illustrated sturgeon fishing in Nantes and other areas of the French coast, with the women carrying the large fish in flat vessels on their heads.

Three further images were drawn and engraved by Angelique Moitte, illustrating sardine fishing in Brittany, one of the poorest areas of France. Plate 1.43a shows men and women carrying the catch to a salting shed. The poverty of the women in particular is underlined by their short, ragged skirts; they wear wooden clogs on their feet, and their lower legs are exposed in a

manner only occasionally seen in the representation of working women's bodies (see Antoine Raspal's 1760 painting of a seamstresses' workshop in Arles, in Crowston 2001, 123). One woman balances her basket on her head while she holds her small child by the hand. When the sardines were sufficiently salted, women workers strung them onto sticks and piled these "brochettes" onto litters covered with a straw mat (Duhamel, 434). In 1.43b we see how the barefoot women carry the litters to the water, where they wash the salt from the sardines, then return the fish to the shed where they are drained. The women wear their skirts, or more likely just a shift, tucked up between their legs, exposing their lower limbs in a way that, we have emphasized, was unusual in representations of women in the period; they must clearly have suffered from moving repeatedly in and out of the cold Atlantic water. Plate 1.43c illustrates the pressing

shed; the buildings would have been closed against the weather, but the convention in these illustrations is to remove a wall to allow us to view the action inside. Two women—again barefoot in contrast with the better-clad men in clogs, smoking their pipes— are not mentioned in the plate legend; they are presumably sorting the washed sardines before they are added to the barrels ranged against the walls where the pressing machines are located. It would take the cargo of four litters of sardines (as pictured in 1.43b) to fill one pressed barrel, weighing over three hundred *livres* when full. We are told that each of these pressing sheds would employ seven or eight women and a few men. Normally, the owner would sign a contract with each worker for the fishing season and pay them at the end; where the women were not engaged for the season, they were paid for each filled barrel (Duhamel, 432–34). This plate is almost identical to that

Pl. 1.43a, b, and c. Salting and pressing sardines. Duhamel, *Traité des pesches*, 2nde partie, [T. II], 3ème section, Pl. [XIX] marked XVIII. Eng. Angelique Moitte.

Pl. 1.44a and b. Preparing and pressing herring. Duhamel, *Traité des pesches*, 2nde partie, [T. II], 3ème section, Pl. XII. Eng. Angelique Moitte.

published in the *Encyclopédie* (*Ency. Planches,* vol. 8: "Pesches de mer," plate 12).

The work of preparing herrings was very similar to the preparation of the sardines, if on a larger scale, with pressing yards located somewhat further from the shore: plate 1.44a illustrates an urban setting with the well-dressed master and his wife directing operations (on the left). In plate 1.44b we see women and men arriving from the shore with the large hods on their backs, while one woman empties the contents into a half-barrel to check the condition of the fish. The women washed the fish in a great vat, removed the gills, separated those that had been gutted at sea from those that had not, and brought them to the salters in baskets. When the herring had already been salted at sea, arriving in barrels, they were washed in their brine (plate 1.44a), and the women then repacked them into barrels. These women were called *caqueuses,* from the French word for the action of removing the gills, and plate 1.45 offers a detail of such a woman with the herring in her hands. Unlike many of the plates illustrating crafts from the *Encyclopédie,* these images are full of movement and give an impression of the bustle and teeming life in such locations: we see one woman taking a drink from a flagon and small children and dogs playing around the vats (plate 1.44a). Similarly, in plate 1.46 we see the women gutting and washing mackerel, which are then salted and packed into barrels.

The section on the preparation of cod in Normandy is interesting because the work was described in detail to the author (Duhamel) by his nephew, Fougeroux de Bondaroy, also a member of the Académie des Sciences, after a visit he made to the district of Tréport (part 2, vol. 2, sect. 1: 74): the text tells us that the women emptied forty-five or forty-six barrels of cod in brine into a huge vat, and six or seven women worked together around that vat. As is the convention in these images, plate 1.47 shows a smaller number of workers so that we can better see what the figures are doing. They wash the cod

Pl. 1.45. Gutting herring, detail: *caqueuse.* Duhamel, *Traité des pesches,* 2nde partie, [T. II], 3ème section, Pl. XIV. Eng. N. Ransonette.

Pl. 1.46. Washing and gutting herring: *caqueuses*. Duhamel, *Traité des pesches*, 2nde partie, T. III, 7ème section, Pl. IV. Eng. Milsan.

carefully in brine with a little brush, always avoiding damage, which would devalue the fish. Holding the fish by the tail, they then wash them repeatedly in two separate vats of fresh water before passing them to a woman who, with a little knife, removes any blood or other defect "that could prejudice the whiteness or quality of the fish" (Duhamel, 75). The fish were then left in great piles for draining and pressing before the women packed them into barrels, salting each fish carefully as they went: "they are skilled at dispensing exactly the quantity of salt which should go into each barrel" (salt being, of course, a very costly commodity in this pe-

riod). Plate 1.48 illustrates the different treatment given to cod in the "North of Europe," where it is dried as "*stockfish.*" Women spread the flattened fish on the rocks to dry: it has been cut down the middle with the head still intact, a practice not followed in France.

Plate 1.49 illustrates a carrier's yard, where fresh fish is washed and packed for rapid transport to the point of sale. Again, we see women arriving from the shore, and others packing the fish into large baskets, most of which will be carried by horses. The packing required great care, and the women who did the work are described as

skillful (Duhamel 1769: part 1, vol. 1, sect. 3: 24): it was their task to sort the fish by size into baskets so as to avoid damage in transit. Skate, for example, might be used in combination with finer fish, such as turbot, both to cushion them and to help maintain a cool temperature. Once full, the baskets were covered with straw and then sealed in various ways with a tool for threading string through the basket weave, depending on the type of carriage to be adopted: plate 1.50 illustrates some of the finished baskets in detail. The largest, most precious fish were packed singly and sewn in a straw package (as shown at letter E in plate 1.50).

Pl. 1.47. Washing and salting cod. Duhamel, *Traité des pesches*, 2nde partie, [T. II], 1ère section, Pl. XII.

Pl. 1.48. Drying cod or stockfish, northern Europe. Duhamel, *Traité des pesches*, 2nde partie, [T. II], 1ère section, Pl. XIX.

Pl. 1.49. Washing and packing in the carrier's yard. Duhamel, *Traité des pesches,* 1ère partie, [T. I], 3ème section, Pl. IX. Eng. Angelique Moitte.

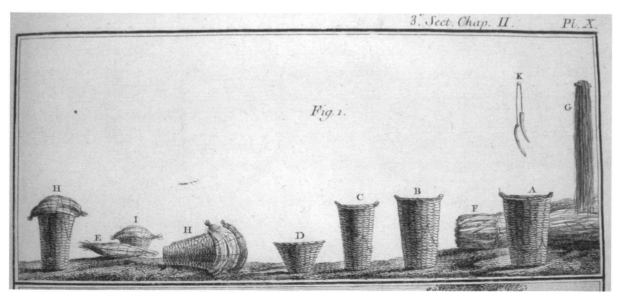

Pl. 1.50. Packing, baskets: detail. Duhamel, *Traité des pesches,* 1ère partie, [T. I], 3ème section, Pl. X. Eng. Marie-Jeanne Ozanne, femme le Gouaz.

Plate 1.51 shows women similarly packing fresh herring out on the seashore.

The section on the preparation of mackerel gives us some detail on the method of payment for the workers in the salting and packing yards: most of them, with the exception of the washers, were not paid by the day but rather by the filled barrel. Thus, their skill and speed contributed to the amount of their earnings. In addition, the women packers (*paqueresses*), along with the master cooper, were each entitled to take six herrings at the end of the day: this would have represented a valuable income supplement to a woman trying to feed a family. The practice was frowned on by the authorities, because the women would naturally choose the best fish, thus diminishing the

Pl. 1.51. Preparing herring for transport. Duhamel, *Traité des pesches,* 2nde partie, [T. II], 3ème section, Pl. IX.

overall quality going to market, and for this reason, we are told, "women have been forbidden [by regulation] from entering the fishing boats": the skippers were supposed to send the catch to market without sifting out the better fish, a rule more honored in the breach than the observance, according to Duhamel (Duhamel 1769: part 2, vol. 2, sect. 3: 399).

Two images give us detail of the women's participation in the work of smoking fish. Plate 1.52 gives an interesting insight into gendered notions of status within what is essentially the same occupation for men and women: it is in two parts. The top section depicts a smoking unit for the preparation of kippered herrings (with a cross-section of what would obviously have been a closed building). We can see that it is in the main a male activity, though women—termed *inqueresses*—do the stringing of the fish onto rods. The men climb up to hang the rods of herring on racks and retrieve them when smoked for packing into barrels. The text calls particular attention to the man tending the fire, who must be "experienced" and sleep only fitfully as he must ensure the herrings are not blackened, over-dried, and so on (Duhamel, 410). The lower section of the image (see detail) represents a smaller smoking unit where a different type of semikippered herrings are prepared. The texts tell us that only women (*les craquelotieres*) are employed in this preparation, which is essentially little different from the process shown in the upper section but results in a prized product: "the true *craquelot* prepared by women alone is esteemed for its delicacy" (Duhamel, 414). The tending of the fire is extremely important here, as the person watching it must know, among other things, when to use dry wood shavings and when to use green wood to color the fish, but the text attributes neither skill nor experience to the woman doing this work. We can see that the women climbed like their male counterparts, and, in reality, to avoid accidents they must have found some better solution than climbing with skirts around their ankles as the designer—Catherine Haussard—has depicted them here. This is a good example of how gender distinctions, always conferring superior status or respect on the male worker, are based on issues extraneous to the tasks and activities actually performed: in this case the distinction is made on the basis of the scale or size of the

Pl. 1.52 and details. Smoking herring. Duhamel, *Traité des pesches*, 2nde partie, [T. II], 3ème section, Pl. XV. Eng. Catherine Haussard.

Pl. 1.53. Smoking sardines. Duhamel, *Traité des pesches*, 2nde partie, [T. II], 3ème section, Pl. XIX. Eng. Angelique Moitte.

undertaking and has little to do with either the product or the production, but the women were paid less (Duhamel, 414).

Plate 1.53 illustrates the smaller hangar used for the smoking of sardines, a practice not very common in France in this period, as most of the sardines were sold salted. Again we see the women stringing the sardines onto rods; the fish were then washed once in seawater and again in fresh water before being brought to the smokehouse. The women here seem to be wearing a type of

breeches, such as we saw in plate 1.30, and clogs and are almost indistinguishable from the men, probably a more realistic portrayal (by Angelique Moitte) than the one we saw by Haussard in plate 1.52. This plate is closely related to the *Encyclopédie* plate "Pesches de mer, XIII" (*Ency. Planches,* vol. 8).

Women have always been known as fishmongers in a major or minor way: two images recall this age-old activity. In plate 1.54 we are shown a merchant-salter buying small fish—herrings or

anchovies—directly from the wife of a fisherman at the shore. She has covered her fish with straw or seaweed to keep them fresh. Plate 1.55 illustrates a marketplace where the women sitting in the large vat, surrounded by their baskets, are selling fish. In the foreground the skippers or fishermen are selling the larger specimens themselves; one is selling a crab, which traditionally belonged to the man in whose net it was caught. The laws and conventions covering market trade could be elaborate, with police

Pl. 1.54. Trading herrings and anchovies. Duhamel, *Traité des pesches*, 2nde partie, [T. II], 3ème section, Pl. XXII. Eng. Catherine Haussard.

Pl. 1.55. The marketplace. Duhamel, *Traité des pesches*, 1ère partie, [T. I], 3ème section, Pl. IX. Eng. Angelique Moitte.

inspectors designated in many towns to oversee the quality of fish sold: for example, in Metz, the female fishmongers were not allowed to sell on the market before midday, the morning being reserved for master fishermen (Duhamel 1769: part 1, vol. 1, sect. 3: 23). This was ostensibly intended to combat rising prices associated with the resale of fish, but clearly, it would also have served to depress the women's income.

2

Artisanal Trades

HE IMAGES IN THIS SEC-
TION reflect a wide range of the
artisanal trades of France in the
eighteenth century. Family-based
workshops produced everything
from the basic requirements of
everyday life—food items, pins,
candles—to the most prestigious
items of luxury for which Paris in
particular was renowned, from
fans to the finest embroidered
garments. These workshops varied in size, from the smallest family unit, involving one master or
mistress with help from immediate family, to large-scale enterprises such as those common in
the hatter's trade, involving perhaps forty journeymen, apprentices, and casual workers (Garden
1970, 322). Some of these larger
enterprises might have been included in the section on manufactories, but I preferred to place
them here because trades such as
hatmaking, waxworks, candle
making, and the fabrication of

pins and nails also operated on a
smaller scale, corresponding to
the traditional artisanal mode of
organization.

The majority of trades described here correspond to the
dominant pattern of male sworn
trades in the major French cities
in the eighteenth century. Although there were many variations in regulations from region
to region, and the situation was
more open outside the main cities
where guilds dominated, in the
majority of trades, by the period
that concerns this study, mastership could pass only from male to
male and not through the female
line (see Davis 1986, 186).
Women were specifically barred
from the training route of apprenticeship, which gave formal
access to skill and status, and they
could not become masters other
than as widows.[47] A widow was
debarred, in many trades, from
taking any new apprentices—

thus ensuring she would eventually have to pass her business to a male substitute—and from running a business if she remarried outside the trade. Throughout this chapter I have recorded many specific examples of these practices as they affected women. It has previously been posited that the imposition of these restrictive trade structures steadily eroded women's access to high-status work, and in particular their access to independent authority within a trade, over the sixteenth and seventeenth centuries (Hufton 1996; Shahar 1983, 189–200; Hudson and Lee 1990, 11). I have endeavored to track some of these changes in regulations for the trades included in this study through the documents recorded by Lespinasse (1897), Savary des Bruslons (1762), and Franklin (1884). In many instances I have identified a clear shift from a level of gender equality in accessing trade rights, with women having entry routes to positions of some authority, to a much more restricted model where prerogatives were strictly tied to the family and kinship ties to men (see Crowston 2000). There is evidence that before the seventeenth century, children of both sexes (*enfants*) could access privileges in the guild as apprentices and skilled workers including the gold beaters (*batteurs d'or*, Lespinasse

1892, 2: 61), metal gilders (*doreurs sur métaux*, 2: 140), *passementier*-button makers (*passementiers-boutonniers d'or et d'argent*, 2: 154–55), embroiderers (*brodeurs-chasubliers*, 2: 162–80), pin makers (*aiguilliers-aléniers* and *épingliers* 2: 560–75), potters (*potiers de terre, carreleurs*, 2: 763–72), ribbon makers (*ouvriers en soie: tissutiers-rubaniers*, 1897, 3: 1–32), wool carders (*cardeurs de laine*, 3: 87–91), and feather dressers (*plumassières*, 3: 296–302). As will be highlighted in the entries for these individual trades, the mention of women's specific rights is progressively eliminated, so that where the daughters in early statutes were admitted to apprenticeship, or full membership in the trade, in eighteenth-century statutes only sons of masters were acknowledged. A good example is the trade of feather dresser (described later in this chapter), which Lespinasse even listed in the feminine. Their statutes of 1599 (arts. 14, 22, and 26, Lespinasse 1897, 3: 297) clearly indicated that daughters were admitted to apprenticeship and could become mistresses, but in the statutes of 1644 (art. 18, Lespinasse 3: 301), only sons of masters were mentioned as holding such rights; moreover, the widow of a master could no longer take on any new apprentices (art. 26). Another telling case

is that of the embroiderers, which will also be detailed later in this chapter. The result of such changes was that women's only privileges became indirect, with widows in the later period forced, sooner rather than later, to pass the authority in their business to a male relative, or see it dwindle with no apprentices. Likewise, daughters, who might have worked in their father's shop throughout their youth, were no longer entitled to apprenticeship or admission to the trade; they were entitled only to transfer mastership rights to a husband (see for example the fan makers' statutes of 1678, art. 9) without retaining any independent rights in their capacity as single women. The full extent and import of these shifts across the economy would require further detailed research on the original statutes, which are often only summarized by Lespinasse, but our limited study serves to corroborate the progressive institutional shift in gender relationships to a family-based model. It is worth noting that the corporate customs reserving organizational activities to men prevailing in the century of enlightenment also served to exclude women from the wider political institutions such as municipal government.

What also becomes clear, however, from the evidence of

our pictures, is the degree to which, despite such changes in their official status, women continued to dominate as workers in many of the same trades with which they had traditionally been associated, whether making pins or ribbons. A person relying on the formal rules and regulations with regard to many of the trades reflected in the images in this section would therefore get a totally false impression concerning women's actual participation in the workshops. Even when we turn to other, more informative sources of evidence concerning female participation in particular industries, the written texts can be imprecise or misleading—as will be shown—with regard to the nature of the tasks performed, the gender division of labor, the actual power relationships within the work situation, or how women related to their fellow workers. Whereas research on the family economy over the last twenty years has helped to create a much more nuanced picture than heretofore of the enduring role of women in the artisanal family in the early modern period (see, for example, Hafter 2001 and 1995; Musgrave 1997; Crowston 2001), the images I have gathered in this section add a new and original dimension to an understanding of some of the key issues. It is clear that in this period

the family business took precedence over all else, and the children—including the daughters—were drawn in to help as soon as they were capable of performing some basic task, which might be as young as eight years of age. It would indeed be surprising if things were otherwise, when shop and family home shared the same quarters—often just a couple of rooms—the journeymen and apprentices traditionally lodging with the family, at least up to the middle of the eighteenth century. In practice, a master taught his trade both to his sons—sanctioned by the regulations, who would become masters in their turn—and to his daughters, whether this was sanctioned or simply tolerated. The latter effectively worked as craftswomen, but as they lacked the privileges of their male counterparts, they could not teach the trade to apprentices or to their husbands in this period, as I have already indicated (see Hudson and Lee 1990, 12). Examples abound in our images of young women—some daughters of tradesmen, we can legitimately suppose—who have acquired proficiency across a broad range of crafts.[48]

Nevertheless, women's occupational identity was, in Natalie Zemon Davis's phrase, "thinner" than that of the men in their milieu (Davis 1986, 169), and how-

ever expert they may have become within the home workshop, they lacked the status of qualified workers that would have allowed them to seek work outside the family sphere. Roberts has argued that women's activities "were primarily viewed as the social obligations of a wife rather than as the 'occupation' of a married woman" (1985, 144). In "the economy of makeshift" of eighteenth-century France, as Olwen Hufton describes it, the artisan's wife was not a homemaker in the modern sense: for such a woman, "cleaning, washing or mending clothes with any frequency, even cooking and child-rearing, were fairly marginal aspects of her existence in the demands they made upon her time" (1975, 11). The wife's contribution as worker was essential, and frequently, her children were put out to wet-nurse so that her labor would not be lost to the business, despite the fact that death rates among infants put out to nurse were almost twice as high as among those nursed by their mothers (Tilly and Scott 1987, 58). There were undoubtedly many married women among those featured in our sample of images, sometimes doing the kind of ancillary, unskilled work into which women's productive energies were drafted as the circumstances demanded—working the bellows (plate 2.47) or warming bone over the cinders (plate 2.38)—but also, as will be shown, performing skilled work, running shops, and selling to the public. The extent to which artisans' wives were involved in the family business was indirectly underlined by the frequency with which journeymen, who would not dare challenge a master, directed their invective instead—often with scatological remarks—at the master's wife (Sonenscher 1983, 249–50; Darnton 1985, 75ff.) For her part, she could assert certain types of power: Cynthia Truant (1988, 131), in her research on journeymen, has remarked that, even in male-dominated trades, "a licensed or tolerated 'disorderliness'" was sanctioned in the behavior of masters' wives or widows, who could "aggressively defend their shops, husbands and workers." Archival sources such as guild inspection records and police reports across a number of areas likewise offer evidence of the constant presence of women in and around the workshop, and of the way in which they involved themselves where there was any perceived threat to the family business (see Crowson 2000, 352; Sheridan 1992). Such sources also highlight how, even in heavy crafts such as building, a wife was often a craftsman's main assistant (see Ogilvie, 1990, 82–83), recall-

ing the heavy physical labor that, as I have emphasized, was undertaken by women across areas of the traditional economy.

The presence of women in the plates is particularly striking in the high-status luxury trades, which occupied an extremely important place in the Parisian economy: in such specialist areas, masters could command high prices for admitting a young (male) apprentice to training (Kaplan 1983, 283). The gender breakdown in many of the images reproduced here from these male sworn trades may therefore seem all the more surprising, but the lack of comment or explanation for it in the texts suggest it was accepted as commonplace by the contemporary observing eye. Everywhere we see women performing tasks that required training, ability, skill, and dexterity, though such qualities are rarely explicitly mentioned in the texts: thus, the *Encyclopédie* series on fan making illustrates the delicate work of the fan painters and mounters (plates 2.4 and 2.5), while another plate details the intricate work of the feather dressers (plate 2.6). Young women work alongside the men in the delicate work of gold and silver filigree, ornamenting snuffboxes (plate 2.7), or damascening steel swords (plate 2.13). The evidence we repeatedly en-

counter of the skill with which they operate across such a variety of trades—some more, some less traditionally associated with women—adds a significant new dimension to our understanding of female work activities under the *ancien régime*.

There were, nonetheless, some all-female guilds in French cities in this period. In her study of Rouen, for example, Daryl Hafter identifies a number of such guilds (linen drapers of new and used clothes, stocking makers, and seamstresses) as well as four mixed guilds that admitted women in their own right, including those of the spinners and ribbon makers (1997, 3). In Le Havre a seamstresses' guild was established in 1722 (Crowston 2001, 198). Daniel Roche estimates that at the beginning of the century the clothing trades accounted for more than 40 percent of all Parisian employers and workers, or some 35,000 souls (1989, 265–67): Cynthia Truant (1988) and Judith Coffin (1996) have described the important place of women in this sector, and their monopoly of the Parisian guilds of the linen drapers and the seamstresses, which acquired significant control within the vast market. Although the making of clothes was dominated by male tailors in rural areas, with women admitted, at best, as subordinate guild members, Crowston identified some fifteen towns, from Marseilles to Le Mans, where women were so admitted (2000, 340; Musgrave 1997, 159). At the most humble end of the guild hierarchy, hemp merchants and Parisian fresh-flower sellers (*bouquetières*) were also incorporated as exclusively female (Crowston 2001, 180, 193).

The oldest and most powerful female guild, that of the linen drapers (founded in 1485, though the women had established rights to sell in the *Halles* long before this: Franklin 1884, "Lingères," 6), was vigilant in preserving its independence from any encroachment by male heads of households, and its statutes forbade the husbands of mistresses from taking a role in their wives' businesses (Coffin 1996, 28–29). In this and in the seamstresses' guild (more recently established by statute in 1675) single women had almost unique access to formal training in the eighteenth century, with the guild's apprenticeship regulations favoring the daughters of mistresses. Truant's (1988, 133) research suggests that up to 40 percent of the guild members (there were 659 mistresses in 1725: Franklin, 12) may have been single women, and their position was bulwarked by a regula-

tion requiring that two of the four officers in each guild be single women, or "*filles majeures.*" The high membership of single women may be one of the reasons why only a small number of new entrants to the seamstress trade were daughters of mistresses; Crowston has highlighted how successful mistresses probably sought to marry their daughters into a position superior to that of manual labor. She concludes, "Despite their independent corporate status, mistress seamstresses thus appear to have accepted the wider cultural preference for the family economy over female economic independence" (2001, 329–30). Such choices notwithstanding, the all-female guilds did provide singular opportunities for Old Regime women "to exercise decision-making power in a formal way" (Truant 1988, 133).

But despite their numerical and political importance, few images in our collection reflect the activities of these all-female workshops. Only the retail end of the linen draper's business is recorded in our section on commercial activity (plate 5.6), as are the activities of the influential *marchandes de modes* (plate 5.5) operating outside guild structures up to 1777. This was just the high-end, most public face of a

business that extended from those making and selling linens to the aristocracy, to the poorest linen workers in the *Halles* who were widely perceived to be also peddling sexual favors (Coffin 1996, 27–28); women from the middle to the lower end of this scale are not represented in the prints. Likewise, we glimpse seamstresses working for the tailor (plate 2.25) and the *marchande de mode* (plate 2.27), but in the two main collections, there were no images portraying a workshop filled with powerful, independent women workers, mistresses in their own guild. Panckouke spotted this glaring omission and remedied it with one new print in his *Encyclopédie méthodique* in the 1780s (plate 2.26). It would appear that these women who broke with the dominant patriarchal forms tended to remain invisible to the "technological" writers and researchers: again, skill, knowledge, and commercial acumen were easily overlooked when they were solely the province of women. Likewise invisible are poor seamstresses, at the lower end of the scale, who sewed for others in their own homes.

But not all our images have to do with the much-vaunted luxury trades. The trades that dealt with food preparation tended to have more masters than workers of any category and depended very heavily on the whole family participating; they are represented here by the images of the vermicelli maker (plates 2.41 and 2.42). Since we know that women filled in the time remaining from their other tasks in the traditional economy by assisting in artisanal activities associated with their families, it is not surprising to see women performing a task such as dressing pots in a rural pottery workshop (plate 2.39). More surprising to the modern eye are the images reflecting the participation of women in trades working with base metals, though many of the tasks represented were commonly associated with women, not just in France, but throughout Europe: women were employed as pin makers and nailers (plates 2.48 to 2.50); they were involved in the casting of lead shot and printing type (plates 2.51 to 2.53) and in the polishing of pewter (plate 2.40). Small manufacture like pin making could be undertaken as a cottage industry; Simonton notes that in the Pays d'Ouche alone the number of pin makers increased tenfold between 1700 and 1789 as merchants transferred work to the countryside in search of cheap labor (1998, 43). In other images, we glimpse women operating in trades not usually associated with

them by historians, such as that of the edge-tool maker (plate 2.56) or the manufacturer of catgut (plate 2.55). Trades for which, alas, I found no images, but in which we know from other evidence that women worked alongside men, are leather-currying, where they could become apprentices but not mistresses, and the making of nails or studs for leather goods, where wives had the formal right to work with their husbands without any apprenticeship (Guilbert 1966, 23–24). Guilbert speculates that the presence of women in such trades was far more extensive than historians have been able to establish (24).

Some of this work was both dangerous and dirty, despite ideological arguments concerning the "protection" of women, particularly pregnant women, used when men sought to exclude them (see Shahar 1983, 199): in a number of images we see evidence of the exposure to antimony fumes, which was known to cause serious health problems (plates 2.51 to 2.53). It is interesting that Diderot, who would likely have been aware of the influential work of Ramazzini, *De morbis artificum diatriba*, published in Modena in 1700, and which drew the attention of the medical and scientific world to the harm done to work-

ers by such fumes (Farge 1977, 993), chose to deny these effects in his *Encyclopédie* article "Caractères d'imprimerie." His attitude toward the health of the workers appears cavalier, no doubt due to his own prejudice against guild solidarities and "secrets":

[These] workers are advised to protect themselves from the fumes of regulus, which is regarded as a dangerous poison, but this is a prejudice: the use of regulus does not expose the typefounders to any illness specific to them. At most the fumes are only dangerous for cats. On the first occasions that the latter are exposed to these fumes, they are attacked by a giddiness of such a singular nature, that having been prey to it for a while in the room where they are forced to breathe the fumes, they throw themselves out the window. I have seen this happen twice in one day.

In this instance, the traditional wisdom of the workers was based on valuable experience and observation concerning the noxious effects on their health, evidence rejected by Diderot with a curious disregard for the implications of his own anecdote concerning the effects of these same fumes on animals.

The great number of women who worked within what we generally refer to as the proto-industrial economy are reflected only rarely in the prints, which concentrate on the relatively public workshop rather than the private space of the home. One exception is the image on lace making (plate 2.28), showing two lace makers in a domestic interior: lacework was commissioned and sold by both the Mercers (a male guild) and the Linen Drapers (a female guild). Huge numbers of women throughout France were involved in its production in the eighteenth century, mainly outside the workshop structure; Abensour (1923, 193) estimated there were 5,500 young lace workers in Alençon alone, and in the mountainous areas around Le Puy, by the start of the next century, there were some 30,000 workers, young girls and elderly women alike (Sweets 1995, 67). The article on lace making (*Ency.*: "Dentelle") was written by Diderot, who declared it was possible to learn the techniques of the trade in a week using his description, as he claimed to have done himself. We can safely assume that from an intellectual understanding to the actual production of a piece of specialist lace there is a gap he is not acknowledging; this was a highly skilled hand-

craft, passed on, typically, from mother to daughter, or through training establishments for young women. Réaumur showed himself to be more realistic when he remarked in his draft preface to the *Descriptions* that to be an artisan "experience must be linked with theory" (Houghton MS Typ 432.1 [1] #1, f. 2); but Diderot's comment, which might be dismissed as naïf arrogance, is nonetheless interesting as a reflection of the widespread assumption that women's trades, operating outside the apprenticeship system, did not involve comparable levels of skill.

In addition to the rural-based cottage workers, many women in the cities worked within their own domestic space or "chambre" and were known as *chambrelanes*. For example, in the Académie treatise on hatmaking mention is made in of the *éjarreuses,* who removed small pieces of flawed fiber from beaver hats with a tweezers: the work was brought to them in their homes, and they were paid 24 *sous* for a dozen finished hats (Nollet 1765, 63). They do not feature in the images related to that trade. Kaplan emphasizes that, even in Paris, there were always more workers operating outside than inside the trade organizations under the *ancien régime* (1988, 363), and studies of

the trades in a town such as Nantes confirm a similar pattern, with the numbers of illegal workers increasing as the century progressed (Musgrave 1997, 162). Fairchilds has shown that the consumer demand for luxury products such as fans, parasols, or decorative snuffboxes was so great, even on the part of the artisan classes themselves, that the official guild workshops could not possibly keep the market supplied; so even masters, despite the regulations, availed themselves of additional labor, which was illegal but by no means unskilled (1993, 231, 239–40). In Lyon women worked outside the guilds covering buttons and enjoyed enough success in the market to lead them to poach young girls from legitimate workshops to work on their behalf (Hafter 2001, 27).

Many of the women who worked as *chambrelanes* had no legal status or protection as workers. They suffered from a double standard whereby they could be harassed and threatened by both police and guild officers when the occasion dictated, especially at times of economic recession: there are many such examples, from illegal seamstresses whose handiwork was seized by officers of the tailors' guild (Coffin 1996, 33), to poor (and possibly illiterate) widows sewing quires for binders in their homes who could be arrested if found with subversive material in their possession (Sheridan 1992, 63). Official documents issued on behalf of the guilds deplored the "innumerable crowds of young girls" in "apartments, rooms and garrets" who were outside the control of a master or mistress, and therefore seen as likely to fall into debauchery.[49] Both men and women outside the established structures were frequently portrayed as "libertines" (Kaplan 1981, 261). Some idea of the difficulties that faced a woman living and working on her own can be gleaned from a police report quoted by Fairchilds. This gave an account of the widow of a master painter, Mme Godet, who worked in her rented room all day as a subcontractor painting fan mountings, as she was entitled to do; but she barely survived in poverty, though she worked from dawn to dusk. To add to her woes, her landlord's wife invaded her room two or three times a day looking for illegal lodgers—or, we can assume, lovers; and the jealous wife of a master from whom she took work accused her of having an affair with her husband, though the police found no evidence to substantiate such a claim (Fairchilds 1993, 240–41). A case such as this allows a rare glimpse of the tough working conditions and vulnerability of

women trying to survive independently of family or master's establishment.

There is some evidence, however, that in the second half of the century unmarried women in the luxury trades were increasingly gaining independence from family and guild master. Garden shows in his study of the capitation taxes in Lyon in 1788 that many hundreds of single embroiderers, seamstresses, and so forth were living independently, though still working for the masters of the city (1970, 187). Some of these single women, who never got to use their earnings for a dowry, left mutual legacies to sisters in the same trade, or to nephews and nieces (228–29). Throughout Paris large groups of fan makers, mainly women, lived close to each other: in the 1770s the police reported that in the rue Quincampoix, where the Fanmakers' Guild had its headquarters, twenty-four male and female fan makers lived together and practiced free love (Benabou 1987, 40–41). The women fabricating such luxury goods were reasonably well paid, though they received less than the men with whom they worked and formed liaisons; Benabou suggests that it was in this social group above all others that relationships of *concubinage,* outside traditional marriage, were established on the

basis of friendship and shared work, foreshadowing the widespread practice of workers in nineteenth-century France (287). Certainly, there is evidence that illegitimacy rates began to rise in France from the 1750s (Tilly and Scott 1987, 97).

In the Faubourgs and other privileged areas of Paris, such as the great abbeys like Saint Germain des Près, large numbers of women and men worked independently beyond the control of the guilds: as many as 10,000 for the Faubourg Saint-Antoine alone (Kaplan 1988, 360). These artisans could well have learned their craft in official workshops; Parisian masters were often happy to buy their products and sell them on to their clients under their own trademark (359). Although the workers of the privileged areas were officially banned from bringing their products across the boundary into Paris, many women were found illegally selling their wares on the streets of the city, especially at the poorer end of the market for fans and small items (Fairchilds, 1993, 240). These workers were the subject of constant complaint by the guilds, who repeatedly tried to get the privileged protection withdrawn from the Faubourgs and other enclaves.

Kaplan has shown how the arguments advanced by the workers

of the Faubourg Saint-Antoine in their own defence in 1716 anticipate the liberal theses on the primacy of the market that came to the fore in 1776. They present the Faubourg as "a kind of utopia, an enclave of liberty (but not licence)" (1988, 360), a bulwark against poverty and degeneration, where "all the poor workers of the Kingdom can freely practice their crafts and trades."[50] Were single women in these free zones any more emancipated from the patriarchal tutelage of family and master, to whom the "unbridled female," in Natalie Zemon Davis's phrase, was always a subject of concern? (1986, 185) Unfortunately, little is known of their lives and activities, and much research remains to be done in this area.

Do some of the women in our images reflect the existence of these armies of *chambrelanes?* Such may well be the case of the embroiderers in plate 2.23; the young woman on the left of the image might be showing her work to an employer, or illegally addressing herself directly to a consumer. She appears to the modern eye to have an unsettling "poetic" quality: unusually for this corpus of images, she looks directly out at the reader, as though appealing for recognition for her work and defying the silence of history in relation to such humble subjects

and their lives. Likewise, the *Encyclopédie* images of women painting and mounting fans in a domestic setting may well evoke similar realities, but without attracting any comment in the texts (plates 2.4 and 2.5).

Overall, the corpus of images brought together in this section breathes fresh life into our understanding of the wide range of artisanal activities in which women continued to be active throughout the eighteenth century.

::

ORNAMENTAL AND LUXURY PRODUCTS

The *bimbelotier* was the fabricator of knickknacks, in particular children's toys. Plate 2.1 was intended for the *Descriptions* but was never published; it was almost certainly commissioned by Réaumur, who referred to this trade in a letter to the abbé Bignon in July 1719. In his reply, Bignon remarked that in his youth, the term used was *Blinblotier* rather than *Binblottier,* as Réaumur had spelled it, and congratulated the scientist, who had left Paris on personal business, on finding the time to collect "so many unusual little pieces to give us pleasure."[51] It appears that a description, or even a sketch of a toy maker's shop sent by Réaumur, was one of the original elements to which Bignon refers

here. The original drawing for this image by Bretez is bound alongside the print in the Institut album (ms. 1064, f. 10); a manuscript note gives the title and confirms that it was drawn from life in a provincial workshop in 1720—"Les Blinblottiers Levé à Saumur." This is a rare example that allows us to identify a specific geographical location for the actual workshop illustrated. The relevant article in the *Encyclopédie* ("Bimbloterie") tells us that the trade of toy making was divided between the guilds of Mercer and Mirror-Lensmaker: the former had the right to trade in toys made of wood and textile, such as dolls, or horses and carriages, while the latter held the rights to toys cast in lead and pewter. The workshop figured in our image is mainly involved in casting, although an elaborate horse and carriage, possibly made of wood, is featured on the shelf: outside of Paris the distinction between the trades would have carried less weight, and it is unlikely that there was any relevant guild in Saumur. The two women pictured here, in what was probably a small family workshop, appear to be finishers, filing and sanding blemishes off the newly cast pieces and polishing them (plate 2.1 detail). This charming image does not show the stove where the molten lead for casting would have given off

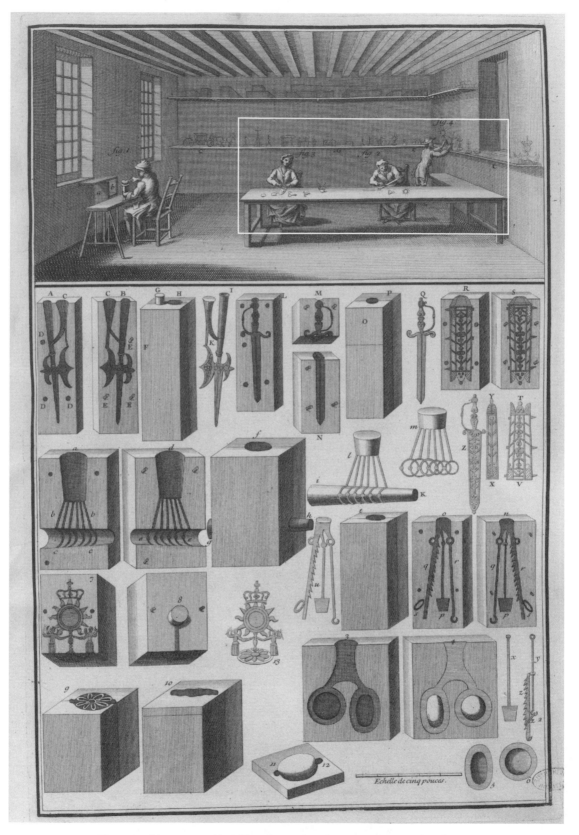

Pl. 2.1. Making toys and knickknacks. Institut de France, ms. 1065bis, f. 107
[Bimbelottier]. Des. Bretez, 1720.

noxious fumes (but see plate 2.52).

Among the favorite children's toys were miniature sets of tableware, such as plates, ewers, and vases: the *Encyclopédie* illustrates the casting of these objects in a series of plates entitled "Potier d'Etain Bimblotier" (*Ency. Planches,* vol. 8). Miniature versions of church artifacts were also in demand, as indicated in our image: crucifix, chalice, monstrance, or censer. The text of Diderot's article "Dragée" offers an interesting comment on these items in children's play of the period, describing them as "trinkets in lead and tin with which children decorate the chapels built for them in some private houses, and in which they are allowed, in a ridiculous fashion, to imitate the ceremonies of the church." Unsurprisingly, swords and other miniature weapons were also great favorites, as we see from the molds illustrated in the bottom section of this plate. "To appreciate the extent of the trade in these bagatelles, we need only remind ourselves of the prodigious quantities sold from one end of the year to the other, and especially the huge consumption that occurs at New Year" wrote Diderot (*Ency.:* "Bimbloterie"); presumably, all members of the artisan's household would be called on to assist in periods of peak demand.

Plate 2.2, prepared for the *Descriptions* in 1717 but never published, shows a fan maker's workshop, with four men and four women working side by side. Of rather poor quality, the engraving was not used by Diderot and offers an interesting contrast with the rationalized series of processes in the plates later produced by Goussier and Defehrt for the *Encyclopédie* (see plates 2.3 to 2.5). This may be a more realistic view, showing, as it does, most of the stages in the mounting of a fan taking place in one workspace. The women glue the paper onto the frame and trim and smooth the edges while the master folds the fan ready for mounting. The images in both collections emphasize that this was a trade with a large percentage of women workers, despite the fact that the Guild of Master Fan Makers (*Eventaillistes*) excluded them. When the popularity of fans grew in the wider population, throughout the first half of the century, the cheap labor of women was available to supply the swelling consumer market. The women pictured here may be employed in a legitimate workshop (wives, daughters, so-called domestic servants), but we have seen that many others worked on the fringe, making fans illegally.

Fairchilds asserts that the system "was so riddled with illegalities that whole neighborhoods in Paris where fans were made and sold lived outside the law" (Fairchilds 1993, 239).

The *Encyclopédistes* chose to represent an "enlightened," rationalized workspace and set of processes for the same trade, with an entirely female workforce. The first image (plate 2.3) represents a breakdown of the steps within production in an empty, clinical environment: the workers are separate ciphers of the task allotted to them, with no sense of community. Each is described by a specific term relating to her task. The woman seated on the left at the table is the *colleuse,* whose function, as her name suggests, is to glue two sheets of tissue paper together, using the small sponge and bowl of glue. The woman seated to the front, the *leveuse,* peels off the now double sheets from the pile supplied to her—from this gesture she gets her name, which is a term also used in papermaking—and, wetting the sides, spreads them on the hoops or frames of the appropriate size. The worker standing behind them has the sole function of taking the hoop and hanging it up to dry; she too takes her name—*l'étendeuse*—from papermaking, where a woman typically performed the

Pl. 2.2. Fan making. Institut ms. 1065bis, f. 203 [Eventailliste]. Eng. Lucas, 1717.

Pl. 2.3. Steps of manufacture in fan making. *Ency. Planches*, vol. 4. "Eventailliste, colage et preparation des papiers; Pl. I." S94.

task of hanging the paper on the treble (drying rack). The *coupeuse* removes the now dry paper from each hoop, and passes the pile to the *arrondisseuse,* who rounds off two of the corners with a scissors. Shown at the front right is an inert object: a stone block and beetle or mall, similar to that used by bookbinders, which might be used to smooth or beat the papers, especially in gilding or silverizing the top-quality fans. The women in the image are almost as inert as the stone block: they lack individualization in features or demeanor, and they look away from each other with no gestures implying communication: we do not, for example, see the *leveuse* pass the hoop to the *étendeuse.*

Plate 2.4 portrays the room where the fans are painted, probably with gouache, and where, we are told, two workers could operate, though we see only one in the image. Unlike the last image, this well-lit room looks more like a domestic interior than a workshop: the tables and chairs have carved legs, in contrast to the plain wooden benches of the previous plate. There are decorated panels on the walls, and, most impressively, drapes with ties on the windows. No comment is made on this rather striking change of décor in the notes, but we need not be too surprised by it: in this period an artisan's workshop or small manufacture of this kind would most frequently be located on the same premises as the master's dwelling, and this room might have doubled as part of the domestic interior. The woman performing this task would very likely be a member of the master's own family, wife, sister, or daughter: this would undoubtedly be seen as the "plum" activity in comparison to the type of work we have seen illustrated in the previous plates, carried out in a workshop in which (the notes remind us) a stove for making glue from hide clippings would typically have been installed. The glass-fronted case supported by a stand contains a model of the design the worker is to copy. The cardboard ruler (labeled "fig. 9"), in which holes have been punched at the appropriate distances, is fixed by a nail at the bottom of the paper, and a pencil is inserted in the holes in order to draw two arcs, one the exterior edge of the leaf, one marking the inner arc of the leaf. The edges of the paper, glued to the board, will subsequently be cut off along these lines. No trivial detail is omitted from the description, which shades into prescription: the worker, we are told, holds the brush in her right hand, and the paint in a shell (fig. 5) in her left as she copies the model in the glass case onto her paper. Figure 4 is the *coquillier* or shell cabinet for holding the little saucers or cups of pigment (*godets*).

With the third plate in the series (plate 2.5) we are back in a workshop, where the relatively skilled work of assembling the fan is carried out. The first worker is marking out the lines along which the leaf will be folded. For this she uses a walnut form or block, on which twenty radiating grooves, equidistant and at acute angles from the base, have been deeply etched. The skill of the *monteuse,* indeed, her "duty," as we are told, is to place the paper on this form in such a way that none of the principal features of the painting—typically more ornate on one side than the other—disappear into the folds of the fan: on this depends "the perfection of the piece." She then steadies the paper with a marble weight, and, holding the paper with her left hand, uses a flat piece of silver or brass, similar to a 24 *sous* coin, to press the paper into each groove, thus marking where the first folds are to be made. The paper is folded along the lines marked, and then folded accordionwise in the other direction along the mid line between the previous folds. The second worker uses the copper needle or rod to insert between

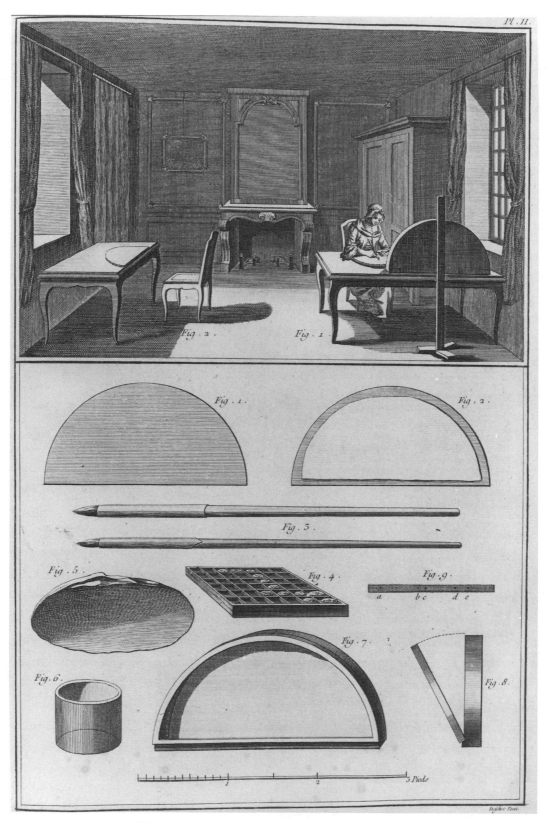

Pl. 2.4. Painting of fans. *Ency. Planches*, vol. 4. "Eventailliste, peinture des feuilles; Pl. II." S95.

Pl. 2.5. Assembling of fans. *Ency. Planches*, vol. 4. "Eventailliste, monture des éventails; Pl. III." S96.

the two sides of the paper along-side each fold, so that the sticks of the fan can be fitted into the spaces. The ends of the sticks are trimmed, and the leaf is then edged with a border of paper glued to both sides. This series is remarkable for its analytical presentation of the work tasks: each skill involved is highlighted separately, in contrast to the Académie's picture of an integrated workshop in which the steps in production are not so clearly differentiated.

The trade of *plumassier-panachier*, or feather-dresser, gives rise to a splendid picture

(2.6): a male sworn guild in this period (see *Ency.*: "Plumassier"), it had been an all-female guild in the middle ages, which is reflected in the fact that Lespinasse uses the feminine form (*Plumassières*) in the title of his article on this trade (1892, 2: 296–302). The statutes of 1599 still refer to "Masters and Mistresses" of the trade (art. 26), and to the rights of daughters to apprenticeship (art. 22). But the statutes of 1644 refer exclusively to masters and masters' sons, and the only privileges featured for women are those of widows (2: 301). Yet all the workers shown in this plate are women, operating in

what was at once workspace and shop. This was a high-end fashion industry, the plumes of a head-dress or "panache" being an essential element in court etiquette for all members of the nobility and the royal administration. The women's attire distinguishes them from the lowly workers of the majority of our images: they wear their hair fashionably dressed, or perhaps sport wigs, in contrast to the bonnets of the more menial working girls. Though the legend refers to them simply as "*ou-vrières,*" these women, who appear relatively mature in years, are likely to be members of a suc-

Pl. 2.6. Feather dresser. *Ency. Planches,* vol. 8. "Plumassier-panachier, différens ouvrages et outils; Pl. I." S221.

cessful merchant's household attached to the workspace: the singularly well-dressed child, who is the only male figure featured, presumably being part of their family group. Ostrich plumes and peacock tails hang from the ceiling; these, along with other, more prized plumes, such as those of the heron or egret, would be degreased, washed, dyed, or bleached in another area of the workshop, and then thinned, curled, or crimped as required. The knives lying on the table in front of the woman second from the left would serve for thus dressing the feathers, which she

then sews together with a large needle. The woman on the left is preparing a headdress for a duke on a ceremonial occasion; the woman in the center is working on a splendid panache for a horse to wear for the entry of an ambassador to Paris, while the woman on the right adds feather ornamentation to a gown. This was all skilled and intricate work. In 1788 Louis Sebastien Mercier mocked the "*têtes emplumées*" of fashionable women who wore feather headdresses, no longer the preserve of the nobility; the feather dressers, he claimed, had made a fortune from this trend (1788, ix:

233–34).

In plate 2.7, luxury snuffboxes and other small items of value are being fabricated in the workshop of a "*Piqueur et Incrusteur de Tabatière.*" The Guild of *Tabletiers-Peigniers* laid claim to the fabrication of many fashionable luxury items, from combs to gaming tables, but masters tended to specialize in one area, as seems to be the case in the workshop featured here. The women and men in our image do the same fine work of decorating tortoiseshell with inlays of gold and silver filigree wire. The person at the far end of the table on the right may

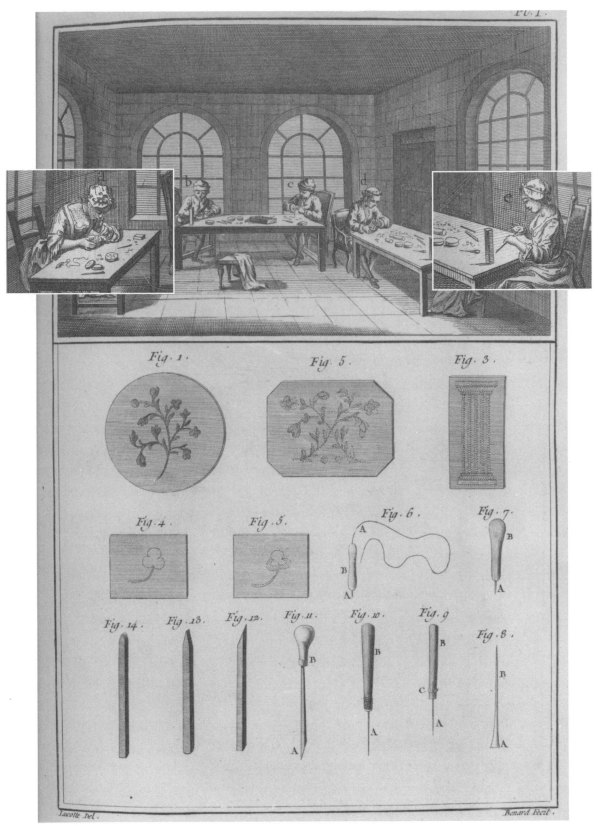

Pl. 2.7 and details. Decorating gold and silver snuffboxes. *Ency. Planches*, vol. 9. "Piqueur et incrusteur de tabatiere, ouvrages et outils; Pl. I." S132.

Pl. 2.8. Making artificial pearls. *Ency. Planches,* vol. 4. "Emailleur, a la lampe perles fausses; Pl. II." S26.

well be the master—distinguished by his wig—with a mixture of apprentices and family members working with him: the plate legend makes a reference to "the genius of the artist" in applying these techniques, which remark would appear to apply in this rare example to both genders. The two young women are using different skilled techniques: the woman on the far left (see detail) is engraving the design (of which examples are shown in the lower section of the plate) into the surface with an etcher's needle or *burin* (the tool shown at "fig. 7"), before inserting the gold or silver filigree into the groove. The worker at the far right undertakes the "*brodé,*" a composite of three other tech-

niques of incrustation (detail). These skilled young women may well be the master's daughters or sisters, trained in the family workshop but denied the benefits of formal apprenticeship in this male trade.

Plate 2.8 shows an enamelling workshop for making artificial pearls, which, the related text tells us, were so realistic that they were in high demand and fetched a good price (*Ency.:* "Perles"). In the first image, the person at the right is about to cut a tube of glass into small pieces, which will then be blown by the man at the table on the left into the required bead shape (round, oval, etc.). The young woman beside him smooths any rough edge left

where the glass was separated from the tube. They each work with a lamp, kept burning by a foot-operated bellows beneath the table: the room is darkened so they can see the fine detail by the light of the lamp. The two characters in the background are involved in a separate process: the man is melting glass and drawing it into a very fine thread, which is then wound onto a reel by the young woman: this glass thread was used for making an ornament for women's attire called an "*aigrette,*" presumably because the pieces of glass thread, cut and arranged in a bunch, bore some resemblance to feather ornamentation.

In another part of the same

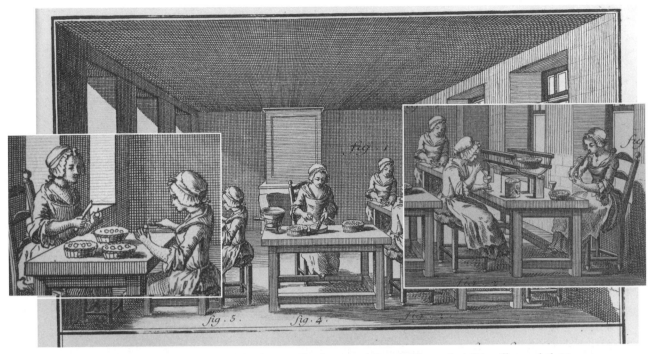

Pl. 2.9 and details. Filling and finishing artificial pearls. *Ency. Planches,* vol. 4. "Emailleur, a la lampe, perles fausses; Pl. III." S27.

workshop (plate 2.9), six young women complete the fabrication of the pearls. The woman at the far end of the table on the right is descaling a fish called the *ablette* (bleak), found in abundance in the Marne River, whose scales are the color of pearl. The scales were then ground to powder and mixed with liquid; the second woman is sucking a drop of this compound into her mouth through a glass straw, while the third is shown blowing it back into a glass bead, which thus acquires the appearance of a pearl (detail). This can hardly have been pleasant work! The pearls are placed in a basket on the cradle in front of them: this is a type of jigger, which the third woman is operating with her foot

as she works so that the constant oscillation spreads the liquid evenly around the inside of each bead. The woman at the center is filling the inside of each pearl by sticking it onto a piece of wood and dipping it in a basin of melted wax; the women on the left insert a tiny roll of paper into the pearls while the wax is still soft so that they can then be strung through this funnel. Large numbers of women were employed in this type of operation, which required patience and dexterity.

Plate 2.10 offers an image of the same processes; it was prepared some fifty years earlier (almost certainly between 1715 and 1720) but never published. It is very clear (particularly from the

bottom section of the plate, where the materials and techniques are illustrated) that it served as a model for Diderot; it is possible, given the information highlighted by Mme Gardey in 1964a (168), that the identification written in black ink—*"Fabrique des fausses perles"*—on the copy in the Bibliothèque de l'Arsenal (Gr. Fol. 435ter [17], f. 3) is that of Diderot himself, who had many of the Académie plates in his possession. This is a good example of a workshop where, already at this early period, the process has been broken down by task to create an industrial-style manufacture of a craft product. In this image the workshop is clearly situated in a rural

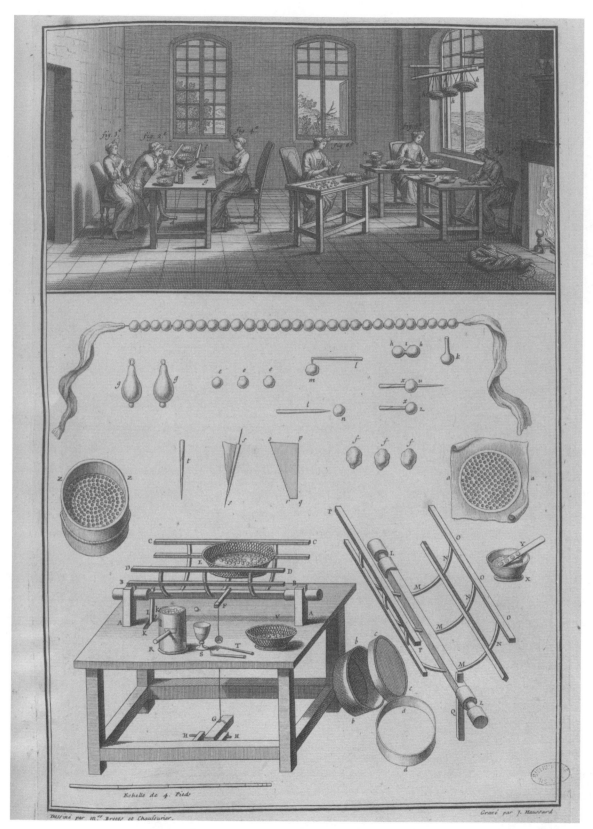

Pl. 2.10. Enamelling workshop: filling and finishing artificial pearls. Institut ms. 1065bis, f. 170. [*Perles fausses*].
Des. Bretez and Chaufourier, eng. J. Haussard.

Pl. 2.11 and detail. Making and stringing artificial pearls. Institut ms. 1065bis, f. 169. [*Perles fausses*].
Des. Bretez and Chaufourier, eng. J. Haussard.

setting, as were many of those drawn for Réaumur, but this detail is stripped out of the *Encyclopédie* version, which features a more clinical, perhaps urban environment, and where the young man on the right is replaced by a woman to create an all-female workforce. The similarities between the plates give us some authority to remark on the continuity in the processes across the century, and the female-identified nature of this trade, which, if anything, appears to have been more accentuated in the later period. A companion plate in the unpublished Académie series corresponds closely to our plate 2.8, with the added detail of a woman stringing the pearls (plate 2.11 and detail).

The image depicting the fabrication of artificial flowers (plate 2.12) stands out from our corpus of *Encyclopédie* images in a number of ways. It gives a more realistic impression of the hustle and bustle of a crowded workshop, with twelve people working in close proximity, than the more "rationalized" images, such as the series on fan making discussed earlier, where processes are broken up into a series. Materials (vellum, linen, etc.) hang overhead or lie on the floor. The legend refers to the "male workers, female workers and children" who all work together, probably drawn from a number of families, and the designer suggests communication between them: the women watch or talk to the young girls who are learning the trade (detail), and the man who is winding green vellum onto wire (for the stems) is no doubt directing the "little boy" who turns the wheel for him. One young man cuts out petals from a sheet of material using a puncheon, and the women and little girls assemble them into flower buds and arrangements (anemones, buttercups, roses etc.). A woman at the far end of the table at the left uses a machine to crimp and flute materials as needed, while another at the right of the detail uses a goffering iron to apply finishes.

Damascening was the art of

Pl. 2.12 and detail. Artificial flower fabrication. *Ency. Planches,* vol. 4. "Fleuriste artificiel, plans d'emporte-pieces de feuilles de fleurs; Pl. I." S126.

inlaying gold and silver in patterns on steel (known as Damascus steel), a craft imported into France from Italy in the Renaissance period, like many such decorative trades. Sword hilts (illustrated in the bottom section of plate 2.13), candlesticks, and muskets, among other objects, were decorated with precious metals. The steel surfaces were chased with an intricate pattern (using the tools shown in detail), into which gold or silver thread was laid; the piece was tempered over a brazier, then burnished and polished. Though poor in artistic quality, this engraving from 1718,

drawn on instructions from Réaumur and undoubtedly based on a visit to a workshop, is extremely interesting because it offers evidence of women working with tools on metals. The later, roughly equivalent *Encyclopédie* plate does not show any women involved in this trade (*Ency. Planches,* vol. 4: "Ciseleur Damasquineur," plate 1). The woman on the right (detail) appears to be using one of the engraving chisels illustrated in the bottom section, and the woman on the left a brush such as that shown as *M,* no doubt part of the finishing process. A proof of this

plate, hand corrected with notes by Réaumur, is conserved in the Bibliothèque de l'Arsenal (Gr. Fol. 435 ter doss. 11, f. 3), but the accompanying text is missing.

An image from a silver plater's workshop gives another interesting detail of a woman working metal: she is scoring or cross-hatching a metal (possibly copper) plate, with a special knife (see tools in bottom section) so that the silver leaf will cling to the surface when it is heated. The physical effort required is signalled by the way in which she braces her foot against the bench for extra strength (de-

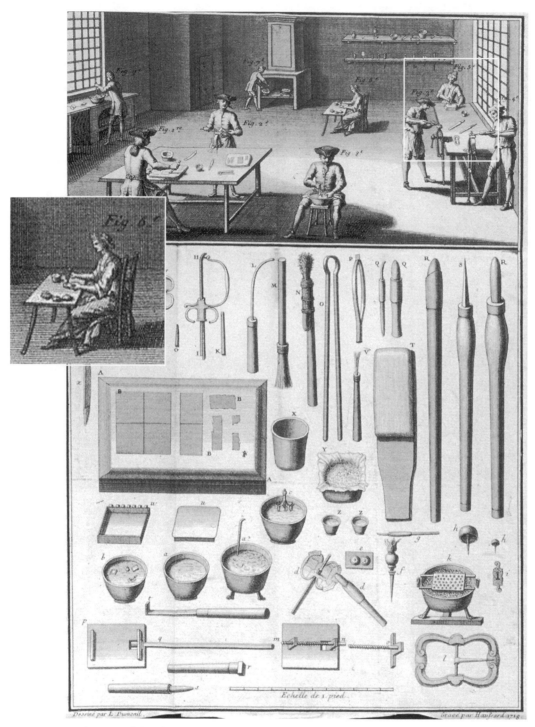

Pl. 2.13 and detail. Damascening with gold and silver. [*Damasquineur*]. MS Typ 432.1 #10, Department of Printing and Graphic Arts, Houghton Library, Harvard College Library. Des. L. Dumenil, eng. Haussard, 1718.

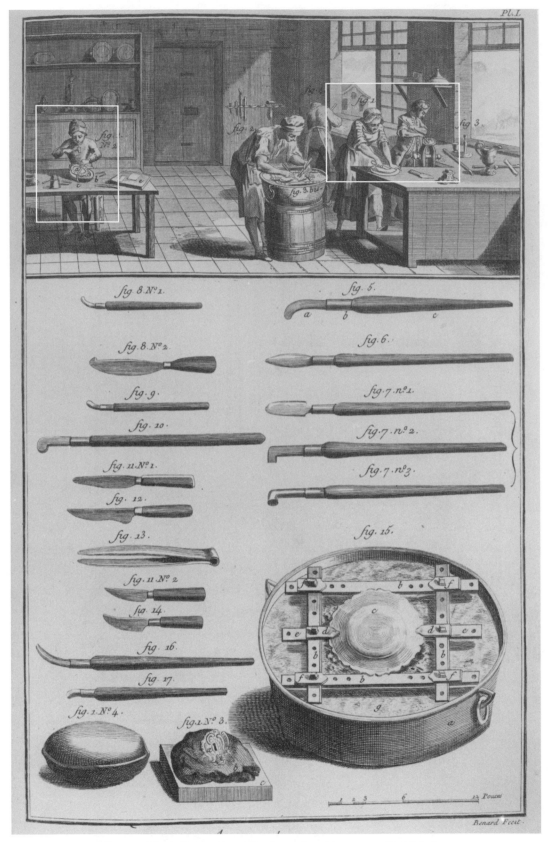

Pl. 2.14. Silver plating. *Ency. Planches*, vol. 1. "Argenteur; Pl. I." S284.

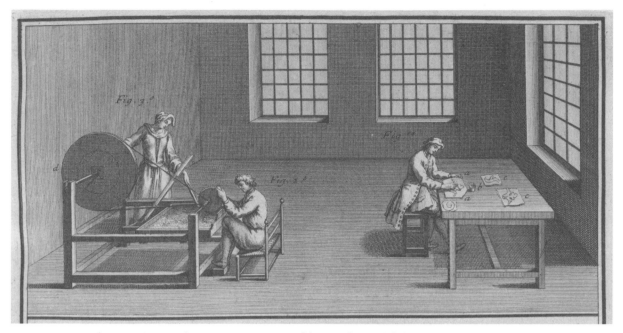

Pl. 2.15. Mirror making. Institut ms. 1064, fol. ci (B) [*Miroitier*]. Eng. L. Simonneau, 1713.

tail).

A drawing for the engraving of the mirror maker's workshop (intended as the third in a series) was approved by Réaumur in December 1712 and engraved shortly thereafter. In fact, two versions of the same scene (both drawing and plate) exist in manuscript collections, but the other version was not approved and is less detailed than the one reproduced here (plate 2.15).[52] The person on the right appears to be making drawings or templates for the ornaments (typically made of wood and gilded) which would decorate a mirror frame; the man at the left is cutting or polishing the pieces on the wheel, while the woman both turns the wheel and controls the tension and speed

with the notched stick in her left hand. While her work clearly demands skill and constant attention, it was undoubtedly seen as ancillary to the work of the "craftsmen": her presence in the workshop would typically remain unrecorded in guild or administrative documents.

The Gold-beaters' Guild represented one of the luxury trades, restricted to only thirty master-merchants in Paris (*Ency.*: "Batteur"): preparing the fine gold leaves was a complex and labor-intensive process, whose secrets—such as the use of finely stretched ox gut (*baudruche*) for burnishing—were jealously guarded (*Ency.*: "Battre l'or"). In the *Encyclopédie* picture (2.16) four of the workers appear to be

young men, family members or apprentices, but the two young women are simply referred to as "*ouvrières.*" To them falls the delicate work of peeling sheets from a beaten pile with special pincers and trimming them with a knife (on a pad covered in calf-kin held on the knees). They then divide each sheet into four and reassemble the smaller sheets into piles carefully and skillfully, separated by the appropriate pieces of vellum, parchment, or skin. A plate illustrating this trade was prepared for the *Descriptions* as early as 1693, but never published (2.17); it allows us to see the same gender breakdown in the workshop over half a century earlier, with a woman separating out the gold leaves and using the same

Pl. 2.16. Gold beating. *Ency. Planches*, vol. 2. "Batteur d'or; Pl. I." S43.

Pl. 2.17. Gold beating. Institut ms. 1065bis, f. 87 [*Batteur d'or;* 1693].

tools and techniques. In the statutes of 1699, recorded by Lespinasse (1886, 2: 61), it is implied that a master's children (*enfants*) of both sexes could be registered as apprentices, but by 1749 the statutes provide only for masters' sons (*fils de maîtres*) functioning as guild members. For the eighteenth century the images provide valuable evidence of the continuity of the work roles of the women, despite the erosion of their position in the statutes.

In the *Encyclopédie*'s image of a wood gilder's workshop we see how the gold leaf is applied to the wood, particularly picture

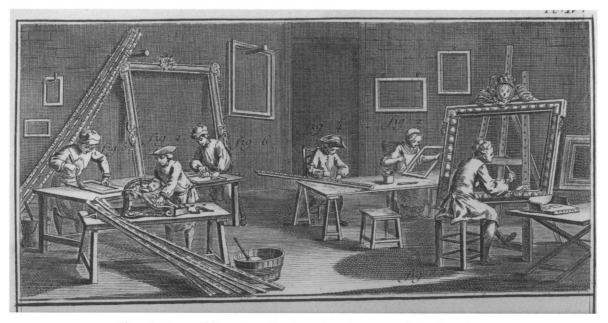

Pl. 2.18. Frame gilding. *Ency. Planches*, vol. 2. "Doreur sur bois; Pl. IV." S269.

or mirror frames: the man on the right applying the gilt is probably the master. This is a good example of an image where the presence of the woman is contradicted by the plate legend; the person second from right is described as an *"ouvrier,"* though she is clearly female. We cannot know whether this was a simple printing error or perhaps an example of the gender-blindness of a commentator so used to the ubiquitous presence of women in this role that he thought it irrelevant. The woman, whose existence is thus recorded only at the level of the image, is priming a frame with vermilion, a task typical of the kind of preparatory or finishing activity attributed to women in craft workshops.

The two plates on book binding that we reproduce from the *Descriptions* were prepared in the 1690s, with meticulous care, by Jacques Jaugeon and his colleagues, the first group charged with the work of recording the "technologies" of France. In the first (plate 2.19), a stitcher (*brocheuse*) is sitting at a frame for sewing the printed quires of a book together. She will stitch the quires by hand onto the cords or thongs that are on the frame; the cords will eventually show as raised bands across the spine of the book, or they will be sunk into slots sawed into the folds of the paper to give the book a flat back. This work required skill and patience, compared with the tasks being carried out by the two male

workers in this picture, one of whom is beating the folded book flat with a mallet and block, while the other is trimming the edges of the book. However, we know that the woman's task was regarded as the lowest category of work in this trade. The work of sewing, identified with women and the domestic sphere, was consistently undervalued across the spectrum of trades: *brocheuses*, who were often widows of deceased workers, were paid a pittance and exploited by unscrupulous publishers, despite the high status of the book trade in general under the *ancien régime* (Sheridan 1992, 63). The corresponding *Encyclopédie* plate, published in 1772, clearly used this one as a model (vol. 8, "Relieur," plate 1), with the same

Pl. 2.19. Bookbinding. Dudin, *L'Art du relieur doreur de livres*, Pl. VIII. Eng. L. Simonneau.

Pl. 2.20. Bookbinding: gilding. Dudin, *L'Art du relieur doreur de livres*, Pl. XI. Eng. L. Simonneau.

layout and gender distribution of tasks.

In the two parallel series on bookbinding we can compare the respective images illustrating the gilding of book edges and leather bindings. An interesting switch occurs: the 1697 image (plate 2.20) shows a woman with a brush in her hand priming the cut edges of the book before gilding, while a man in the center lays the gold leaf on the spine of the book, obviously one of the most important steps in the finishing of the

Pl. 2.21. Bookbinding: gilding. *Ency. Planches,* vol. 8. "Relieur doreur; Pl. V." S273.

binding. In the *Encyclopédie* version (plate 2.21), gender roles have been swapped, and now it is the woman who lays on the gold leaf. Was this change due to observation by the editor or designer in the 1770s? We cannot, alas, be sure: we know that Diderot was forced to camouflage his effective plagiarism of the Académie's plates after he was visited by their inspectors (see p. 8), and the changes made in this plate might simply be a result of his concern in this regard. But it is likely that such tasks were interchangeable in a small workshop, especially where family members worked together. The techniques described in both versions are es-sentially the same; the third (male) worker is using a roll for tooling the flat covers.

The *Encyclopédie* shows us a woman doing the job of *découpeur et gaufreur* (plate 2.22). This was a skilled trade involving techniques of pinking and perforating materials to allow the fine materials of underclothes to show through an outer garment; known as slashing in its most extreme form, it was fashionable in the sixteenth and early seventeenth centuries and was maintained by the Swiss Guards in France in the design of their uniforms into the eighteenth century (Franklin: 1884, "Brodeurs-Chasubliers, Dé-coupeurs," 7). It also encom-passed the embossing of complex designs on the rich materials used in fashion—for example, in the making of cuffs, or the embellish-ment of skirts—or in *passe-menterie* for decoration on beds, carriages, and so forth. These arts had fallen out of fashion in the eighteenth century, and the *Ency-clopédie* article "Découpeur" tells us that where there was formerly a flourishing guild of over sixty masters, only eight remained.[53] The bottom section of the plate il-lustrates the selection of pinking and goffering irons, tools the young woman might use: the de-signs produced by irons *A-G* on the bottom left are illustrated on the sample piece of material (la-

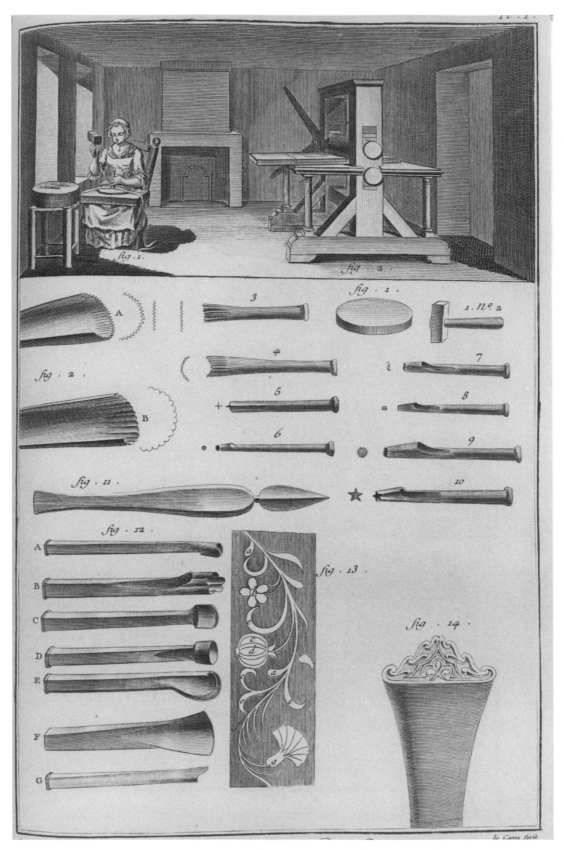

Pl. 2.22. Pinking and perforating. *Ency. Planches,* vol. 3. "Découpeur et gaufreur; Pl. I." S200.

beled "fig. 13"), with corresponding letters. In the vignette, the worker uses one such iron with a lump hammer to emboss a bell-shaped design on the strip of material, which is clearly destined for use as a border. The material is placed between several sheets of paper and rested on a lead plate (fig. 1) to avoid damage to the expensive textile. The press on the right of the vignette is used for embossing designs on cardboard. This is all skilled work, requiring training, but strangely, only this woman features in the set of three plates on this supposedly male trade. In 1776 the *Découpeurs* were united by edict with the Seamstresses' Guild, the latter complaining to the Crown that the choice of such a male guild was inappropriate (Crowston 2001, 212). Our image suggests one possible explanation for the decision if the work was, in fact, frequently performed by the women of a household; moreover, there was a complex relationship between this group and the *Brodeurs,* a guild where, as will be shown, the majority of the workers were, in fact, women.

The Guild of Embroiderers ("Brodeurs, Découpeurs, Egratigneurs, Chasubliers" in the 1704 statutes) is an interesting example of a guild that was mixed, and predominantly female from the middle ages into the seven-

teenth century. When the *communauté* was first established in 1295, *maître* and *maîtresse* had equal access, girls and boys could be apprenticed on equal terms, and one of the officers (*jurés*) was always a woman (Lespinasse 1886, 2: 162). Of the ninety-three names of initial members registered at the top of these statutes, only a dozen were men; a significant proportion of the women were married to men in other professions, so they were here acceding to mastership as independent persons (Franklin 1884, "Brodeurs-Chasubliers, Découpeurs," 1–2). Their position was explicitly bulwarked in the statutes of 1566 (4). But by 1648, women's rights were clearly being curtailed: only sons and sons-in-law are mentioned in the regulations with regard to the mastership (Lespinasse 2: 178, art. 2); a widow who remarries another embroiderer cannot instruct her own children in the trade (art. 8); and widows cannot take on any new apprentices (art. 13). In the statutes of 1704 a major shift has taken place: there is no longer any reference to women acceding to apprenticeship, mastership, or any other rights (2: 180). The privileges of daughters are now reduced to those of transferring mastership to a husband, and the possibility of "being employed" in the trade, but they have no route to becom-

ing qualified independently.

The *Encyclopédie* plate on embroidery (2.23) suggests not a sterile workshop space like so many of the other vignettes in this collection but a home: we note the frill in front of the grate, the pictures on the wall, and personal items on the mantle shelf. There are two young women working in this space: the woman on the right is bent over the frame, one hand above the material pushing the needle through, the other hand pulling needle and thread from below; the woman on the left is holding a frame and gestures to the pattern of a waistcoat to be embroidered that has been sketched on the material. These young women may be working within the domestic space of a master's establishment, either as members of his family, daughters of another master, or as servants; or they are possibly illegal workers operating from their family home, or a shared room, as outworkers, selling their services to master tradesmen who commonly contravened their own trade regulations. Women in the garment trades working outside the confines of a shop were commonplace, especially in the privileged zones in the Faubourgs or Saint Germain des Prés, and these women might equally well be involved in underground sales networks. The bottom section of the

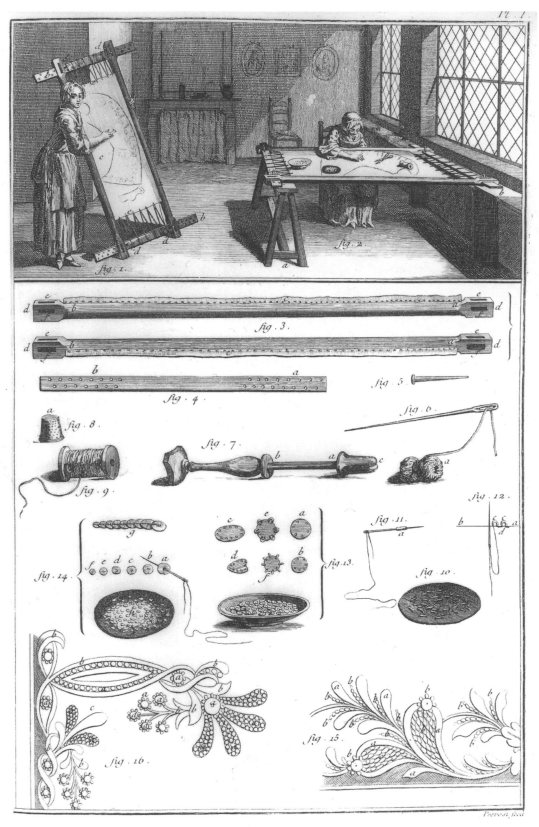

Pl. 2.23. Embroidery. *Ency. Planches*, vol. 2. "Brodeur; Pl. I." S150.

plate illustrates the fine work these women accomplish using threads, beads, and sequins. The direct appeal of the woman on the left looking out at the viewer and communicating the significance of her work, sets her apart in our corpus from the majority of silent, docile workers with heads bent to their task.

Although the majority of embroiderers in the eighteenth century, as in earlier centuries, do appear to be women, the *Encyclopédie* article "Brodeur" gives a chilling reminder of their lack of status and economic power: "We only include under the title 'embroiderers' [male] workers who work with heavy materials: fine linen embroidery is done by women, who belong neither to the embroiderers' guild nor any other." But the guild masters broke or manipulated the rules when it suited them: plate 2.24 from the Académie's collection gives the lie to the text just quoted, as we can clearly see that women are working on heavy church vestments. Patterns suited to such heavy materials are illustrated in the bottom section. Two young women—are they masters' daughters or illegal employees?—work at a frame (detail), and the text specifies that one is right-handed, and the other left-handed: as they sit on opposite

sides of the frame, this allows for maximum speed of production. The material could be wound on as they complete each section.

The text of the *Encyclopédie* article "Broderie" does refer to the esteem in which some embroiderers are held—those of Saxony in particular—and to the "judgement" the women use in choosing the effects wrought through the techniques of their trade. The bottom of plate 2.23 illustrates some of these effects, along with the embroiderer's few tools (an advantage for poorer women), and the various types of sequins used. The Académie text remarks that this was one of the better-paying activities for a woman, at 25 *sous*, but adds, "Men are paid more, in proportion to their talent and skill" (Saint-Aubin 1770, 9). By way of comparison, skilled masons or carpenters were paid between 40 and 50 *sous* a day, but it is true that most women were paid far less (Sonenscher 1983, 152). As these skilled women no longer had any status within the official guild structure, their talent and skill were taken for granted and apparently attracted no additional economic reward.

The trades that dealt with the making and decoration of all types of clothing employed women. The most prestigious guild in the field was that of the

tailors, a male guild whose regulations repeatedly tried to keep women out of the workshop, with the exception of daughters of masters who had the right to make clothes for children up to the age of eight (*Statuts de 1660:* see Franklin 1884, "Couturières," 1).

For a long time tailors tried to retain the exclusive right to make bodices, and in the Académie's image (plate 2.25) we see one male tailor fitting a bodice on the client. But fashion increasingly favored the "*robe*"—an example of which hangs behind the women workers—rather than the bodice and petticoat, and the tailors had to compete in a market flooded by large numbers of clandestine workers (Coffin 1996, 31–34; Roche 1989, 140–45). Despite repeated bans by the guild (Coffin, 25), the master tailors were happy to draw on the pool of poorly paid women workers, in addition to the female members of their own households, especially if they could keep them under control within their own workshops. This image shows the clear segregation of tasks: as women took over more and more the work of sewing in the eighteenth century, the tailor's guild defined it as "accessory" and inferior to the work of cutting. Sewing was not regarded as a "skill" unless it was being done by men (Coffin 1996,

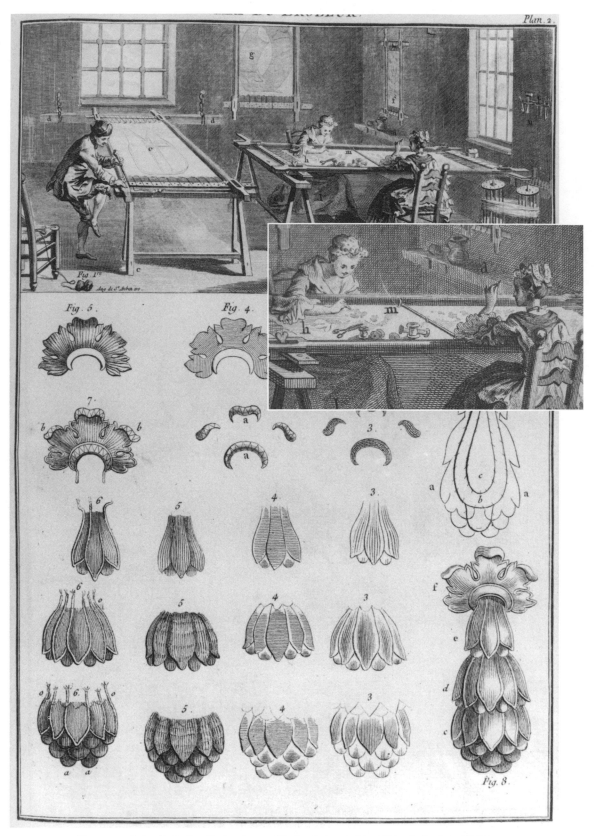

Pl. 2.24 and detail. Embroidering heavy fabrics. Saint-Aubin, *L'Art du brodeur*, Pl. II.

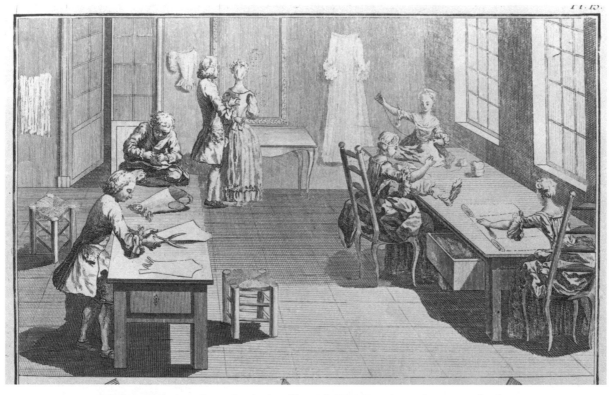

Pl. 2.25. Tailoring. Garsault, *Art du tailleur*, Pl. XVI. Des. Garsault, eng. Berthault.

24). The woman with her back to the viewer is referred to as a *couturière*, a seamstress; her relatively superior status vis-à-vis the other two young women (simply *filles*, girls) is indicated by her fashionably dressed hair. We may also note the abundant lace on the women's sleeves: workers in the garment trades liked to emulate the style of their clients. Unusually, this and the next plate were designed by the author of the treatise, Garsault, who was very well versed in the operations of the trade, and his eye for detail adds to the ethnographic value of the images.

In 1675 the seamstresses (*cou-turières*)—who had previously sold their services, unprotected, to a number of trades—succeeded in forming their own all-female guild, with the right to dress women and children of both sexes up to the age of eight (Garsault 1769, 48); the founding edict referred to cultural conceptions of modesty, deeming it to be "suitable to the demureness and modesty of women and girls, to allow themselves to be dressed by persons of their sex" (Coffin 1996, 30). Crowston has emphasized how the model established by this edict "suggested that a woman's sex should determine all aspects of the work she performed, from

the products she made to the people she worked with to the clients she served" (2001, 174). There were 100 to 150 new mistresses admitted every year over the eighteenth century, though the regulations allowed mistresses to take only one apprentice in an effort to keep down numbers qualifying (Coffin, 31). The tailors fought bitter legal battles throughout the eighteenth century to keep the seamstresses and the female linen drapers from encroaching on their territory. Images of these women who had acquired power through the guild system are rare: the *couturières* do not feature as independent arti-

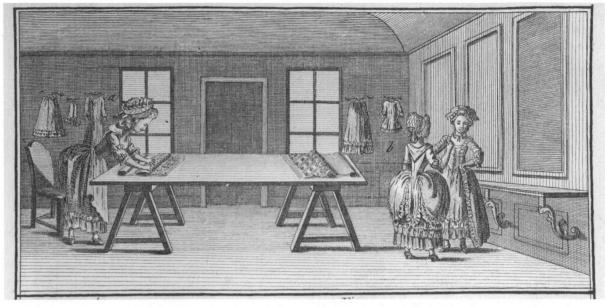

Pl. 2.26. Seamstress's workshop. *Encyclopédie méthodique. Recueil de planches; 2ème division des arts et métiers,* vol. 6. "Couturière." © Bibliothèque Sainte Geneviève, Paris. Photo N. Boutros.

sans in either of our two main collections. Noting their absence, Panckouke had a new image engraved for his *Encyclopédie méthodique* (plate 2.26), with a textual description by Roland de la Platière, who also worked on the Académie collection (1782–91, *Deuxième division des arts et métiers méchaniques,* 223–26, a subsection of the *Encyclopédie méthodique*). This plate shows two seamstresses in their workshop. The woman on the left is preparing to line a piece: we can see the two separate bolts of material. The seamstress on the right is measuring a client for a dress: she herself is fashionably wearing a *polonaise* to which the plate legend specifically calls attention. In his

text, de la Platière emphasized that the tailors had priority in the fabrication of many women's garments, but he chose to group the latter together under the entry for the seamstresses because this seemed more "natural" to him, and because "some seamstresses also made them" (223).

Garsault included the "Marchande de mode" in his treatise on the *Art du tailleur* somewhat reluctantly, because, he declares (with some justification), these women have arrogated the right to make some garments that should properly fall within the province of the seamstress. "They belong to no trade guild," he continues, "and can work only in the shadow of their husbands, who, to

confer this faculty on them, must belong to the Guild of Merchant Mercers. They call what they do a 'talent'" (54). With the same scathing tone, he points out the fashion-dependent nature of the trade: the work of trimming in muslin, ribbon, fur, embossed fabrics, net, and lace demands imagination and novelty, qualities he clearly considers frivolous despite the fact that they were central to Paris's reputation for luxury goods. The position of these tradeswomen was strengthened when they were given guild status in 1776 (Roche 1989, 293). The garments that the *modistes* make are short capes (such as the client is wearing in plate 2.27), fur-lined wraps (*pelisses*), and head-dresses

Pl. 2.27. Fashion shop: "Marchande de mode." Garsault, *Art du tailleur*, Pl. XIII. Des. Garsault, eng. Aveline.

(*coeffes*).

This plate presents a space that is both shop and workshop: the women on the left are finishing garments, while the *maîtresse* on the right shows her wares to a client (who is presumably being chaperoned by the young man behind). The hierarchy in the shop is highlighted by the women's *coiffure*: the mistress's hair is fashionably dressed, as is that of the mature woman working on the headdress (though her clothes are less elaborate, and she is presumably in a subordinate position); the two seemingly younger assistants wear the more modest bonnet. The mistress also

sports a double layer of lace on her cuffs. A revised version of this plate was published eight years later in the supplement to the *Encyclopédie* (see plate 5.5): the bottom section was directly copied from this image, underlining the relationship between the two.

Lace making has been included in this section because its highly prized products were central to the luxury and fashion trades, although their production allies them more with the proto-industrial textile trades, as most lace was made by women in their homes; only occasionally was the manufacture concentrated in

workshops, as was the case in Caen. Described in the *Encyclopédie* ("Dentelle") as "very beautiful and very precious ornaments," lace was the most costly commodity in Europe: Hufton estimates that by the mid-eighteenth century silk sold for about 10 shillings per yard, while an equivalent amount of lace cost about 20 pounds. But the wage of the lace maker was among the lowest of all women workers, barely enough to provide a couple of pounds of bread for a day's work. This is another example of how "skill" as we understand it had no objective value independent of the worker's gender and relationship (or lack of it) to the corporate system. In default of any guild order, convents (in Flanders) and pious laywomen (the *Béates* in the Velay region of France) organized training and residential work for girls to help them acquire a dowry from their meager earnings (Hufton 1993, 24). Some women, to reduce their living costs, lived together in rented rooms, what Hufton refers to as "clustering" (1984, 362; see Collins 1989, 454). This is perhaps reflected in plate 2.28, where our two young lace makers are described as working in a *chambre*, "travail en chambre" being the expression used in this period for outwork. Also, the curtains on the windows and the elaborate tables suggest a domestic setting rather than a workshop, though these are highly stylized and suggest a standard of furnishing (the carved table and mantelpiece) that would scarcely have been available to such women.

Hufton underlines that "the value [of lace] lay entirely in the handiwork, and many years were required to learn the skill" (1993, 23). Plate 2.28 shows one woman using the technique of bobbin lace (made on a "pillow" shown as Fig. 6), which came from Flanders and dominated in this period, while the other (on the right) copies the design of a piece of lace onto vellum so that it can be re-

produced. The majority of lace makers made lace according to the traditional styles and patterns of their area, but some worked new patterns supplied to them by the merchants who competed for success in the world of high fashion, and this work attracted higher payment. Nearly half the heads of the lace establishments in Le Puy in the late eighteenth century were women (Sweets 1995, 68).

In the *Encyclopédie* image illustrating the trade of the *boutonnier passementier* (2.29) we see a very similar bobbin technique in use by a woman for the making of garter, frog, or watch cord; the curved pad on her knee is called a *boisseau*. Her male companion uses a related technique to make round cord. In the left half of the image a man is covering buttons with silk thread while the woman sews bullion piping or other ornamentation onto the buttons. Originally, all buttons were made with hand-sewn silk or other precious materials within this trade, which was united with that of the *passementiers* (see also images 3.25 to 3.29) as early as 1558. But from the seventeenth century onward, the guild was under constant pressure from the sumptuary laws forbidding the use of gold or silver in *passementerie*, and from the competition posed by buttons made from lesser materials (matching the material of the garment, for

example), from buttons made on frames, or buttons made in molds from horn (Franklin 1788, "Passementiers-Boutonniers," 7–8). As late as 1653 the statutes of the corporation record the right of the wives and daughters of masters to be employed within the trade (Lespinasse 1886, 2: 154–55), though they had no access to independent roles within the guild. The plate legend here takes pains to point out that normally six workers would sit around this hexagonal table, but just two are shown in the interest of clarity, as one would otherwise obscure the work of the other, and the details would be too small in scale: the didacticism of the plate supersedes its documentary function. In a very rare reference to the workers' conditions, the author specifies that the workspace has been divided by a windowed partition "so that the workers [. . .] may be more at ease." Given what we know of eighteenth-century workshops, it is more likely that this reflects the writer's utopian aspirations than any observed reality.

Precisely the same bobbin techniques are illustrated in plate 2.30, which was engraved in 1718 for the Académie and allows us to see, in the lower section, some of the finely detailed work of these *boutonniers-passementiers*. Interestingly, in this plate, the task per-

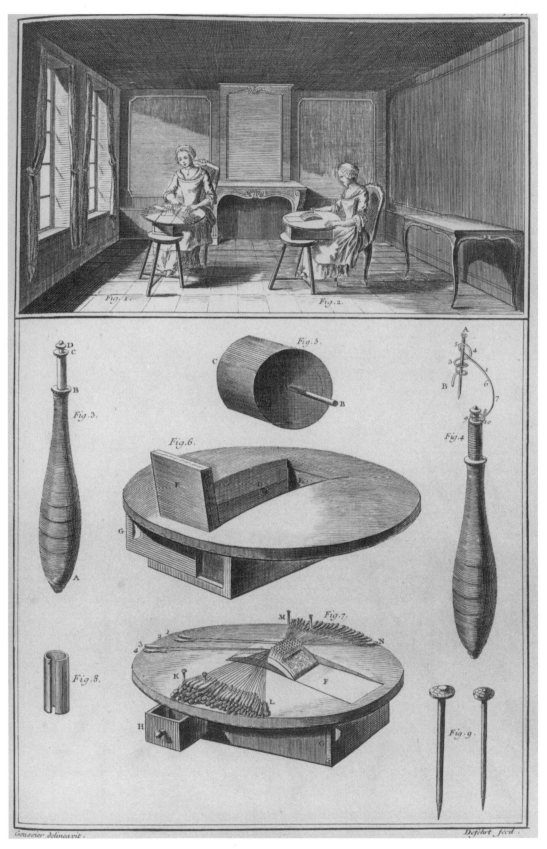

Pl. 2.28. Making bobbin lace. *Ency. Planches*, vol. 3. "Dentelle; Pl. I." S204.

Pl. 2.29. Making cord and decorating buttons. *Ency. Planches,* vol. 2. "Boutonnier passementier; Pl. IV." S138.

formed by the woman in *Encyclopédie* image (plate 2.29) is performed by a man, suggesting that this kind of work was not strongly gender specific: the tasks would have been interchangeable in a family workshop such as this may well be. A woman at the far left is shown winding gold wire onto a button-mold, while the man beside her applies gold or silver braid ornamentation onto a covered button. The woman at the back is reeling silk thread, again suggesting a small concern where all stages in the process take place in the same workspace.[54]

The beautifully engraved plate (plate 2.31) on the art of the *tapissier* shows an upholsterer's shop, full of clutter, with various types of materials and furnishings on offer in the style of Louis XV. This is a lively image, contrasting with the many highly stilted vignettes elsewhere in the *Encyclopédie*. A porter carries mattresses down from the storeroom above, while the master shows a chair to a prospective client: that this was a high-end, prosperous trade is obvious, not just from the well-stocked workshop, but from the master-merchant *tapissier*'s dress, on a par with that of the consumer. Chair frames, for which customers could choose the upholstery fabrics, are hanging from the ceiling. A lively group of four young women, "*ouvrières tapissières,*" who seem to form a little community of their own (detail), are seated at a worktable, sewing lengths of material for wall-hangings and curtains: again we see how the task of sewing falls to women across a broad spectrum of guild trades.

Plate 2.32 from the *Encyclopédie* shows the "*atelier ou boutique*" of a wig maker, of which there were two hundred for Paris alone: here, male clients were shaved, and both sexes had their wigs made and fitted. The men in this picture are assembling (far left) and finishing (right) the wigs, with the worker in the background warming curling tongs at the fire for this purpose. The

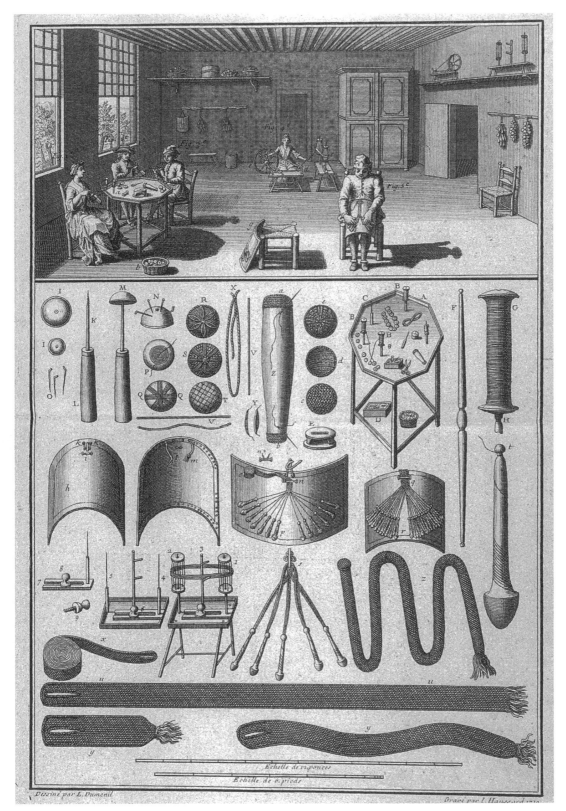

Pl. 2.30. Making cord and decorating buttons. [*Boutons, et cordonets au boisseau*], MS Typ 432.1 (3) #9,
Department of Printing and Graphic Arts, Houghton Library, Harvard College Library.
Des. Dumenil, eng. J. Haussard, 1718.

Pl. 2.31 and detail. Upholstery workshop. *Ency. Planches,* vol. 9. "Tapissier, intérieur d'une boutique et différens ouvrages; Pl. I." S244–45.

women were mainly confined to the work of weaving the hair on the three-stringed wefting frame: tufts of hair, woven and laced together, provided the essential elements that could then be assembled into wigs. We see what appears to be a very young girl sitting at such a frame while an older woman in the background (not mentioned in the legend) picks up or returns a curling iron to the fire. This plate was based fairly closely on a plate in the *De-scriptions,* published just four years earlier, where the skilled and intricate work of the women (called *tresseuses*) is described and the frame shown in detail (see plate 2.33). The accompanying text tells us that male wig makers occasionally wove hair tufts of a certain thickness, but "only women, because of the delicacy and the agility of their hands, control the making of short and fine tufts" (Garsault 1767, 15). The centrality of these women to the trade is reflected in the fact that the 1674 statutes of the guild (art. 23: see Savary des Bruslons 1762, 4: 140–41) required *tresseuses* to have written permission to leave a workshop, in order to forestall poaching of good workers by other masters, as was the norm in the case of journeymen. But despite its importance, this was probably the lowest-paying job in the shop, when it was not done—unpaid—by members of the household, and it was typically

Pl. 2.32. Wig making. *Ency. Planches*, vol. 8. "Perruquier barbier; Pl. I." S119.

the type of work given to impecu-
nious widows of masters. In the
Encyclopédie image the women are
barely there, lightly etched into
the background. Gayne has
shown that many women worked
outside the shop weaving hair for
legal and illegal wig makers, and
that they also took a prominent
role in managing illegal establishments, typically family businesses. She found some evidence
of enterprising women operating
independently as wig makers in
the illegal trade (2004, 126–28).

The work of women in hat-
making is illustrated in detail in

plate 2.34a; the text accompanying this plate in the Académie collection gives much useful detail
on the status and payment of the
workers. Arguably, this trade
might have been located in our
section on large-scale manufactories: at the top end of the market
(making expensive beaver hats,
accessible only to the wealthiest
consumers), workshops were
mainly large establishments that
might employ up to sixty workers
in one location. These were located principally in Paris, Lyon,
Marseilles, and Rouen. But ordinary hats of lower cost "for Ne-

groes, Soldiers, the common people and peasants" (Nollet 1765, 2)
were made in smaller workshops
in other locations, such as the
Dauphiné and Provence. This all-
male guild depended heavily on
female workers, who typically
composed over one third of the
workforce (Sonenscher 1987, 33
and 54).

The abbé Nollet, who wrote
the article in the *Descriptions*,
mentions how he watched the
processes being carried out in the
workshop of "a very good
Parisian hatmaker." Hats were
made from the finest fur of the

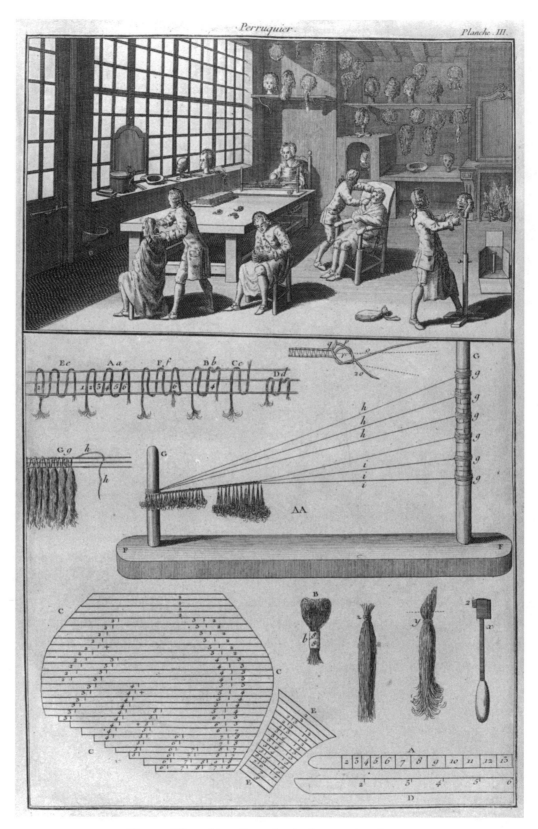

Pl. 2.33. Wig making. Garsault, *Art du perruquier*, Pl. III.

beaver (mainly imported from Canada), the hare, and the rabbit, the beaver providing the best quality material. The author describes how the initial stripping of the beaver fur is done by a male worker (center), using a kind of drawing-knife (the *plane*); he then passes the skin to a woman *repasseuse* (far left), so named because she works back over the same skin, removing the finer fur he has failed to clear. She uses a tool that resembles a shoemaker's knife: the handle has to be bound in cloth, and she must wear a leather thumb shield to protect her skin, "as the fur is tough, and the action of the hand is violent." Her success depends on a powerful wrist movement (Nollet, 12). She is not employed by the master but is attached to the *arracheur,* who pays her an unspecified, but no doubt small amount out of his earnings, which were approximately four *livres* per day. As in the case of activities in agriculture and mining, it is very likely that wives would have performed this function, to avoid part of the household earnings going outside the family.

In the case of the rabbits and hares, the equivalent work was done solely by the women (*arracheuses,* shown at the right rear), who were directly employed, using essentially the same tech-nique as the *repasseuses:* they were paid around 10 *sous* for one hundred skins, though somewhat more in the case of hares (Nollet, 13). The final clearing of the most precious fur from all the skins was done by women called *coupeuses* (shown at the center rear), who normally worked standing at their benches: they were highly skilled in using a special knife (labeled "fig. 10" in plate 2.34b) to shave the pelts in strips, as we see illus-trated in the detail and labeled "fig. 11." The worker keeps a cut-ler's wheel nearby to sharpen her knife regularly. "These move-ments," writes Nollet of the tech-nique, "because of the habit [these women] have formed, are per-formed at great speed" (16). She also grades the fur and separates it out according to quality; she is paid 6 *sous* per pound for beaver and 8 *sous* for rabbit and hare, which are "harder to handle," and can sell the skins of the smaller animals for her own profit to the glue makers. A good *coupeuse* could produce four to five pounds of fur per day, giving her between 1 *livre* 10 *sous* and 2 *livres* in pay (17), an unusually high income for a woman working independ-ently. This is a good example of women undertaking one of the most skilled and important tasks in the workshop; though they earned a respectable payment, it was still less than their male coun-terparts, and they were treated differently from the male workers as regards status and method of payment. Work on the most pres-tigious material (the beaver) was largely reserved for men, and they were paid a set daily rate, while the women were paid by the piece. Michael Sonenscher has studied in detail how status and customary practices among the guild workers were closely tied into the way wages were calcu-lated and paid: "In the hatting trade skill enjoyed a fragile asso-ciation with certain materials, and with beaver fur in particular" (1987, 36). Lacking the bargain-ing power of journeymen, the women received little additional recognition for skill, strength, or danger to their person. In Lyon, it would appear that some of the *coupeuses* responded, after mid-century, by setting themselves up as autonomous artisans directing their own workers (Hafter 2001). We also learn from the *Ency-clopédie* article "Chapeau" (which mentions women workers though they are not shown in the images) that some masters bought the fur already prepared from "*maîtresses coupeuses,*" who were presum-ably just such independent opera-tors. The women in these images are dressed plainly, with no frills or flounces; the woman at the cen-

Pl. 2.34a. Hatmaking: stripping fur. Nollet, *L'Art de faire des chapeaux*, Pl. I.

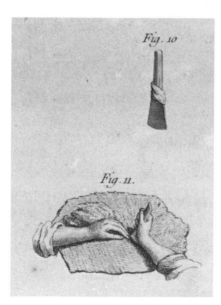

Pl. 2.34b. Stripping fur: hands of *la coupeuse*.

Pl. 2.35 and detail. Saddle and carriage making. *Ency. Planches,* vol. 9. "Sellier-carossier, selles; Pl. I." S21.

ter rear appears to wear a protective leather apron.

The *éjarreuses* were women who did the final tidying of the felt surface of the best quality hats: after the hats had been glazed with a stiffening agent, the women trimmed off any protruding fibers with a type of pincers. These were mainly outworkers operating from their homes and do not feature in our images (Nollet, 63). A hatmaker's shop is shown in plate 5.3.

In the workshop of the saddle and carriage maker (plate 2.35) the *Encyclopédie* shows us one woman, not mentioned in the plate legend, and depicted in the background of the picture. She seems to be sewing or edging long strips of material, probably cut from the bale in front of her, presumably as part of the padding to be incorporated into a saddle or bridle. This figure is typical of the common but unremarked presence of women right across the artisanal trades.

The art of making playing cards yields two images of women. The plate in the *Descriptions,* though published in 1762, was actually prepared in the late 1690s by Des Billettes, who also drafted the description. A version from this period is filed in the albums of the Institut, and another in the Bibliothèque Nationale (Ma Mat 39, f. 47bis); the early material was reworked by Duhamel and his engraver Patte. The text related to plate 2.36 details how the woman does the *épluchage* in a workshop where male workers

Pl. 2.36 and detail. Making playing cards. Duhamel, *Art du cartier*, Pl. I. Des. and eng. Patte

have glued paper together, and separated out the stiffened material to be made into cards. Her work consists of removing—delicately, with a pointed knife—any little pieces of dust or dirt that may have stuck to the surface of the card and could tear it during the polishing process. This essential work was slow and tedious: Duhamel remarks that an "*ouvrière*" could scarcely complete more than three gross of cards in a day (1762a, 12).

We are told that, in accordance with the statutes of the Merchant Cardmakers, this work is given only to the widows or daughters of masters in poor circumstances: it constitutes a "small

resource" for families who have not prospered in their business, a kind of charity (Duhamel 1762a, 11). It is clear that these women were very poorly paid: as they were not regarded as independent wage earners, but as additional contributors to a family economy, their labor was not valued on any comparable scale with that of the male workers sitting alongside them.

Similarly, in an *Encyclopédie* plate on the same trade of making playing cards (plate 2.37), we see a woman whose lack of value is aptly communicated by the way in which her presence is crudely sketched into the background: she is described in the plate legend as

"a female worker who carries the cardboard sheets to the cutter," and, if she were not a family member or domestic servant, probably fell into the same category of cheap guild-associated labor as the women in plate 2.35.

Finally, a plate depicting the trade of the *tabletier cornetier* (plate 2.38) again shows a woman in the role of general aide in a workshop. This trade—which was allied to that of the comb maker—involved the making of gaming tables, chess and checkers pieces, and many other objects that used horn or bone. The woman here is warming the bone over the cinders to make it more pliable; the male workers are

Pl. 2.37. Making playing cards. *Ency. Planches*, vol. 2. "Cartier; Pl. I." S244.

Pl. 2.38 and detail. Manufacture of objects from horn and bone. *Ency. Planches*, vol. 9. "Tabletier Cornetier, Préparation de la Corne; Pl. I." S137.

Pl. 2.39. Pottery: finishing tasks. Duhamel, *Art du potier de terre,* Pl. III. Des. and eng. Ransonette.

using various techniques for rough-hewing and pressing the horn into the required shape.

::

ESSENTIAL GOODS

Duhamel's discussion of the art of the potter in the *Descriptions* includes an interesting account (taken from the *Calendrier Limousin* for 1770) of the village of Saint-Eutrope, south of Angoulême, where almost the entire population of the village—thirty households with twenty-eight kilns—worked in pottery. The text tells us that the women and children prepared and kneaded the clay, found locally, using an iron bar on a block of wood, but, unusually for this collection, the image provided (not reproduced here) belies the account by showing a man performing this work. Women were also responsible for cutting and collecting the scrub wood to feed the kilns, and it was they who finished or "dressed" the pots; in plate 2.39 we see a woman fixing the handle to a vessel. This is a good example of an artisanal trade closely integrated with the traditional economy, where the labor of the whole household is crucial to the enterprise. The Parisian guild *Potiers de Terre, Carreleurs,* like many others we have studied, explicitly recognized the role of children of both genders in the trade in its early statutes (1456), but by 1693 only sons are mentioned (see Lespinasse 1886, 2: 763–72).

The *potier d'étain* made pewter vessels and cutlery for the majority of the population, who could not afford silverware; it was a male-sworn trade (Lespinasse 1886, 2: 525–39). There were workshops in many cities, and the author of this entry in the *Descriptions* was himself a pewter-goods merchant in Chartres. He does not mention women workers, but they feature in the plate on the sanding and polishing of the cast cutlery (plate 2.40); their tasks are

Pl. XXIX

Pl. 2.40. Making pewter cutlery. Duhamel, *Art du potier d'étain,* Pl. XXIX.

ascribed in the text to an *ouvrier* in the masculine, yet another example of how the image eludes the tyranny of the word. The women on the right are using pumice stone and cloth to remove marks left by the previous workers who had cleaned the surfaces with scraping tools; the woman at the table below the window is wiping or wrapping the polished spoons in soft cloth.

Few of the trades to do with food preparation were included in our two collections: one exception is the treatise on the trades of the miller, the baker, and the vermicelli maker. In plate 2.41, the workers in the boulting-room of a *vermicellier* are sifting the grain, using progressively finer riddles

or sieves to remove the coarse flour, which is then either used to bake their own bread or sold to a baker. The woman is using a fine sieve suspended from the ceiling: with a horizontal movement, she shakes the sieve gently to separate the semolina from the bran, which she scoops off the top using a piece of cardboard and deposits in the basket beside her. "Experience is needed to boult semolina successfully," comments the author (Malouin 1767, 99). Semolina was used as the basis for pasta dough, which was then forced through a press (using different molds) to produce noodles of different shapes and consistencies. Plate 2.42 shows a woman (*la vermicelière*) shaping the soft noodles

and laying them on a drying rack; fig. 10 is the cloth she uses to cover the noodles in her basket to keep them soft.

Wax was used for many purposes in the eighteenth century, and white wax was produced in great quantities in many parts of France, though mainly in the north and west. Jacques Savary des Bruslons remarked that Paris consumed more than three quarters of France's production (1762, 1: 900). This trade was under the control of the Grocers' Guild, one of the six most influential corporations. Some of the establishments were on a large scale, particularly those operating by royal patent, independent of the guild system, and could equally well

Pl. 2.41. Making vermicelli. Malouin, *Description et détails des arts du meunier, du vermicelier et du boulenger*, Pl. III.

Pl. 2.42. Making vermicelli: shaping noodles. Malouin, *Description et détails des arts du meunier, du vermicelier et du boulenger*, Pl. IV.

Pl. 2.43. Wax making: blanching works. *Ency. Planches,* vol. 2, part 2. "Blanchissage des cires; Pl. II." S150.

have been included in our section on manufactories: Savary described such a large-scale enterprise at Antony near Paris, established in 1702 and given the royal patent in 1719, which united many aspects of wax and candle production under one roof. Other workshops, however, were smaller, and devoted to just one branch of the trade. Plate 2.43 shows a blanching works, where wax was melted and whitened by a succession of processes. The woman in the background is turning the crank on a cylinder to control the flow of wax into the water, where it will cool in streams whose size is determined by the speed at which she operates. This is the type of work we see performed by women across many different trades. Although the woman worker is identified by a number in the plate, the writer of the plate legend forgot to note her function, which we can find described as that of a "worker" in the masculine in the *Encyclopédie* article "Blanchir": again, as in plate 2.40, only the image remains to bear witness to the presence of women in this workshop. However, it is clear from the early statutes of the Guild of Candle Makers (1428) recorded by Lespinasse that women had been commonly employed in this trade for centuries (as *ouvrières* and *chandelières*: 1886, 1: 540), although the statutes evolved to an exclusively male-gendered guild.

Pl. 2.44. Sealing-wax manufacture. *Ency. Planches,* vol. 3. "Cirier, en cire à cacheter; Pl. I." S159.

Pl. 2.45. Sealing-wax manufacture. *Ency. Planches,* vol. 3. "Cirier, en cire à cacheter; Pl. II." S160.

Savary des Bruslons (1762) described the employment of girls in the manufactory at Antony to carry the hot wax to the cooling vats (1: 911).

Plate 2.44, also from the *Encyclopédie,* represents a workshop where sealing wax is prepared: a furnace for melting the material is kept burning in the chimney. The woman in the foreground (an *ouvrière*) is stirring the "viscous composition" as it melts over a little brazier (undoubtedly uncomfortable work in the summer months); the woman behind her takes this warm wax in handfuls and measures it into equal quantities for the drawers. These men roll the wax on a brass plate, also kept warm by a brazier, into little sticks of equal length. In the next plate (2.45), a woman is covering common wax with high-quality sealing wax. To do this, she first melts the wax between the grills of the little furnace (fired by coal); she then dips the melted stick into the box of powdered, high-quality wax on her right. The stick is returned to the heat to melt this coating onto the surface, following which the male worker beside her rolls and polishes the stick on a marble slab. The tasks shown here would appear to be interchangeable in terms of the effort and skill they required, yet they were probably

designated on the basis of gender.

Candle makers (*chandeliers* or *ciergiers*) formed a separate guild from the wax makers (*blanchisseurs de cire*), although the description given by Savary des Bruslons (1: 912) suggests that all these activities were brought together in the Royal Manufactory at Antony. The image from Duhamel's *Art du chandelier* (plate 2.46) shows a woman performing the kind of tasks strongly associated with female gender in all the textile trades, as we shall see. She unwinds the skeins of cotton for the wicks, reeling them if necessary (typically three threads at a time) onto a simple reeling machine (shown in the background behind her). When she has enough balls of cotton—four being a common number, but varying in accordance with the size of candle being made—she sits at the bench, on which a cutting apparatus is mounted. Adjusting the distance between the spindle (on the right at *e*) and the cutting blade (on the left at *d*) as appropriate, she winds the four threads around the spindle, doubling them, then cuts them and twists them together. In our example she will then have a wick of twenty-four cotton threads. These wicks pile up along the spindle, and when it is full, she transfers them onto a rod. Duhamel emphasizes that "the

quality of the candle depends as much on the perfection of the wick as on that of the tallow" (1764, 11), so the reeling and twisting of the cotton is crucial to the process. The text underlines that this is always a woman's job, as is substantiated by Savary des Bruslons' description of Antony, where the reeling is done by girls employed directly, or by female outworkers in the village.

The art of the cutler was well described for the *Descriptions* by a master of the art, Perret, whose sumptuous shop in Paris was illustrated in a plate (plate 5.7). However, Fougeroux de Bondaroy followed up with a description of the *Art du coutelier en ouvrages communs* based on his own study (in 1763) of a manufacturer in Saint-Etienne en Forez, southwest of Lyon: this workshop would be typical of those producing goods, mainly knives and chisels, for the wider urban and peasant populations. Fougeroux comments, in his introduction, on the different consumer needs for knives according to wealth and social status; ingenious practices have evolved, he suggests, to ensure the speedy and cheap production of simple knives required by the common people (1772, 1). Indeed, this sector tended toward large-scale manufacture—with up to thirty or forty workers together—and the separation of

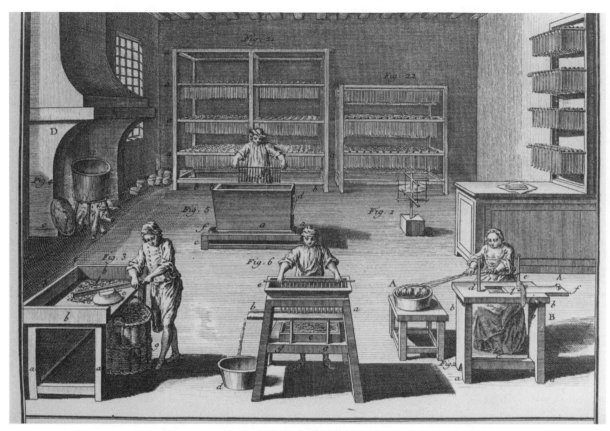

Pl. 2.46. Candle making. Duhamel, *Art du chandelier*, Pl. II. Eng. Patte.

Pl. 2.47. Cutler's workshop. Fougeroux de Bondaroy, *L'Art du coutelier en ouvrages communs*, Pl. II.

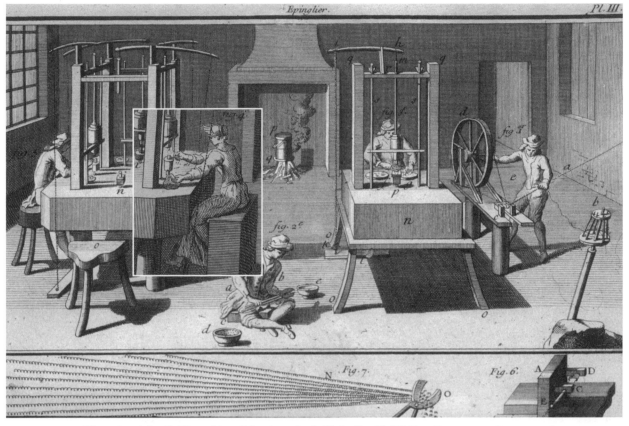

Pl. 2.48 and detail. Pin making. Réaumur, *Art de l'épinglier,* Pl. III. Des. Bretez, eng. Lucas, 1718.

tasks, as the profits were minimal on each item (1772, 2). In our image (plate 2.47) we see a woman working the bellows for the coal fire, essential for heating the iron, while her companion hammers out the blade of a knife on the anvil. The fuel used is coal; the text (1772, 7) tells us that this particular task—termed in the local trade *"tirer la vache"*—is normally done by women, or alternatively by young boys, whoever was available, most likely, from the members of the tradesman's family.

Plate 2.48, engraved for Réaumur in 1718, shows the work of putting heads onto pins: this manufacture was famously used by Adam Smith in Book 1 of *The Wealth of Nations* as an example of the advantages of the division of labor, following Delaire's comment in the *Encyclopédie* that one pin underwent eighteen operations before being sold to the consumer (*Ency.:* "Epingle"). In fact, however, Réaumur had remarked on the same phenomenon some fifty years earlier, in a draft preface for the *Descriptions,* never actually published: "A pin, to which we pay no attention, passes [. . .]

through more than 20 different hands, and every hand shapes it" (Houghton MS Typ 432.1 [1], f. 2). The original statutes of the *Aiguillers-aléniers* (1599) indicated that children of both genders (*enfants*) could be received into the guild, but when this guild was united with that of the *Epingliers* in 1695, there was no mention of any access for women (Lespinasse 1886, 2: 560–75).

Of note in the image is a large cauldron on a tripod in the chimney, used for tinning the copper pins, yet another indicator of the unhealthy atmosphere pervading these workshops. The pin heads are made from wire, which is first twisted (right), then cut (center), and they are hammered onto the pin shanks by the workers at the benches. This work requires dexterity and speed: the worker places a head on the anvil, inserts the pin shank, then drops the puncheon onto it four or five times, all the while rotating the shank. The puncheon is dropped by the operation of a foot pedal beneath the bench (see detail). Réaumur's text specifies that this work is done almost exclusively by women or children ("Epinglier," 33), but the image does not accurately reflect this. The later additional text drafted by Perronet for the *Art de l'épinglier* details the payments made to the *frappeurs,* those putting the heads on the pins, in the masculine only: they earned on average, he states, 7 or 8 *sous* for producing 10,000 to 12,000 pins per day, but out of this they were obliged to furnish the puncheons and anvils for their machines themselves (34). Given the confusion concerning the gender breakdown, and the lack of clarity in the texts, we cannot be sure how much the women received for the same work. Réaumur's assertions are backed up by evidence from other European countries that this task was widely performed by women and young girls: Arthur

Young, in his *Six Weeks Tour,* described a "great number of girls" working in a pin manufactory near Bristol in 1767, and operating "little machines, worked by their feet" (qtd. Pinchbeck 1969, 277). Pinchbeck shows that in some areas of Britain, they began this work as young as five years of age (273). Strangely, Diderot shows no women in the corresponding plates of the *Encyclopédie;* in the article "Epinglier" he comments that the master pin makers of Paris no longer fabricate the product because of the costs attaching to the labor but get their pins from Normandy, where they are produced more cheaply. It may well be that Réaumur's picture recorded a workshop activity that could no longer be directly witnessed in Paris fifty years later.

The women pictured in the two plates 2.49a and b are putting the heads on small nails, part of the trade of the pin maker rather than the nailer, who made the heavier nails; the description of the work is given with more precision and correctness in the *Art de l'épinglier,* written by Réaumur around 1718 (53–54), than in the *Encyclopédie.* Plate 2.49a was engraved by Patte for the Académie in 1761, under the direction of Duhamel du Monceau (who edited Réaumur's manuscript work).

The plate legend underlines that this work was done by female workers, in this case as part of a small, two-person operation. The woman featured here has the required lengths of cut wire for the shanks, which have been pointed, in the wooden bowl in front of her: she uses a special vise held in a larger bench vise in front of her. For each nail she opens the vise with her left hand, knocking the finished nail into her apron and placing the next piece of wire with her right hand. A slight tap of the hammer produces a nail suitable for shoemaking; a second, harder blow is administered to create a larger flat head suitable for carpenters, sculptors, and the like. To make the round-headed nails used by case and box makers, after the first light tap on the wire she takes a puncheon with which she hammers the shape into the head: this is the action performed by the woman in plate 2.49b, from the corresponding *Encyclopédie* plate, which features a larger workshop. "The best workers make 10 to 12 thousand [nails] a day," Réaumur's text tells us.

There were many types of needles made in this period: plate 2.50 shows a workshop, staffed mainly by women, making hook-shaped needles for a stocking frame. The wire from a roll is drawn through the device shown

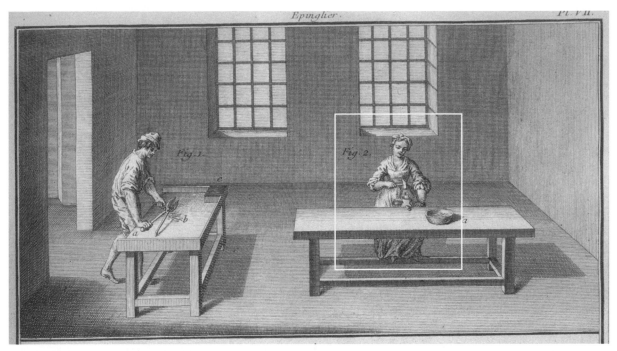

Pl. 2.49a. Making small nails. Réaumur, *Art de l'épinglier,* Pl. VII. A 10.10.15F (v. 18), Houghton Library, Harvard College Library. Des. and eng. Patte,1761.

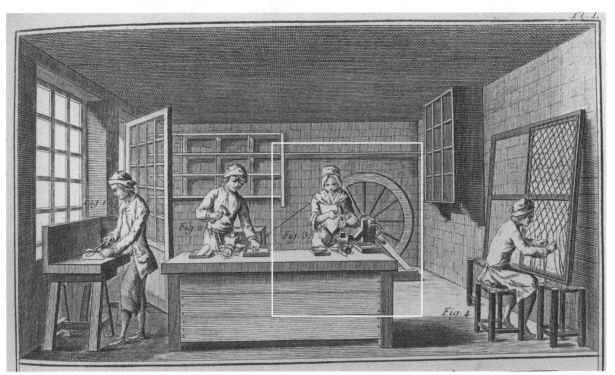

Pl. 2.49b. Making small nails. *Ency. Planches,* vol. 2, part 2. "Cloutier d'epingles; Pl. I." S168.

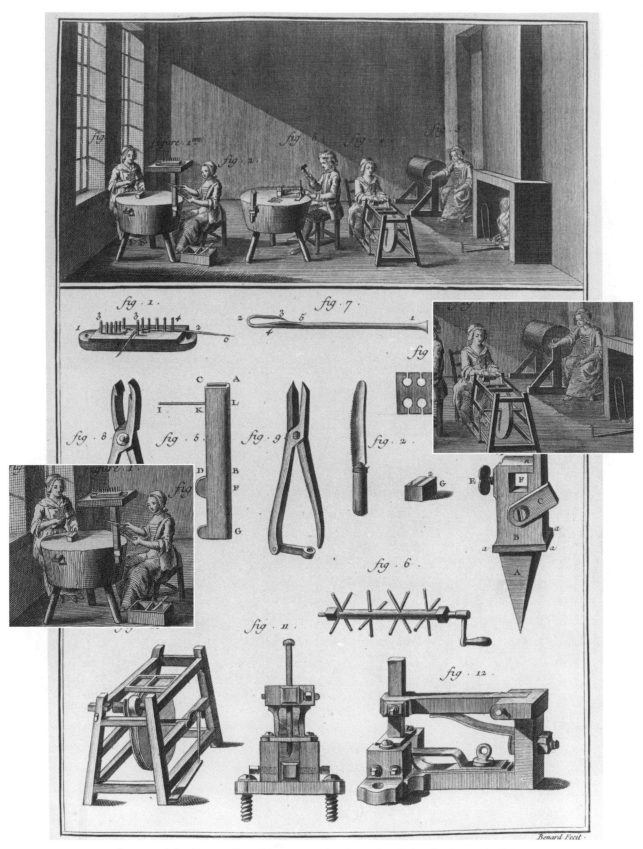

Pl. 2.50 and details. Needle making. *Ency. Planches,* vol. 1. "Aiguiller-bonnetier." S114.

Pl. 2.51. Making shot. *Ency. Planches*, vol. 5. "Fonte de la Dragée Moulée; Pl. III." S204.

as fig. 1, then cut into the appropriate lengths. The woman second from the left sharpens one end into a point (detail 1); the needle is then heated in the fire (presumably before being bent into its required shape), the shank is flattened by the person at the far left, and a hole punched in it by the person at the center. The next worker (second from the right) polishes the needles on an emery wheel before they are washed in soap and dried in a drum—of which the person at the far right rotates the handle—with bran and breadcrumbs (detail 2).

The casting of lead shot for hunting rifles fell, oddly enough, within the province of the *bimbe-*

lotier, the maker of toys and knickknacks, a trade in which we have already seen women active (plate 2.01). The workshop in plate 2.51, from the *Encyclopédie,* is referred to, unusually, as a *laboratoire,* because here the lead was melted in the stove and poured into the mold being handled by the worker in the background. Note the wide-open window and large hod over the stove, for the purpose of allowing the noxious fumes to escape: the preceding plate legend refers specifically to "the dangerous vapours which arise from lead, and especially from orpiment," with which it was sometimes mixed. The woman—*la coupeuse*—cuts the

shot from the stems with pincers, letting the pieces fall onto the leather apron in front of her before collecting them in the large wooden bowl shown on the bench. She keeps a wet sponge in the other bowl to dampen the cutting edges of the pincers. The jets are remelted in the stove.

Another workshop where the stoves were used to melt lead and other alloys (particularly antimony) was that of the typecaster: in the first of two plates on this trade from the *Encyclopédie,* we see workers of both genders operating very close to the furnace. As the workers of the time were well aware, exposure to antimony through inhalation caused a vari-

Pl. 2.52 and detail. Typecasting: smoothing new type. *Ency. Planches*, vol. 2. "Fonderie en caracteres; Pl. I." S156.

ety of health problems, including dizziness, headache, vomiting, and insomnia, though Diderot chose to deny these effects in his commentary (as has been discussed previously). In plate 2.52 one woman breaks off the jets of metal from the newly cast type letters; the woman beside her at the bench then rubs the flat surfaces of the shank of each letter smooth on the circular stone in front of her (see detail). The second image (plate 2.53 and detail) shows a woman setting up the cast letters in a long stick or frame where they are firmly clamped; her companion then scrapes excess material from the set with a knife, while the worker on the left

uses a plane to insert a uniform groove along the row of letters. The same *Encyclopédie* article tells us that typecasting was a "free" craft, with no mastership or guild visitations, though the typecasters—of which there were only a dozen running operations for the whole of France, half of them in Paris—were regarded as part of the "Corps" of printers, and benefited from many of the same privileges. The absence of guild visitation helps to explain how women could play a prominent role here, whereas they were pushed to the margins in other areas of the printing trade, particularly the prestigious activity of pulling the press (Sheridan 1992).

Both metal and fabric buttons were mounted, sewn, or embroidered onto wooden bases or molds, then supplied to the passementerie trade and the goldsmith by the mold maker as featured in plate 2.54. This vignette, never published, was prepared by Réaumur, probably around 1718, the period when the Haussard family was engraving for him. The work of description was taken up again by Fougeroux de Bondaroy around 1763, but remained in manuscript (Houghton MS Typ 432.1 [9]): Diderot, however, undoubtedly used the Académie's plate showing this trade—which he describes as "a very minor trade" (*Ency.:* "Bou-

Pl. 2.53 and detail. Typecasting: setting up new type. *Ency. Planches,* vol. 2. "Fonderie en caracteres; Pl. III." S159.

ton , Moule de")—as the basis for his own vignette, which followed it closely (*Ency. Planches,* vol. 2: "Boutonnier, faiseur de moules, Pl. I"). The persons on the right cut up planks of oak, into which the worker in the background on the left bores the shape of the button mold with a tool powered by a wheel that takes two men to turn. The workers in the foreground at the left finish the process with a similar tool, powered by a bow (detail), and knock the molds out of the casing. Holes are then bored through the mold to take the threads. The manuscript text tells us that the woman who is powering the bow grasps a stick

on the bench (*i*) "to hold herself steadier and bring more force to bear with her other hand" (Houghton MS Typ 432.1 [9], p. 12). It would seem that the processes and practices described and presented here changed little over the century; Diderot commented that speed of production was the workers' only hope of eking out a living (*Ency.:* "Bouton, Moule de"). In this unprofitable trade, family collaboration would have been of crucial importance in keeping the business afloat.

The making of catgut for rackets and musical instruments—supplying the material for luxury trades—was in itself

an unpleasant activity sometimes carried out in open hangars because of the awful smells that attended it. There were eight masters in Paris, and all the workshops were located in the Faubourg St. Martin near the slaughterhouses (*Ency.:* "Boyaudier"). The gut used was that of lamb or sheep; it was first cleaned, washed, and dried on frames outside the workshop (plate 2.55, far right), then degreased, the outer fibers removed, and left soaking in water again. The job of taking the wet guts from one tub (see detail) and sewing them together using the soaked fibers in a second tub for thread, was reserved for

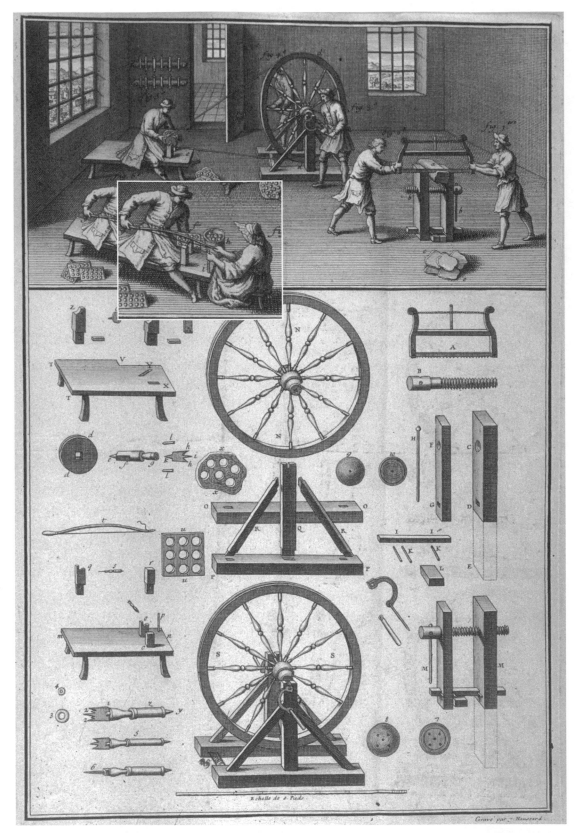

Pl. 2.54 and detail. Making button molds. [*Faiseur de moules de boutons*]. MS Typ 432.1 (9), Department of Printing and Graphic Arts, Houghton Library, Harvard College Library. Eng. J. Haussard [c. 1718].

Pl. 2.55 and detail. Making catgut. *Ency. Planches*, vol. 2. "Boyaudier." S142.

women. The gut was then spun, stretched, and polished as shown on the right.

The workshop of the edge-tool maker is another male-gendered area where we might not expect to see women working. Plate 2.56 is again an early plate prepared by Réaumur in the period 1714–20, when the designers Bretez and Chaufourier and the engraver Lucas were working with him: manuscript notes tell us that all three had a hand in this one. The original drawing is in the Bibliothèque de l'Institut (ms. 1064, f. xcv [A]), and a proof, with notes and corrections in Réaumur's own hand,

is in the Bibliothèque de l'Arsenal (Gr. Fol. 435ter, f. 21[1]), allowing us to study the painstaking development of the image from conception to completion. We do not have the finished descriptions that would have accompanied it, but it is clear that the right-hand image depicts the preparation of the skin for a gold beater. The male worker on the far right stretches the membrane taken from the outer gut of beef onto a frame to dry; the woman appears to be mixing some product in a bowl, possibly glue for sticking the membrane to the frame. Réaumur's notes made it clear that he had visited the

workshop described and that he intended to return there to correct a number of details in the plates: "we must return to the maker of the gold-beater's skin," he wrote, specifying that he wanted to take back from that visit a partially made pipe so he could "give it to Mr. Chaufourier to draw it from life." In the left-hand image, where the workers are presumably grinding metal to make some tool, a woman—very likely the master's wife—is arranging items in a store cupboard. The later, unconnected set of images on this trade drawn for the *Encyclopédie* show no women; we owe the record of

Pl. 2.56. Edge-tool making. Institut ms. 1064, f. xcv (B). [*Taillandier*]. Des. [Bretez and Chaufourier], eng. Lucas [c. 1714-20].

their presence here to the meticulous care taken by the Academician and his personal observations of the workshop scene.

We have already remarked that Réaumur frequently visited workshops outside of Paris, where the mix of workers may

well have been different from the more tightly controlled Parisian trade situation.

3

Textiles

CROSS THE CENTURIES women formed a major part of the workforce in the wide range of activities involved in textile production, and this is reflected in images that record aspects of the production of cotton, linen, silk, wool cloth, and gold and silver thread, as well as the related trades of the ribbon maker and the *passementier*. The plates in this section are drawn from the *Encyclopédie*, from two *Descriptions* dealing with types of woollen cloth by the Academicians Duhamel du Monceau and Roland de la Platière, and from the extensive account of silk making written for the Académie by Jean Paulet, the son of a silk manufacturer in Nîmes. Fougeroux de Bondaroy also took a keen interest in this latter publication and the numerous plates it contained: in the course of his journey to Italy in 1763, he visited many silk workshops in Lyon and made inquiries concerning the techniques of silk manufacture in Bologna (Jaoul and Pinault 1982, 30 and 34). This firsthand knowledge bolsters the value of the plates from Paulet's treatise as a reflection of contemporary practices. Though the descriptions were not intended, as has already been noted, to reflect activities in any one location but rather to represent best practice current in the period, it was nonetheless imperative, to accomplish this aim, that the authors and designers be familiar with manufacturing processes in the most important centers of production for the textile in question. In addition to the plates published in our two collections, this section contains over a dozen unpublished images conserved in manuscript collections: these were prepared for the Académie fifty years before

Diderot ordered the plates for the *Encyclopédie,* which in some instances were based on them. Where two versions recorded very similar images the older and lesser-known of the two has been reproduced.

Wives, sisters, or daughters within the traditional economy worked in their homes as spinners of wool, flax, or cotton, and this was taken for granted as a supplement to their work in farming, fishing, and mining. In the proto-industrial period, they spun for merchants in the towns, contributing to their families while managing to remain within their home communities: Gay Gullickson has shown that in the Canton of Auffay near Rouen, 75 percent of women were spinning for merchants in 1796, the cotton industry there employing almost eight times as many women as men (1990, 209). In general, in the pre-industrial period, spinning was recognized as a female occupation, though, as Goodman has emphasized, "Different textile fibres elicited enormous differences in cultural and social constructions" (1993, 232). Women spinners were rarely organized on a trade basis: Rouen, where women had access to a mixed-gender Spinners' Guild, has emerged as very much an exception. Even here, the status of the women was eroded toward the end of the

eighteenth century, when they lost the right to transfer guild membership to their children (Hafter 1989, 418; Boxer and Quataert 2000, 47). Ogilvie has demonstrated how guild monopolies on other types of work forced women into marginal activities such as spinning (2004, para. 25).

Although the technique of spinning demanded skill and experience, as is shown in the commentary to plates 3.1 and 3.2, the women's work was seen as secondary to that of the male breadwinners, and their wages were not calculated to allow them to live independently. Moreover, as Ogilvie has observed, "By excluding women from *guilded* sectors, guilds increased the supply of female workers in *unguilded* sectors, thereby lowering their wages—a form of 'pre-market' labor discrimination that economists term 'occupational crowding'" (2004, para. 25). Gullickson reminds us that "while it is impossible to be precise about the earnings of men and women in cottage industry, it is important to note that whenever a range of wages is cited, the lowest paid to men are higher than the highest wages paid to women" (1990, 211). She estimates that spinners in the Caux earned somewhere between 9 and 12 *sous* a day in the 1780s, while the male weavers—their brothers or husbands—are

thought to have earned anything between 20 and 40 *sous* a day, depending on experience, skill, and speed. Hufton notes that, even in the boom period of the Languedoc woollen industry, *fileuses* could expect only 8 *sous* a day (1975, 2), and Vardi likewise gauges the earnings of spinners in the region of Montigny at 8, or a maximum of 9 *sous* per day, and that only for the finest cotton yarns (1993b, 134). Gullickson describes how women spinners gathered together in houses in the evenings to continue their day's work in a more social context, while their menfolk frequented the tavern (1990, 213). In some instances in the second half of the century, according to Gullickson, single and widowed spinners did manage to support themselves in their own households (1986, 78), though she suggests that overall, proto-industrialization brought only slight improvement to the lives of women in areas such as the Caux (1990, 222). Nonetheless, where such work was available, peasant families clearly preferred to keep their young daughters employed at home, in preference to having them migrate to the cities (Gullickson 1986, 137).

In many other regions, where cottage industry was not established, the young girls were forced to leave to seek work in urban centers. In cities like Tours and Lyon, the manufacture of textiles such as calico, and above all, silk, drew large numbers of workers: Garden has accounted for around 10,000 women in Lyon alone in the tasks ancillary to weaving in 1789 (Garden 1970, 317). In the wool industry there were large numbers of women employed in carding and fulling (see Lespinasse 1886, 3: 87), though unfortunately, I found no images recording their presence in these activities. Pierre Cayez estimates that 69 percent of all silk workers were female (1978, 44): they unwound cocoons, twisted thread, prepared bobbins, reeled warp, and pulled cords on the looms; all of these activities are illustrated in detail in the plates in this section. Many of them were recruited from rural areas: in the case of Lyon, they came from Bugey, Beaujolais, and Savoy (Hafter 1995, 47). Such was presumably the case for the many young silk workers, ribbon makers, and so forth pictured in our prints; the images record the work of girls who started in the workshops as servants and industrial assistants at the age of ten or twelve and stayed for up to twenty years. Although their availability was the most crucial factor in the production cycle, they were clustered at the bottom of a capitalistically organized

trade: barred from the indispensable apprenticeship, they would never be qualified workers. For girls, as Farge puts it, "in the workshop the lack of work definition led more often to the status of servant than to a professional qualification" (1996, 111). Garden concludes that their condition would never be that of "citizens," and no one even conceived of their being able to mount an organized protest (1970, 572).

Many historians have documented the dreadful conditions these girls faced as they fought for survival. Recruited by agents, or, more typically, brought to the city through relatives or close contacts from their home villages, they were supposed to be given a year-long contract, but in practice, the masters refused to pay them when business was poor, as happened in 1750 (Hafter 1995, 46–47 and 56). Coming from rural backgrounds into city work while still effectively children, most had never received even basic instruction and so could not read their contracts: Garden has shown that 57 percent of women silk workers could not sign a marriage contract in 1728–30, and the situation had deteriorated still more by 1786–88, when the figure was 62 percent (1970, 311). The work was hard; the girls unwinding cocoons suffered damage to their hands (see plate 3.11), and tuberculosis

was rife in the damp, fetid air of the workshops where the girls frequently ate and slept (Hufton 1975, 8). As late as 1834, when Villermé undertook a survey of textile workers in France, he described the condition of the silk winders—filthy and generally in bad health—as so "wretched" it would be hard to imagine; they also endured great pain in their fingers (1840, 245). Whereas our images illustrate some illuminating aspects of the work activities of these girls, the idealized, stylized nature of the representations—for example their clean, neat dress—falls short of illustrating other aspects of their degraded working conditions. Drawgirls pulling cords for large looms with heavy weights, beneath which they were confined to a narrow working space for fourteen or even eighteen hours a day, were soon exhausted (Guilbert 1966, 27, quoting *Mémoire* by the Intendant Bouillon in 1765): an anonymous *Mémoire* of 1760 describes the "lamentable fate" of these "robust" country girls who returned to their homes after six or seven years with their health broken.[55] In exchange for their labor they would be lucky to get 36 or 40 *livres* in wages per year, their food and board counting for the major part of their remuneration (Hafter 58). And that was of a minimal standard: a young *servante* typically found herself sleeping in cupboards or under looms. She was at the bottom of the pecking order in a situation where the master, his family, and a couple of apprentices all shared one or two rooms; in addition, she was an easy target for the sexual attentions of master or apprentices, running the risk of a disastrous pregnancy (Hufton 1984, 362; 1975, 8). Maurice Garden's statistics illustrate the terrible death toll among these young silk workers, especially in the first two thirds of the century; the average age of the *servantes* of the silk industry sent to die at the Hôtel-Dieu in Lyon was twenty years (1970, 143), but some were less than ten years old. In 1756 alone, 108 *servantes* died there: all were from the Dauphiné, Savoy, or Bugey, and their average age was twenty-one (53). We can presume that many more had been dispatched back to die in their home villages. One sick girl was quickly replaced by another sibling or cousin sent to fill her place (Hufton 1975, 5). The authorities in the silk industry were well aware of the terrible conditions under which these girls worked and lived, described as "*pénible*" and "*rébutant*," such that no Lyon girl would accept them (Garden 1970, 53). The Chambre de commerce in Lyon suggested that one answer to the problem would be

to allow these girls access to journeyman status, which would in turn give them the possibility of marrying, but the masters were firmly opposed to any such moves. They replied that already too many of them married and that the drawgirls should be left "no hope of getting out" of this "appalling" trade, which needed their totally compliant labor to operate (53).

Young women who survived the hardships slowly amassed a dowry of a couple of hundred *livres* over anything from fourteen to twenty years; this was just enough to buy some basic furnishings and cooking utensils to found a home, or at best to help stock a small farm (Hufton 1975, 2–8). These women workers therefore married late: Garden found that in one parish in Lyon in the first half of the century, the average age of first marriage for a woman was twenty-seven and a half years, but for women who came from outside Lyon, it was thirty and over (1970, 91–95). Paradoxically, daughters who worked in their father's business in the city—a master *fabricant* with a couple of looms—frequently found themselves in a worse position when it came to marriage prospects than the working girls from the country. The father's looms—the most valuable part of an inheritance—

were reserved for the sons and were not available to form part of the dowry of a daughter; thus, even though the daughter might have worked for years, contributing to the family enterprise in the kind of workshop situations our images reflect, she would have received no salary and would not have amassed the valuable dowry that a country girl who survived long enough could offer (Garden, 297).

A small minority of these women workers had the chance to better their social position by marrying a master weaver (Garden 1970, 321). The most common form of union for the journeyman silk weaver or new master was with a country girl who typically might have been working for him already (297). Throughout the century the small proportion of women workers—typically the most able of their peer group—who succeeded in marrying a qualified master, and then had the right to work on the looms, was a thorn in the side of the big merchant manufacturers. The officials of the guild complained that this "defection" obliged the big operators to constantly seek new female labor to replace the workers at the bottom (54). Recent research has shown that a certain number of women also managed to hire themselves out to entrepreneurs outside the guild, and even to collaborate together to set up their own businesses: the serious threat such initiative posed to masters was reflected in a special clause in the statutes of Lyon's *passementiers* which attempted to dictate that women must not "associate with other girls in the trade or live together" (Hafter 2001, 27).

In general, women were excluded from the position of weaver; the regulations of 1561 had converted the previously free trade of the *Grande Fabrique* into a guild, restricting women's access; before this, they could become apprentices and journeyworkers. Nonetheless, the statutes assumed that wives would work alongside their husbands at the loom and that both might weave in the shop of another master when the occasion demanded (Hafter 1995, 48). Although the regulations of 1569 forbade women in guild families to work at the loom, they remained a dead letter, and in the eighteenth century the rationale that wives, widows, and daughters could weave, provided they could prove their ties to the master, continued to operate. It was not until 1786, however, that women won the legal right to become master weavers (Hafter 2001, 15).

The wife was nonetheless of crucial importance in a weaver's family workshop. So that she could maintain her position at the loom, her children were put out to wet-nurse, but this resulted in a tragically high mortality rate: as has already been mentioned, as many as two-thirds of the children of bourgeois and artisans from Lyon placed with wet-nurses died (Garden 1970, 139). Whereas a former silk winder might perceive this position of wife and weaver as a promotion, the conditions of work for a girl who had previously worked at the loom in a family workshop could scarcely be seen to have improved. In addition to her weaving, she was now also responsible for organizing the household and providing the food, and we can scarcely imagine the stress of a succession of pregnancies, at least in the earlier years of the marriage, where the mother faced the loss of many of her children (Garden 1970, 296). Moreover, these women later struggled as widows of masters, being incapable—because of their poor literacy levels—of keeping any written account of production.

Nonetheless, given the importance of the role of these female weavers, the following question must be asked: why do none of our many images record women actually operating a full-sized silk loom? The Académie treatise was written, as the reader will recall, by a master within the trade who was undoubtedly well acquainted with this reality. We can only assume that despite the importance of the wife in any such enterprise, her existence was taken for granted and viewed as too banal to record, a lived experience excluded from the dominant categories of organizational thought. Perhaps an outsider—an Academician rather than a master—might have recorded a different reality, but in this instance, the image does not rise above the author's sense of guild order and a fixed concept of work relationships.

As the century progressed and master weavers increasingly fell into the dependent economic situation of hired hands for the large merchants, their wives also worked at weaving as independent artisans—thus extending the guild-family ethos to what was actually a wage-work situation—in an attempt to gain an advantage in the labor market. The merchants succeeded in putting an end to this privilege when the regulations of 1744 prohibited masters' wives from weaving outside their home *atelier* (Hafter 1995, 51), although similar attempts to likewise prohibit daughters were less successful (52). The position of guild-family women was further undermined in the last quarter of the century by the increased recruitment of drawgirls at lower wages to work looms: an *Arrêt du Conseil* in 1786 made weaving legal for hired female workers who had no family ties to silk masters (Garden 1970, 316).

Several images document the work of women in ribbon making, fringing, the making of gold and silver thread, and various aspects of *passementerie*. While we know these sectors drew heavily on female labor, again, the institutional framework was generally male by the eighteenth century: such was certainly the case for the guild of *Tissutiers-Rubanniers* in Paris, though it had previously been a mixed guild (see p. 76). Hafter's research on the guilds in Rouen, where women in their individual capacity could attain mastership in a small number of mixed-gender guilds, including that of the *Rubanniers-Dentelliers-Frangers-Dorlotiers* ("*doreloterie*" being a largely obsolete term for ribbon and fringe making), suggests that women may have retained guild privileges established in the medieval period more successfully, and for a more extended period, outside of Paris (1997, 3); comparable detailed studies for other towns are lacking.[56] Hafter's ribbon makers carefully preserved their rights from encroachment by the closely related (male) trade of the *passementier*. The previously unpublished plates from the early part of the century placing

women in a variety of tasks within wire- and thread-making workshops provide valuable and original evidence of the significance and extent of their roles within these trades, particularly in the making of gold and silver thread (see plates 3.40 to 3.43).

Though a combination of guild regulations, market forces, and traditional assumptions ensured that women's work was classed as "ancillary," and therefore beneath the trade classifications of training and skill, they nonetheless learned a wide range of techniques on the job or in their family environment. The plates in this section on textiles offer many examples of women performing intricate tasks requiring expertise and experience. Jean-Marie Roland de la Platière comments on the importance of the skill and experience of the spinner in the production of wool cloth (plate 3.1), and Diderot marvels at the ability of the fringe maker as she twists each strand with a hook (plate 3.35), but more often than not, only the image itself remains to stand witness to the knowledge, understanding, and dexterity with which women accomplished the many tasks assigned to them in this sector. In the often complex and delicate work of silk manufacture, we can see innumerable examples: plate 3.16 shows a woman performing

multiple tasks at the same time on the four-wheel reeling machine, and plate 3.26 shows a young woman reeling seven strands onto a spinning wheel, twisting the strands evenly at high speed. While the texts continually underline the patience and care required for these tasks, they generally stop short of epithets we might take to be signifiers of "skill," such as *talent* or *capacité*, which would challenge the underlying assumptions about women's place in the world of work. As Hafter has underlined, in the eighteenth century, "skill was often an artificial label that shed more light on the sex and status of the worker than what was produced" (1995, 44). The fact that the highly complex techniques of unwinding and reeling silk were crucial to the quality of the finished product was irrelevant to the status and payment afforded to the workers: as women, they fell into the category of unskilled, cheap labor.

Researchers have indicated some small improvements in the conditions of these women workers' lives in the course of the century. Of the sixty-six silk winders whose deaths were registered at the Hôtel-Dieu in Lyon in 1783, the average age was thirty, showing a better survival rate than in the 1750s, and there were far fewer *servantes* living with masters (Garden 1970, 49). Garden recorded the increasing numbers of single women who lived separately in their own lodgings: in 1792, in one small area of the city of Lyon where 105 *dévideuses* were entered on the rolls, 47 were single women living alone in fifth-floor rooms. We have seen that some spinners in Auffay similarly managed to head up their own households. Hufton highlighted the phenomenon in many French cities of spinster clustering, single women renting accommodation together and pooling their meager income, thus creating a substitute family where, for at least some of their time, they escaped from the tyranny of a master and mistress (1984, 362). The older women among them sometimes ran their own little workshop, employing a couple of other workers and fur-nishing material to the masters (see Berg 1994, 160).

We understand very little, however, of how the thousands of anonymous women in the clothing trades who pass through our images actually related to their work, and to each other: unlike male journeymen, they lacked institutional identities and have therefore left little trace of their attitudes and experiences in the court records of the period. It was only when the women began to drop out of the world of textile production and crossed over into prostitution that they appeared in police records (see Benabou 1986). One rare document recorded by Sonenscher does detail the complaints of an eighty-year-old woman in Reims about fourteen or fifteen spinners working in the room above hers, who offended her by "dancing and leaping about in an outrageous manner," particularly on the feast day of Saint Blaise, patron of those involved in the wool trade.[57] Any evidence of such self-expression, or high spirits, unsurprising on the part of a group of (probably) very young women, is absent from our images, where the workers are ideally disciplined, subdued, and obedient to the demands of production.

::

Many images illustrate the largely female occupations of spinning, pulling cords, and warp reeling. The first two are drawn from a treatise on the preparation of dry-spun, short-napped wool. In plate 3.1a, we see a woman using the "small wheel" technique of spinning: she tucks the end of the long distaff into her belt, and it lies across her chest "like a cross-belt." She can then turn the wheel

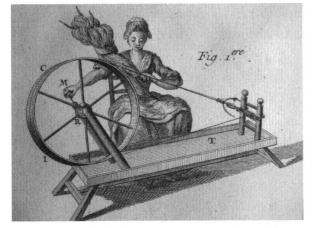

Pl. 3.1a. "Small wheel" spinning technique. Roland de la Platière, *Art du fabricant d'étoffes en laines rases et seches, unies et croisées,* Pl. III. Des. Fossier, eng. Bénard.

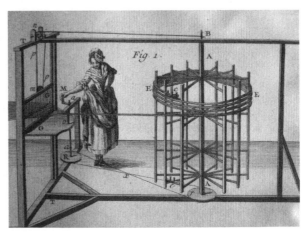

Pl. 3.1b. Reeling warp. Roland de la Platière, *Art du fabricant d'étoffes en laines rases et seches, unies et croisées,* Pl. V. Des. Fossier, eng. Bénard.

with her right hand while pulling the wool thread with her left. The writer points out that although there are regional variations in technique, this is the most common one, and the only one practiced in Picardy. "It is on this very precise repetition [of the movements], the result of a great deal of practice, that the perfection of this part of the operation depends. And since the beauty and quality of the cloth (as far as the manufacturing aspects are concerned) depend entirely on this perfection, we realize that there is no process more important" (Roland de la Platière 1780, 14). This is a rare recognition of the contribution made by "women's work" to a manufacturing process, and of the skill involved in an apparently simple technology, which was so often just taken for granted.[58] In plate 3.1b we see a woman reeling warp, with a technique used in the making of many textiles, including broadcloth (see plate 3.7) and silk (plate 3.19).

Plate 3.2, from the *Encyclopédie,* is a representation of the art of spinning all types of fiber that women practiced in their homes; it is a paradigm, not a realistic image. It represents a range of practices, from the older technology of the handheld spindle and distaff, to the spinning wheel operated by a treadle. "The spin-

ning wheel is a machine that appears simple to us," remarks Diderot; "as we see it everywhere, it never attracts our attention, but it is nonetheless ingenious" ("Fil"). Diderot likewise details, in seven points, the care and skill required of the *fileuse,* whether she spins by hand or by wheel. The women pictured here span the age and social groups: the young woman by the window is clearly, as we see from her dress, of modest origins, possibly a domestic servant within the household. The well-dressed lady on the right might be the mistress of the house. Another stylish young woman, who wears no bonnet (and can again be presumed to be a member of the family), winds the wool into skeins, while the older woman, wearing a shawl, winds the skeins into balls. Thus, all the women of a household contribute to the preparation of yarn that could be used for a variety of purposes, from weaving to knitting. The domestic interior, with curtains and pictures on the wall, clearly differentiates this household-based activity from that of a workshop.

Women spun yarn of all sorts from their homes in town and country throughout France, and in the proto-industrial period, this was one of their main wage-earning activities: Reddy has esti-

mated that the cotton industry in the west of France, the most rapidly expanding sector of the French textile industry, provided work for perhaps three hundred thousand cottagers by 1780 (1984, 24). Gullickson's study of the Caux area (Upper Normandy) shows that, of the estimated 188,207 cotton workers employed by the Rouen merchants in 1782, there were at least eight spinners (almost exclusively women) to every one (male) weaver (1990, 209). The 1796 census for the small village of Sevis recorded that 120 out of the 123 women (over the age of twelve) were spinners. But these women's wages, estimated at something between 9 and 12 *sous* per day, were half, or less, of the male weaver's wage (210–11). Nonetheless, the steady employment offered by the spinning merchants did allow some single and widowed women to maintain their own households: Gullickson records that in the second half of the eighteenth century, a relatively high proportion—between 10 and 15 percent—of the households in the canton of Auffay (Caux) were headed by women, almost certainly spinners (216).

Plate 3.3 illustrates the next stage in the preparation of yarn for weaving, more typically carried out in a workshop; the

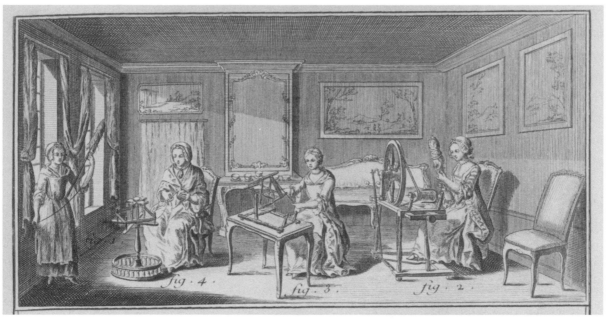

Pl. 3.2. Spinning techniques. *Ency. Planches,* vol. 4. "Fil, roüet, dévidoirs; Pl. I." S119.

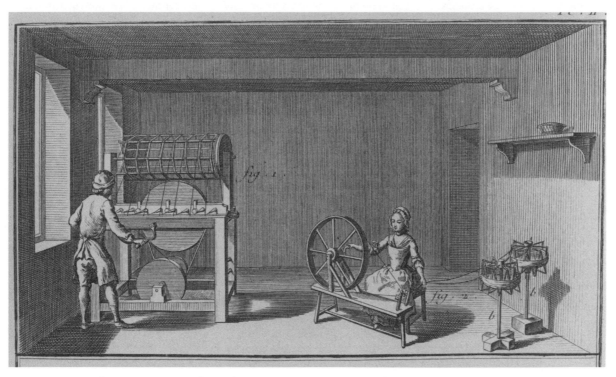

Pl. 3.3. Preparation of yarn for weaving. *Ency. Planches,* vol. 4. "Fil, roüet; Pl. II." S120.

woman on the right twists two threads together—in the direction opposite to that in which they were originally spun—to produce bobbins of strengthened yarn. The man on the left uses a twisting machine to accomplish the same result, with reel and bobbins revolving at different speeds to produce the required tension, representing a more developed stage of technology. This *Encyclopédie* plate is copied almost exactly from one prepared for the Académie in 1718 by Bretez and Haussard, originally intended for a series on the preparation of organzine within the silk industry (Institut ms. 1065bis, f. 112).

The corresponding processes of spinning and winding wool for the preparation of broadcloth were described by Duhamel du Monceau for the Académie; he tells us that the director of the Gobelins manufactory allowed him to visit the workshops, while a manufacturer in Sedan (M. Drouin) gave him a very good *Mémoire* on the subject. He found many engraved images already prepared in the archives of the Académie, dating from the early part of the century, and the first of our two images on this trade (plate 3.4), which has no engraver's signature, may well be one of these. It shows women using two different versions of the spinning wheel: the French version, which had a horizontal table and a metal spindle, and the Dutch version, with an inclined table and a hardwood spindle. Duhamel recommends the latter version, as the spindle does not heat up as much as the metal one. Details of the care needed on the part of the spinner are again given in the text (Duhamel 1765, 36): "the spinner (*la fileuse*) must be careful not to break the raw wool she holds in her hand; she must raise her hand boldly to form it into thread, and only release the correct amount of wool required" (36). This is the rather elegant action pictured in the vignette. The author remarks that some French manufactories supply smaller wheels so that children can spin (37). In the establishments described, the women are paid by the length of yarn produced rather than by the weight, which was the more traditional manner, and consequently, the author remarks approvingly, "they are committed to spinning the finest [yarn] possible." The women were penalized if they fell short on the prescribed length (41). The image also shows a man winding the yarn; unlike spinning, which was almost exclusively female work, the text makes it clear that this work was done by people of both genders.

The woman in plate 3.5 performs an action similar to that of the spinner: she is winding the thread for the weft onto bobbins, which will then be used to weave the broadcloth. "The woman worker who fills the bobbin must be careful to wet the weft thread evenly, and not to tighten her fingers too much as the thread passes through them while it unwinds." The status of the woman "auxiliary" worker vis-à-vis the tradesmen weavers is reflected in her peripheral positioning in the corner of the picture. We will see a very similar technique illustrated in the plates on silk making (3.12).

Plate 3.6, a poor-quality engraving never published, was part of the series prepared for the Académie (in the early part of the century) to illustrate processes common to all the textile trades: it represents the appliance that separated the warp threads for a loom. It is worth reproducing because it underlines the degree to which women were participants throughout the world of textile manufacture. The left-hand side of this image shows a man thinning and polishing reeds to form the teeth, or dents, which the woman then fits between side-pieces to form the reed. In the center is a girl sitting at a heddle frame ("*une jeune fille*") and preparing a half-warp. The two women (*ouvrières*) on the right are finishing the warp:

Pl. 3.4. French and Dutch spinning wheels. Duhamel, *Art de la draperie, principalement pour ce qui regarde les draps fins*, Pl. IV.

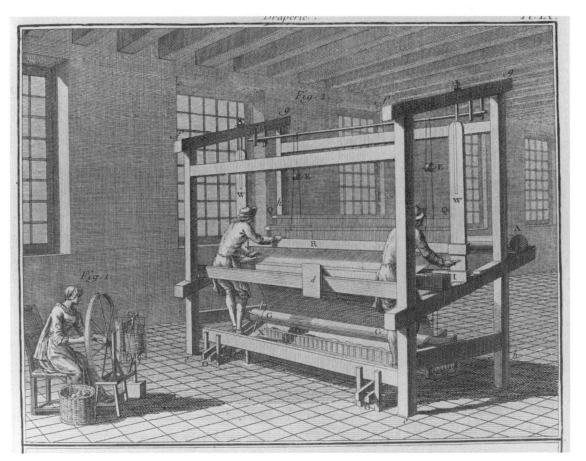

Pl. 3.5. Winding thread for broadcloth. Duhamel, *Art de la draperie, principalement pour ce qui regarde les draps fins*, Pl. IX.

Pl. 3.6. Preparing the warp. [*Lames ou lisses à l'usage des tissutiers*]. MS Typ 432.1 (7), Department of Printing and Graphic Arts, Houghton Library, Harvard College Library. Des. Bretez and Chaufourier, eng. Lucas [c. 1714–20].

the woman in the front holds up the loop for the other woman, who passes the thread through (see Houghton MS Typ 432.1 [7]).

Plate 3.7 shows the work of women warpers—*ourdisseuses*—working with yarn supplied to them by women who have already wound the bobbins. The warper performs the complex task of intertwining the twenty-four threads as she winds them in a flat ribbonlike band around the warping frame (detail). In the lower part of the plate the sticks marked *c* and *d* represent the fingers of the warper, as illustrated more correctly in detail in plate 3.8. When the warp has been wound top to bottom, then bottom to top, it is tied off, re-

moved, and tied in chains (fig. 4) before being passed to the sizers. The work of the warper, "which does not require great strength" (Duhamel 1765, 49), can be performed, we are told, by both men and women. This image was engraved by Elisabeth Haussard, who took over from her father some time after 1720 (see Jaoul and Pinault 1982, 348); the original drawing is in the Houghton Library, Harvard University (MS Typ 432.1 [5] #10), along with a related draft plate (MS Typ 432.1 [5] #8).

Power was provided to textile workshops in different ways, sometimes by watermills or horses, but mainly by human effort. One extraordinary image (plate 3.9), never actually pub-

lished, was signed by Bretez and Lucas in 1719. Intended for a treatise on the making of yarn (*L'Art du filtier*), it was incorporated into a later manuscript on the same topic by Fougeroux de Blaveau and Fougeroux de Bondaroy, who studied workshops in Amiens, Le Plessier, and other locations (Houghton MS Typ 432.1 [5] #7). A manuscript note on the back of the engraving identifies the machine as a "square mill for twisting yarn, wool etc." The accompanying commentary simply states, "Movement is communicated to it [the mill] by a wheel, one or two persons, as we see here, place themselves between the cross-bars.[. . .] They push [the wheel] at a walking speed and make it turn in the appropriate di-

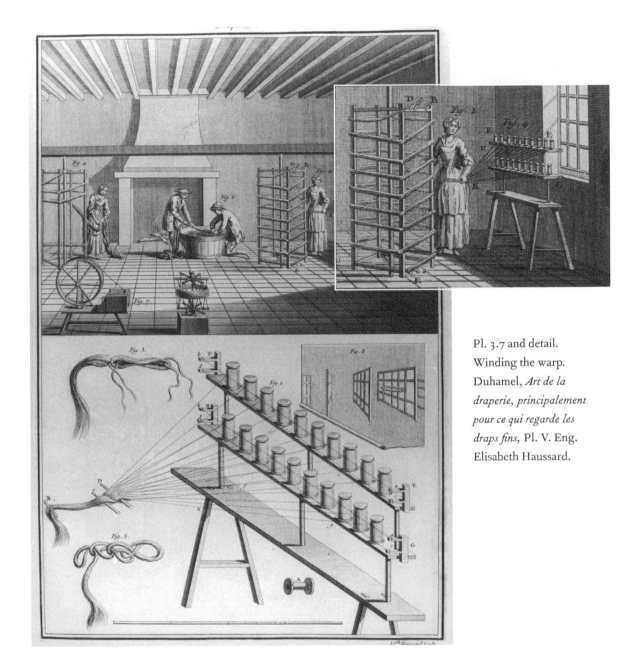

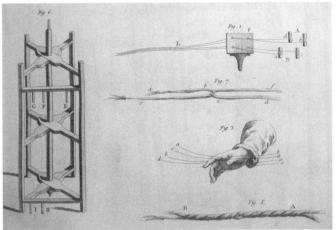

Pl. 3.7 and detail.
Winding the warp.
Duhamel, *Art de la draperie, principalement pour ce qui regarde les draps fins*, Pl. V. Eng. Elisabeth Haussard.

Pl. 3.8. Fingers of the warper.
Duhamel, *Art de la draperie, principalement pour ce qui regarde les draps fins*, Pl. VI.

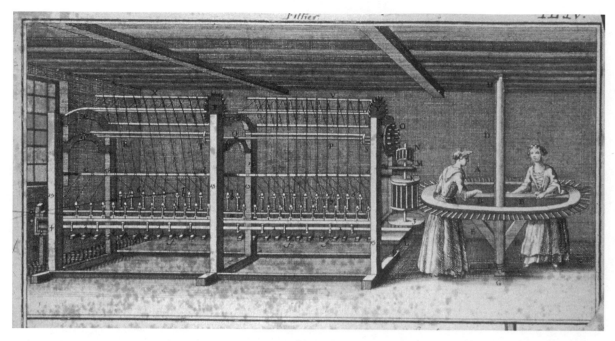

Pl. 3.9. Square mill for twisting yarn. "Pl. IV. Filtier." MS Typ 432.1 (5) #7, Department of Printing and Graphic Arts, Houghton Library, Harvard College Library. Des. Bretez, eng. Lucas, 1719.

rection." Only the picture stands as witness that the work being described was actually done by women, who turned in circles, probably with little respite from the wheel, throughout the long workday current in such an environment. The notes also refer to the *Encyclopédie* article "Fil" and remark that identical letters appear on the corresponding plate in that collection (*Ency. Planches*, vol. 4: "Fil et laine, 2 bis, Moulin carré, détail de ce moulin par coupes et plans"), clearly suggesting that it was copied in part from this original: the *Encyclopédie* version, however, does not show how the mill was powered. A similar type of machine, with twenty-

four spindles, is described in manuscript notes in the dossier "Lainier": too heavy to be turned by children, it is normally turned, the text states, by a man and a woman (Houghton MS Typ 432.1 [5] #8, f. 42). When strength was required in these situations women were called on without question; their bodies are the producers of energy in this world of early mechanization. We can again remark how the conventions of the genre operate here to mask the traces such heavy physical toil would have left on their physique and on their clothing.

A companion image in the manuscript collections (dated 1718) was later reproduced, in re-

duced size, in the *Art du fabricant d'étoffes en laines rases et seches, unies et croisées* published by Jean-Marie Roland de la Platière in 1780. This plate (3.10) depicts a mill used for the reeling of wool thread: a man on the side cranks the axle, and the mill turns around the young woman, whose job involves joining up the ends of the threads, which frequently break (Houghton MS Typ 432.1 [5] #8, f. 77). The woman could spend up to fifteen hours a day stretching thus above her head while the machine spun around her. This and the preceding image foreshadow the domination of machine over human operator that would characterize the next century, while at

Pl. 3.10. Mill for reeling wool thread. Roland de la Platière, *Art du fabricant d'étoffes en laines rases et seches, unies et croisées*, Pl. IV. Eng. Bénard.

the same time recalling the millennial contribution of women in traditional economies as suppliers of both manual dexterity and brute energy.

In our collections there are many fine plates illustrating silk making. From early on, this craft, imported from Italy, employed large numbers of women in urban centers, particularly Lyon. Our images document the many complex stages through which silk passed before being woven into the luxury fabrics that decorated the homes and persons of the affluent.

The first stage was the unwinding of the raw cocoons spun by the silkworm, which were first immersed in a hot solution to dissolve the silk-gum (sericin). In plate 3.11 from the *Encyclopédie*, two women (the *dévideuses*) work in an outside hangar in a silk factory: we see two threads (detail), each made up of separate filaments from a number of cocoons, being reeled onto a machine operated by a hand crank. Known as the "Tour de Piémont" and developed in northern Italy, this type of machine was used right into the next century (Hills 1993, 59–90). The woman seated is taking up the single filament from each silk cocoon in a pan in front of her; the water in it, used to dissolve the cocoons, is kept just below boiling temperature by a little furnace underneath. The bowl on the ground beside her is filled with cold water so that she can cool her hand occasionally. This work was done outdoors in June and July, when the heat built up by the furnace and the boiling water could be more easily dissipated outside. Many women workers, who dominated the silk trade, suffered illnesses, especially tuberculosis, from working in fetid conditions inside workshops, with resultant high mortality rates; they also suffered permanent damage to their skin and hands, which lost sensitivity from being plunged continuously into the hot water. The texts say nothing of these hazards; the bucolic setting and imposing

Pl. 3.11. Unwinding cocoons. *Ency. Planches,* vol. 11. "Soierie, tirage de la soie et plan du tour de Piémont; Pl. I." S138.

gates of this rather charming picture distract from these realities. Although the girls doing this work were very poorly paid, the text of the *Encyclopédie* article "Soie" does highlight the importance and skill of this work, on which the quality of a usable silk thread depended. Women unwound the cocoons, because, Merry Wiesner asserts, "women, or more accurately girls, were viewed as having greater dexterity and ability to concentrate than men" (Wiesner 2000, 111).

Once unwound, the thread had to be reeled in various combinations, depending on the purpose for which it was intended. Paulet, who wrote the Académie treatise, was himself a successful manufacturer from Nîmes, and he was painstaking in his descriptions. He first illustrates the older technologies for accomplishing this task in two images. Plate 3.12 shows one woman (left) using a type of frame to hold the hank of silk thread, which she reels onto the bobbin with a handheld spindle: the end of this spindle rests in a hole in a belt

she wears (compare with plate 3.1 on spinning). The woman on the right has a wheel (*guindre*) to hold the hank of thread, which she reels onto the bobbin with her left hand, turning a crank to spin the bobbin with her right. Plate 3.13 shows two women using the *escouladou,* a frame with a spindle and a wheel for turning the bobbin at speed, and which they hold on their knees. Plate 3.14, from the *Encyclopédie,* shows (on the right) the *escouladou* being used for the "doubling" of the silk, that is, the

Pl. 3.12. Reeling the thread. Paulet, *L'Art du fabriquant d'étoffes de soie. Premiere et seconde sections*, Pl. I. A 10.1015F (v. 16), Houghton Library, Harvard College Library. Des. Goussier, eng. Bénard.

Pl. 3.13. Reeling the thread: *escouladou*. Paulet, *L'Art du fabriquant d'étoffes de soie. Premiere et seconde sections*, Pl. III. A 10.1015F (v. 16), Houghton Library, Harvard College Library. Des. Goussier, eng. Bénard.

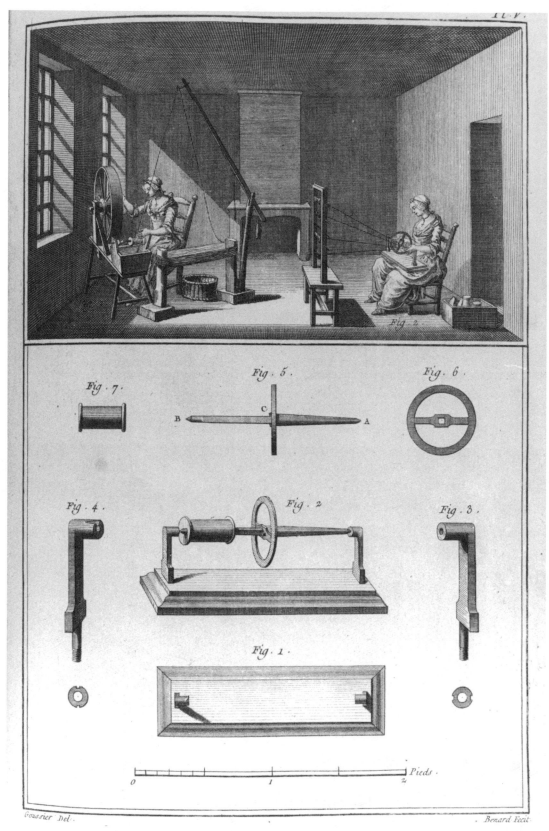

Pl. 3.14. Reeling the thread. *Ency. Planches,* vol. 11. "Soierie, dévidage de la soie sur le tour d'Espagne, doublage et développement de l'escaladou; Pl. V." S142.

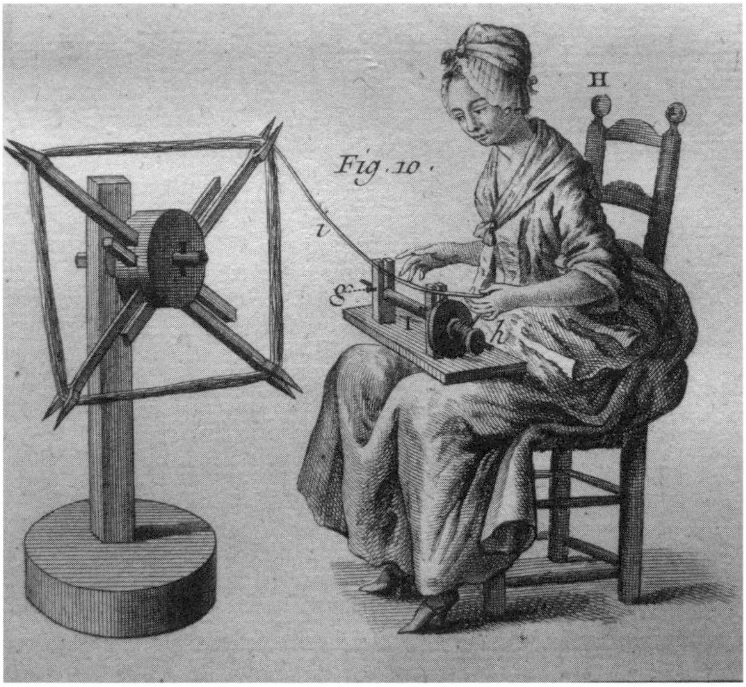

Pl. 3.15. Reeling the thread: *escouladou*. Paulet, *L'Art du fabriquant d'étoffes de soie. Sixieme section*, Pl. X. Des. Paulet, eng. Bénard.

combining of several threads from the bobbins on the vertical frame in front of the worker; the device is illustrated in detail in the bottom section of the plate. On the left a woman is illustrated using the "Spanish wheel," yet another variation on the reeling wheel: the skein of silk is supported on two vertical wooden posts and fed into the worker's left hand through a glass hook on the tall wooden pole suspended above her, appropriately called "the stork." Interestingly, the *Encyclopédie* plates for this "art" were drawn and engraved by the same people (Goussier and Benard) who were responsible for the majority of the corresponding Académie plates: this

explains the similarity in style. A woman is shown using a slightly different *escouladou* in plate 3.15, combined with a vertical, square-shaped wheel: the purpose here is to reel the strong twisted thread (*ligneul*) used by shoemakers and saddlers onto large bobbins. In this case the woman spins the shaft with the flat of her hand rather than with a wheel. Paulet explains that whereas these types of reeling device remained useful for reeling materials such as cotton or wool, they had been superseded by better technology for silk making; with the older methods, the thread came into too much contact with the reeler's heated hand, "sweating or naturally oily," and this de-

tracted from the luster of the finished silk (Paulet 1773, 1: 7).

Plate 3.16 shows a woman using the complex four-wheel reeling machine (known as the "Rouet de Lyon") that took over from the simpler technologies. She is operating the machine with her feet, and the text tells us that she uses her hands for two different operations: with her fingers she separates the strands of the skeins of dyed silk hanging from a bar in front of her face, thus readying them for the wheel, while at the same time, she checks and corrects the operation of the machine, tying broken threads and so forth as necessary. The image shows how she keeps her right hand on the skein

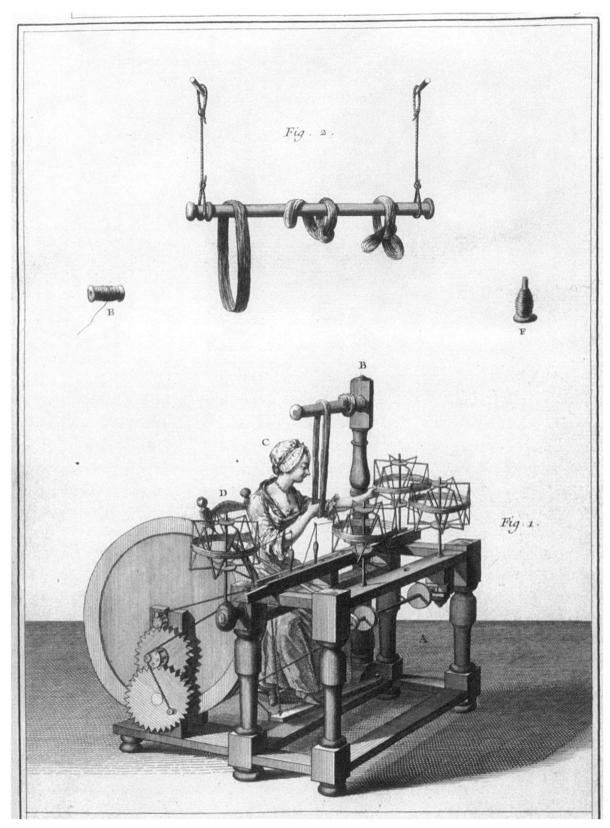

Pl. 3.16. Four-wheel reeling machine. Paulet, *L'Art du fabriquant d'étoffes de soie. Première et seconde sections*, Pl. IX. A 10.1015F (v. 16), Houghton Library, Harvard College Library. Des. Goussier, eng. Bénard.

Pl. 3.17a. Stocking making. *Ency. Planches,* vol. 2. "Metier à faire des bas; Pl. I." S23.

Pl. 3.17b. Stocking making. Drawing in black ink and grey wash by Pierre de Rochefort. Archives de l'Académie des Sciences, Paris, Dossier biographique de Des Billettes.

of silk while adjusting a loose thread on one of the wheels with her left: "It is in order not to lose any time, from which she benefits, that she does not re- move her hand from the skein of silk she is separating" (Paulet 1773, 34). With this technology there is less contact with the thread, and the woman's hand does not become overheated; thus, the silk is of better quality. A woman operating the same machine is shown in the *Ency-clopédie* plate on stocking making

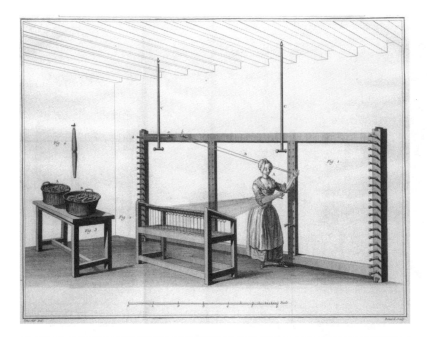

Pl. 3.18. Stretching the warp. Paulet, *L'Art du fabriquant d'étoffes de soie. Première et seconde sections,* Pl. III (2nd series). A 10.1015F (v. 16), Houghton Library, Harvard College Library. Des. Goussier, eng. Bénard.

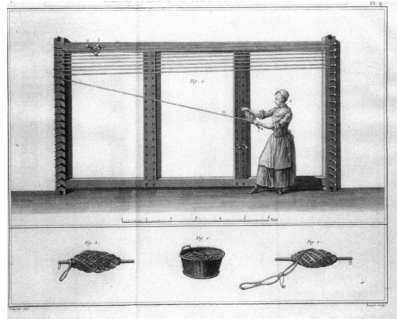

Pl. 3.19. Removing the warp. Paulet, *L'Art du fabriquant d'étoffes de soie. Première et seconde sections,* Pl. IV (2nd series). A 10.1015F (v. 16), Houghton Library, Harvard College Library. Des. Goussier, eng. Bénard.

(3.17a); the conception of this plate corresponds closely with a much earlier drawing by Pierre de Rochefort, prepared sometime between 1709 and 1717 (Pinault 2002, 159) and intended for the Académie's treatise on the stocking frame, never published. In this drawing the

woman uses the more primitive technology of reeling the silk by hand onto the bobbins (3.17b). In both of these images, from the early and later parts of the century, we see a typical small workshop where husband and wife work side by side.

Plate 3.18 is the first of a

rather splendid series of double-sized plates showing women warpers (*ourdisseuses*). The creel in front contains forty large bobbins; the worker draws a thread from each and brings them together as she stretches them on the wall frame. Plate 3.19 shows how she removes the warp, twist-

Pl. 3.20. Warping with a circular frame. Paulet, *L'Art du fabriquant d'étoffes de soie. Première et seconde sections*, Pl. XV (2nd series). A 10.1015F (v. 16), Houghton Library, Harvard College Library. Des. Goussier, eng. Bénard.

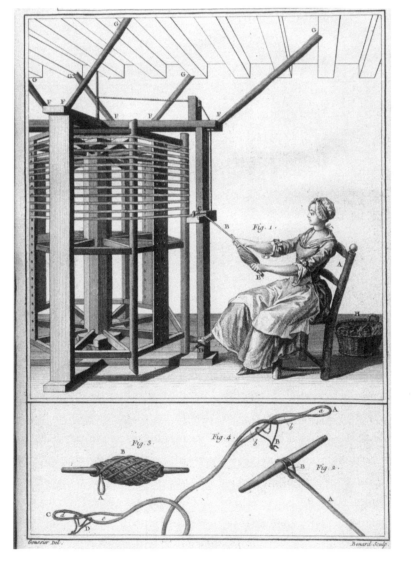

Pl. 3.21. Unwinding the finished warp. Paulet, *L'Art du fabriquant d'étoffes de soie. Première et seconde sections*, Pl. XVI (2nd series). A 10.1015F (v. 16), Houghton Library, Harvard College Library. Des. Goussier, eng. Bénard.

Pl. 3.22. Lyon-style creel with circular warper. Paulet, *L'Art du fabriquant d'étoffes de soie. Première et seconde sections*, Pl. XIX (2nd series). A 10.1015F (v. 16), Houghton Library, Harvard College Library. Des. Goussier, eng. Bénard.

Pl. 3.23. Setting up bobbins: removing the warp. Paulet, *L'Art du fabriquant d'étoffes de soie. Première et seconde sections*, Pl. XX (2nd series). A 10.1015F (v. 16), Houghton Library, Harvard College Library. Des. Goussier, eng. Bénard.

ing it carefully onto a large peg "with all possible force," as is indicated by her posture. Plate 3.20 illustrates the warping of threads of one color, this time with forty bobbins on a vertical frame that are wound onto a circular warping frame. Having attached the threads with the required separators that would serve to interlace

them, the warper (center) sits and turns the axle at the required speed to wind her warp onto the frame; she has to watch carefully and repair or replace any broken threads. Her companion sets up the bobbins for her to use. One section of this image is almost identical to the *Encyclopédie* plate "Soierie; XXIII." Plate 3.21

shows a woman unwinding the finished warp from the same frame: again (as for plate 3.19), the text underlines the physical effort involved; the woman uses her foot to control the movement of the frame, which would otherwise spin too fast. Plate 3.22 combines what is termed the Lyon-style creel with the circular warper, an

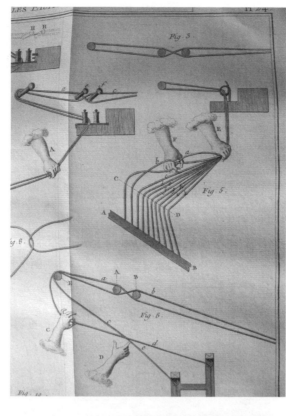

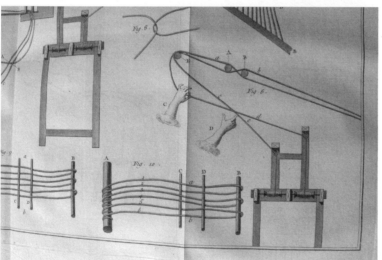

Pl. 3.24a and b. Woman warper's hands, detail. Paulet, *L'Art du fabriquant d'étoffes de soie. Première et seconde sections,* Pl. XXIV (2nd series). Des. Paulet.

image for which a first drawing is preserved in the Houghton dossier on ribbon making (reproduced in Jaoul and Pinault 1982, 354), dating undoubtedly from the early part of the century. Plate 3.23 shows a young worker (on the right) setting up the bobbins for the warping machine illustrated in plate 3.22. The worker on the left appears older; she is removing the warp from the circular frame, this time forming it into loops. Again we see how she controls the frame with her foot and uses leverage to give an even tension to the thread, essential to ensure its quality.

The tasks of the warper were more complex than can readily be illustrated in these images: the

Pl. 3.25. Warping with a large spool. *Ency. Planches*, vol. 11. "Soierie, l'opération de relever; Pl. XXVIII." S170.

ourdisseuse had to separate and interlace the threads in the appropriate manner so that they would be unwound in the right order, and she had to gradate color threads appropriately. Some idea of the complexity of this task can be gleaned from the illustrations detailing the movements of the worker's hands in plates 3.24a and b, images drawn by the expert author Paulet himself. Roland Barthes commented on similar images of disembodied hands in the *Encyclopédie*: "hands, cut off from any body, flutter around the work (because they have an ex-treme lightness); these hands are undoubtedly the symbol of an artisanal world [. . .] but beyond the artisanal, these hands are inescapably the inductive sign of the human essence" (Barthes 1964, 12). This convention of showing hands operating tools can already be seen in Renaissance manuscripts (see Gille 1956, 653: fig. 596), but it is rare that they are represented as being female hands, which is the case here, where they are mentioned only occasionally in the texts for their dexterity and finesse.

The last image of warping (plate 3.25) is from the *Ency-clopédie,* where we see a male worker using what was, in France, the less common methodology of a large spool for winding the warp: in this case the woman performs only the auxiliary task of controlling the movement of the warping frame. Paulet, himself a silk producer who wrote the Académie's trea-tise on silk after the publication of the *Encyclopédie*'s article on the subject, criticized it as being "full of errors" (Paulet 1773, xxi). The images we have seen from his collection may give a

Pl. 3.26. Reeling silk onto a spinning wheel. Paulet, *L'Art du fabriquant d'étoffes de soie. Sixieme section*, Pl. VII. Des. Paulet, eng. Bénard.

Pl. 3.27. Loading silk onto quills from a doubling frame. Paulet, *L'Art du fabriquant d'étoffes de soie. Troisieme et quatrieme sections*, Pl. XI. Des. and eng. Bénard.

more reliable reflection of the dominant role of women in this activity.

The skill of women is further reflected in an image that shows a young woman reeling seven strands of silk onto a spinning wheel (plate 3.26): the text emphasizes how essential it is that the thread be evenly twisted along its whole length and how the worker must never loosen the grip of her fingers as she goes along (Paulet 1773, 6.i: 441). The type of finished silk was determined by the way the thread was twisted: for example, *crepe* demanded a thread that was

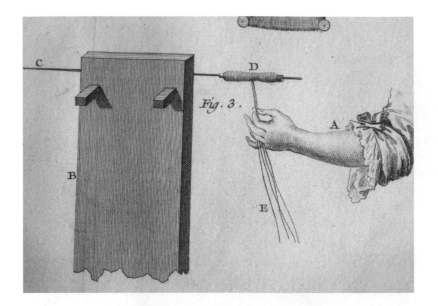

Pl. 3.28a. Guiding the silk onto a quill. Paulet, *L'Art du fabriquant d'étoffes de soie. Troisieme et quatrieme sections*, Pl. X. Des. and eng. Bénard.

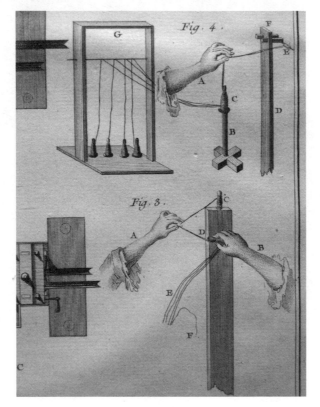

Pl. 3.28b. Rejoining broken thread and returning to quill. Paulet, *L'Art du fabriquant d'étoffes de soie. Troisieme et quatrieme sections*, Pl. XI. Des. and eng. Bénard.

twisted from fifty to eighty turns per 2.5 centimeters (Hills 1993, 68). Paulet emphasizes that the quality of the thread depends on the judgment of the worker (in this case predominantly women) and that "only experience can instruct a worker." Another female worker (plate 3.27) is loading the silk onto quills from a doubling frame: this is described as a delicate operation in which great care must be taken in joining broken threads, and without which "it is logically impossible that these materials would not have some flaws caused by the defect in the quill itself" (Paulet

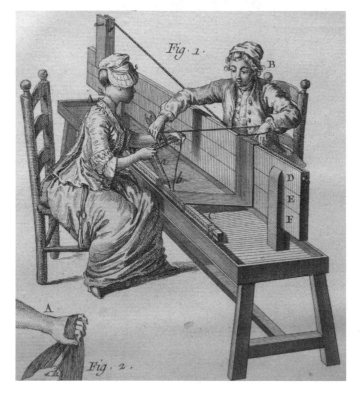

1773, 5: 191–92). The details show a woman's hands guiding the silk onto the quill (plate 3.28a, "fig. 3"); finding and re-joining a broken thread (plate 3.28b, "fig. 3"), and returning the repaired threads to the quill ("fig. 4").

Two last images from Paulet's treatise show the making of heddles, which were used for raising the warp threads of a loom, on two different types of horizontal frame. In both images (plates 3.29 a and b) the young woman catches and pulls up the loops in the correct order (a long one must be joined to a short

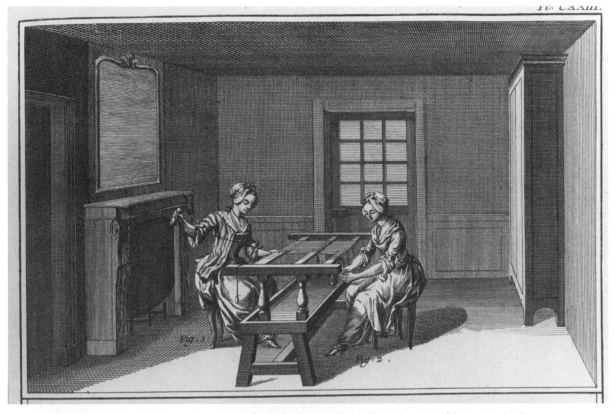

Pl. 3.30. Making heddles on horizontal frame. *Ency. Planches,* vol. 11. "Soierie, fabrication des lisses et le lissoir en perspective; Pl. CXXIII." S278.

one) so the young man (*le remisseur*) can pass the shuttle carrying a warp thread through the loop (Paulet 1773, 5: 348). They are very much a team; in fact, Paulet specifies that "the precautions that must be taken with this work are almost all on the part of the Helper (*Aide*) [. . .] without whom the worker cannot operate" (345). The young men might be apprentice weavers or members of the master's family with a possible future as master craftsmen; the young women had little prospect of bettering themselves. In the corresponding *Encyclopédie* image (plate 3.30), we

see two women (now simply *ouvrières*) working at the frame in what is described as a *chambre;* as was previously noted, this expression could imply that they were outworkers, and the image evokes the way in which masters cut costs by farming out the preparation of heddles to cheap female labor. In the *Encyclopédie* article "Lisses, (Rub.)," referring to the very similar techniques of the ribbon makers (who used silk thread), the author states that the function corresponding to that of the *aide* is typically performed by a child, and that of the *remisseur* by a woman (*ouvrière*). The

"proletarianization" of women is reflected here in the nonspecific terminology—*ouvrière, aide*—applied to them as opposed to the task- and skill-related identifiers more generally applied to male workers.

A number of plates were engraved in the early part of the century for the trade of the ribbon maker, formerly known as the *dorelotier,* who made all types of upholstery trims, fringing, and decorative braid such as was used for livery. Silk, gold, and silver threads were extensively used in these products. In the statutes of 1404 this was a mixed trade,

Pl. 3.31. Ribbon-maker's loom: drawing cords. ["Le metier de la tire"]. MS Typ 432.1 (3) #24, Department of Printing and Graphic Arts, Houghton Library, Harvard College Library. Eng. J. Haussard [c. 1718].

where women were registered as mistresses and apprentices on an equal footing with men and where the daughters of a master or mistress had an automatic right to accede to the mastership on completion of the chef d'œuvre (Lespinasse 1886, 3: 13–20, arts. 2, 3, 4, 6). By 1514 the rights of women in the guild had been severely restricted: there is no mention of female apprentices, and it is now only sons who retain privileged access to the mastership, with daughters' privilege now reduced to that of working in the trade and conferring access rights on their husbands (25, arts. 10, 21). Again in the 1585 statutes it is clear that the children of a master ("*enfants,*" implying both sexes) can work within the trade, but only the boys can advance within the guild (32, art. 6). In our images for this trade, we see many women operating in the workshops.

Réaumur and Fougeroux de Bondaroy both drafted text for a treatise on ribbon making at different periods, but it was never published. Some of the accounts and images were, however, clearly used by Diderot, particularly in his plates on *passementerie,* the trade that brought these products to the market. Again, we know from the

Pl. 3.32. Weaving at a small loom for making braid. ["Métier a faire du gance"]. MS Typ 432.1 (3) #28, Department of Printing and Graphic Arts, Houghton Library, Harvard College Library. Eng. Cl. Lucas: 1714.

Houghton manuscript collections that the information was based on detailed *Mémoires* sent from Lyon, Saint-Chamond, St. Etienne en Forez, and even Bologna (MS Typ 432.1 [3] #24), as well as knowledge of the trade in Paris. The early date of these plates, which remained hidden in manuscript collections, adds to their interest. Plate 3.31, dating from around 1718, shows the ribbon maker's loom with two people drawing cords: the woman is drawing the cords of the semple forward to activate the warp threads. The action of her hands is featured in detail on the right of the image. She then had to tug hard on the semple to pull down the next row of the pattern. This task of the drawgirl was performed from the start by women as well as boys throughout the silk industry, and Hafter has underlined how every contemporary description of the activity stressed its rigors: the problem was caused

by weights at the base of the loom, which made each tug on the semple very arduous (1979, 57). This ribbon-making loom was smaller than the average silk weaver's, so the task may have been somewhat less exhausting than that of the silk drawgirls, whose working life was short. The woman pictured here, in what to the modern eye is rather splendid garb—she is wearing the Fontange headdress, popular in the period—seems an unlikely candidate for this grueling labor of drawing cords; the working girl is likely to have worn a simpler dress than the one embellished here by the designer's imagination. Women from Lyon families avoided tasks such as this, infamous for the drudgery involved, but drawgirls were attracted into the silk industry from the impoverished regions of Savoy and surrounding regions.

Plate 3.32 shows a girl ("*une fille*") working at a small loom or

dobby for making braid, alongside a man working a somewhat larger loom. This is one of the rare instances where a woman is shown actually weaving. She uses the weft thread from the roller beam at the back of her loom to thread through the warp on her frame, the cords being drawn by means of the foot pedals she operates. We can see the braid as she winds it onto the beam in front of her.

The woman on the left of plate 3.33 is repairing the faults in a wide, flat ribbon; she cuts any protruding warp threads with the pointed implement illustrated in the bottom section of the plate (*A*). She winds the ribbon from one roller to the other as she works. The two men in the middle pass the ribbon or braid through a roller press, which gives an even appearance to the surface; presumably, the splendidly dressed man to the front is the master. The woman on the right is reeling

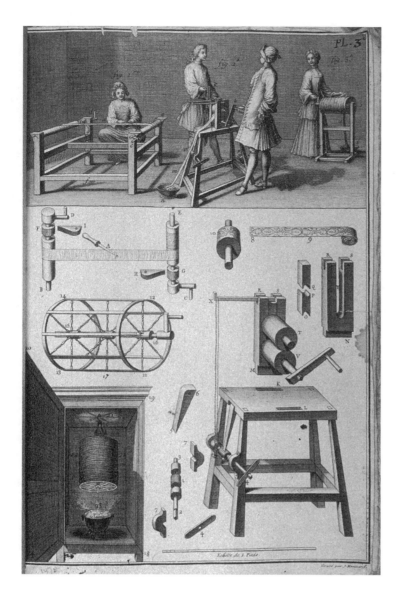

Pl. 3.33. Ribbon making: finishing techniques. "Art du Rubanier, Pl. 3e." MS Typ 432.1 (3) #28, Department of Printing and Graphic Arts, Houghton Library, Harvard College Library. Eng. J. Haussard [c. 1718].

the ribbon onto a large spool (called a *lanterne*), which is then smoked over a brazier in a special cupboard (see bottom left). The purpose of this exercise was to enhance the color of the gold and silver thread—a temporary improvement the text declares to be one of the "tricks of the trade" (*supercherie*) widely practiced to attract the gullible customer (Fougeroux de Bondaroy,

Houghton MS Typ 432.1 [3] #27, f. 71). Different materials were used to produce the smoke; partridge feathers were reputed to be the best. In the *Encyclopédie* these activities are shown in two plates with all male workers ("Passementerie; Pls. XIII and XIV"); again, we may give more credence to the careful and close documentation of the Academicians, which mentions the women

workers in text as well as image, but it is likely that these tasks were interchangeable between genders.

Plate 3.34 illustrates the making of the Nonpareil, the narrowest type of ribbon, and the one most commonly used for the decoration of ladies' fashion items. It was not woven but composed of sixty silk threads fused together by heat and glue. The

Pl. 3.34. Ribbon making: nonpareil. "Art du rubanier, Pl. 2ᵉ." [*La nompareille*]. MS Typ 432.1 (3) #28, Department of Printing and Graphic Arts, Houghton Library, Harvard College Library. Eng. J. Haussard [c. 1718].

woman on the right performs the heating operation: working on her knees, she pulls the strands of silk through a kind of pressing mill with two cylinders, the lower one of which, made of copper, has been heated over charcoal. This smooths the fibers and adds a sheen to the surface of the ribbon; thus, "the material becomes as beautiful as it can possibly be," writes Fougeroux de Bondaroy (Houghton MS Typ 432.1 [3] #28, f. 69). This work can be done, he suggests, by "a woman or a small boy," but he continuously underlines the care that must be taken to ensure that

the cylinder is at the right temperature—the operator must slow the speed with which the ribbon is pressed as it cools— and to ensure that the ribbon does not get creased or entangled (fms Typ 432.1 [3] #27, f. 54–56). The worker must also sort the ribbons correctly according to color and the amount of heat required for their finish (rather a lot to expect of a young child, it would seem). The worker second from the right guides the ribbon through a bowl containing a substance used to firm up the ribbon and contribute to its shiny surface; the nature of the mixture

used in this process was again one of the "secrets" jealously guarded by the trade, which Fougeroux assures us is nothing more than gum Arabic and hot water (MS Typ 432.1 (3) #27, p. 49). The next worker uses a piece of wire to knock off surface gum and leave a smooth finish, while the woman winds the crank of the folding frame to wind up the ribbon. Next to the frame is a brazier used to dry the ribbon as it is folded.

The trade of the *passementier* was a branch of textile work that employed many women. Plate 3.35 illustrates the technique for

Pl. 3.35 and detail. Passementerie: making braid and *cartisane* decorations. [*Ouvrages des cartisanes, et les cordons à la jatte*]. MS Typ 432.1 (3) #10, Department of Printing and Graphic Arts, Houghton Library, Harvard College Library.

making the round cord widely used in *passementerie*, which we have already seen in the closely related illustrations of the art of the buttonmaker-*passementier* (plates 2.28 and 2.29): the man on the left is using the *jatte* (which is shaped like a basin with a hole in the middle) through which the core string passes and around which he braids the decorative thread.

The workers at the table (detail) are using a technique known as *cartisane* whereby small pieces of cardboard are covered with silver or gold thread and used as raised ornamentation on upholstery materials. The woman on the left is winding the gold wire or silk thread onto the cardboard, which the next worker (second from left) then sews onto the piece to be decorated

(see detail). The exact function of the two women is, unfortunately, missing in the manuscript notes filed with the images in the Houghton Library collection, but the woman seated second from the right does appear to be preparing the cardboard for the worker at the far right. Réaumur, who drafted these descriptions, queried the nature of their tasks (Mémoires no. 26,

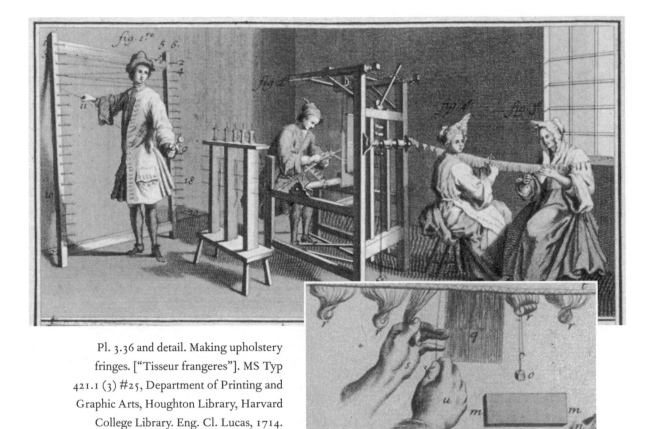

Pl. 3.36 and detail. Making upholstery fringes. ["Tisseur frangeres"]. MS Typ 421.1 (3) #25, Department of Printing and Graphic Arts, Houghton Library, Harvard College Library. Eng. Cl. Lucas, 1714.

Houghton MS Typ 432.1 [3] #10): presumably, his question was addressed to the designer who drew the workshop scene, or a tradesperson on whom he relied for the information. This was the kind of meticulous research that characterized much of the work on the *Descriptions* and was frequently lacking in the *Encyclopédie*.

Plate 3.36 shows the making of upholstery fringes or bullion. The men reel the thread and work the loom; the women do the intricate work of "*guipure,*"

using a little crochet hook. Exactly the same technology is described in the *Planches* of the *Encyclopédie* over half a century later, in a plate that closely follows this one ("Passementerie; Pl. XV"), showing four women performing the same task: this was a highly labor-intensive occupation. The fringing comes off the loom with the cords bunched together; the *guipeuse* separates them and twists each strand with a "violent" movement, using the hook between her thumb and index finger to give it just the

right degree of finish with a little kink at the end (detail). "The beauty of the *guipure* depends on the skilfulness [*habileté*] of the woman worker," remarks Diderot in a rare example of recognition of skill in a female occupation (*Ency.* "Guiper").

There are three further plates in the *Encyclopédie* featuring women working in trades related to *passementerie*. The first (plate 3.37) is on the making of reeds. There were many types of reeds, depending on the size of loom for which they were intended:

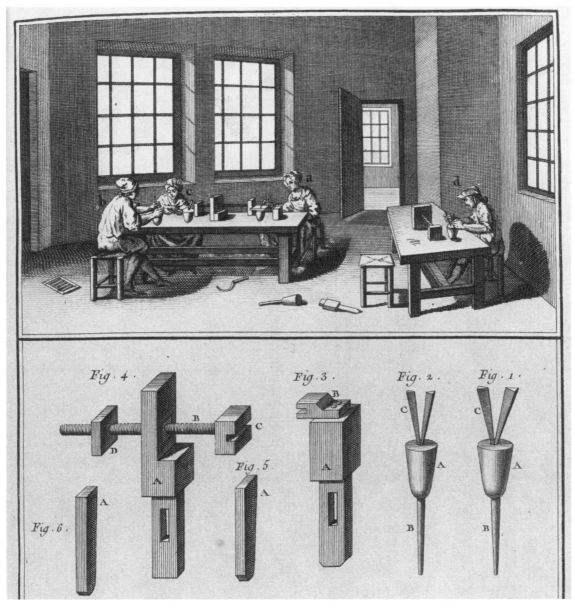

Pl. 3.37. Passementerie: making reeds. *Ency. Planches*, vol. 11. "Passementerie; Pl. XXIII." S48.

the reed is a comblike device for "beating" the weft thread into place; the warp threads pass between the teeth of the reed. In the instance in this plate, they were made with reeds or cane from Provence. The worker on the far right and the two workers on the left are preparing the natural reed to form the dents, and the woman in the center is assembling the finished slay that holds the reeds.

Plate 3.38 shows women working at two different styles of warping frame, presumably used for the weaving of different types of braid or ribbon. One is the more typical two-person frame, where one worker pulls up the heddle eyes for the other to pass the shuttle; the woman on the right operates the smaller frame on her own.

Pl. XXVII

Pl. 3.38. Warping frames. *Ency. Planches,* vol. 11. "Passementerie; Pl. XXVII." S52.

Pl. 3.39. Finishing laces with brass tips. *Ency. Planches,* vol. 11. "Passementerie; Pl. XXIX." S54.

Pl. 3.40 and detail. Drawing, reeling, and laminating gold wire. Institut ms. 1065bis, f. 82 ["Tireur d'or"]. Des. and eng. L. Simonneau, 1713.

In the last of this series (plate 3.39), we see two women working on the finishing of laces, used to tighten the bodices worn by women and children. The laces were generally made from hemp—we see bundles of them on the floor and hanging on the wall—and the ends were finished with tin, or, as in this case, brass, hammered and pinched into place. The man on the left is cutting the pieces of brass; the woman on the right prepares each piece for fit-ting; and the woman at the center hammers them into place. With the lack of care so often found in the *Encyclopédie*, the plate legend refers to this woman in the mas-culine as an *ouvrier*.

An impressive set of plates from the manuscript collections detail the making of gold and sil-ver wire and thread; engraved in the period 1712–14, these were not accompanied by textual ex-planations, but, fortuitously, much of the *Encyclopédie* article "Tireur d'or et d'argent" refers to these very images. This is an-other clear example of the now well-established plagiarism of the Académie's plates by Diderot. Presumably, he had originally in-tended to produce a set of plates on this trade based closely on those of the Académie; but after the accusation of theft was made against him, he changed his plans and produced a set of plates (and plate legends) that do not corre-spond to the references in the ar-

Pl. 3.41. Covering thread with gold or silver. Institut ms. 1065bis, f. 85. ["Tireur d'or"]. Art and eng. L. Simonneau, 1708.

ticle written by the chevalier de Jaucourt and published in the textual volumes. De Jaucourt therefore repeatedly refers the reader to details of plates that cannot be identified in the *Encyclopédie* but correspond very closely to the plates we reproduce here. *Tireur d'or* was a male sworn trade both in Paris and Lyon (Savary des Bruslons 1742, 4: 1011), and the images highlight how the earlier stages of the process of reducing the metal bars to a size where the wire could be drawn were a male preserve. Women were employed, however, in the later stages of the manufacture: plate 3.40 illustrates the wire being drawn through smaller and smaller holes in a drawing plate, first by what appears to be a

young boy on the left, who draws the thicker wire (*la gavette*), then by the woman (center), who draws it to its thinnest (*le trait*). The woman at the back of the picture reels this wire from the cylinder onto a bobbin; both of these female workers are referred to, in the *Encyclopédie* text, as *"filles."* The woman at the right (detail) uses a kind of mill to laminate the wire, which is fed though two wheels of polished steel. The pressure on the wire (increased by the weight at *o*) flattens it into a very fine strip, which can then be used to cover silk thread. Elements of this plate are closely followed in the *Encyclopédie* (*Ency. Planches*, "Tireur d'or; Pl. III").

Plates 3.41 and 3.42 illustrate the impressive machine used for

covering silk thread with the laminated gold or silver. This version has twelve bobbins; another version, featured in the *Encyclopédie*, has sixteen bobbins (*Ency. Planches*, "Tireur et Fileur d'or; Pl. VI–XII"). De Jaucourt enthusiastically remarks (in the corresponding text, *Ency.*: "Fileur d'or): "The workings of this quill winder are so ingenious, that with just one crank the man or woman who operates the machine puts more than one hundred separate components into motion." Two sets of bobbins hold the silk thread and the laminated metal, and the action of the machine wraps one around the other as the woman turns the handle. The woman in the center of plate 3.41 is operating a laminating mill similar to the one seen in plate 3.40.

Pl. 3.42. Covering thread with gold or silver. Institut ms. 1065bis, f. 86 ["Tireur d'or"]. Art and eng. L. Simonneau, 1712.

Pl. 3.43. Making gold wire.
Institut ms. 1065bis, f. 83
["Tireur d'or"]. Art and eng. L.
Simonneau, 1712

This plate has no identifying letters or numbers; these would have been added later had the plates been readied for publication. The woman on the left of plate 3.42 is winding the finished gold thread onto a bobbin. Judith Coffin (1996, 26) asserts that in Paris, all trades that used this gold thread as a primary material were exclusively associated with women.

Lastly, a plate that probably depicts an earlier stage in the process of making gold wire (or possibly imitation gold wire), but for which no description is available, offers yet another example of a woman cranking a wheel and providing the power in a predominantly male workshop. This was indeed ancillary work, but it was physically demanding given the long workdays prevalent in the workshop environment.

4

Manufactories

HE TERM *manufacture* can refer both to a phase of development in the handicraft workshop industry preceding that of modern machine production and to a model of production. Maxime Berg has highlighted the usefulness of the term and the dangers of over-applying the model: "the model of manufactures was useful in highlighting the features of some of eighteenth-century industry, but it was a model and as such excluded the complication and variety of production processes. It was also a linear model, looking forward and back and not to either side, thus failing to place this manufacture in its own wider historical context" (1994, 65). In the French context *manufacture* was sometimes used to refer to proto-industrial production (termed *manufacture dispersée* in the *Encylopédie's* anonymous article "Manufacture"), but it was most com-monly applied to the large enterprises often supported, and sometimes fully capitalized, by the royal administration. In part, the type of goods being manufactured dictated whether a *fabrique* fell under this heading, which was reserved in particular for textiles, carpets, glass, ceramics, beaver hats, wax, candles, tobacco, paper, and soap; but the classification was also related to the size of the enterprise, the level of investment associated with it, and the royal administration's perception of the importance of the enterprise in terms of national economic development (Savary des Bruslons 1762, 3: 1188). Louis XIV's minister Jean-Baptiste Colbert established the statutes for the creation of the most important manufacto-ries of France, to which, Savary des Bruslons asserted in 1762, the kingdom now owed its great prosperity (3: 1188). The advantages to the master "entrepreneur" of setting up such a manufactory were substantial: help with capital from the royal coffers in the form of interest-free loans; grants of lands; the right to brew beer for his workers; and sometimes exemption from visitation by officials of the guilds. His (male) workers were also granted royal privileges: exemption from the *taille* and other taxes; naturalization if they were foreigners; and even masterships in the guilds if they had worked for a specified period in a related manufactory (Savary des Bruslons 3: 1189). In addition, some enterprises were granted patents as Royal Manufactories; such was the case, for example, of the prestigious Gobelins factory, which wove tapestries (see plate 4.8), or La Savonnerie, where Turkish carpets were fabricated (plate 4.9). Such high-status concerns mainly employed men, while the manufactories producing cheaper goods *en masse* depended heavily on women as labor (plate 4.10). It is tempting to see some of the manufactories reflected in our plates as the direct predecessors of the factory as it developed in the nineteenth century, and certain aspects did closely correspond to the later model: the erosion of the distinctions crucial to the guild system in favor of a cheaper and less differ-

entiated workforce, for example, or the division of labor. But it must be remembered, as Jacques Proust has underlined, that the large manufactories of France were a minority phenomenon, artificially created by state support and investment, and that as such, they fall outside the modern model of the industrial factory (1962, 168–70).

Under this heading of *manufactories*, I have included images from a small number of enterprises that were both large in scale and reflected a kind of supervision and work regime different from the artisanal workshop; several of these required access to a centralized source of power, generally a waterway. In reality, as Berg's comment suggests, there was a continuum between "artisanal production" and "manufacture." Thus, hat- and candle making were carried out within a traditional artisanal structure, albeit with a larger than average number of workers. On that basis, I have included these trades in part 2, but there were also manufactories set up around France for these products. Likewise, textile fabrication took place at both ends of the scale, from proto-industrial workers in their own homes to large centralized units of production—often applying the same techniques; I grouped all these

processes together in part 3.

It is clear that for Diderot and his colleagues (as for Savary des Bruslons) these manufactories generally represented triumphant examples of change for the better: the author of the article on the most prestigious of these institutions, the Manufacture des Gobelins, asserted that "it is to this establishment that France owes the progress made by her crafts and manufacture" (*Ency.* "Tapisserie des Gobelins"). The *Encyclopédie* devoted many plates to the modern Langlée paper manufactory near Montargis (about sixty miles south of Paris), a classic case where labor was concentrated within one large institution in a rural location. The splendid premises built in 1738 with the support of the Duke of Orléans were illustrated in the first of the series of plates on papermaking, in their proportion and balance manifesting the high point of classical eighteenth-century architecture (*Ency. Planches*, vol. 5: "Papetterie, Pl. I"). Two great side wings provided housing for the workers and their children: this was a paternalistic establishment, with all aspects of the lives of the hundreds of workers contained within this ideal city.

There is, however, a stark contrast to be noted between the utopian presentation of the pristine factory in the outside view, and the working conditions inside reflected in both sets of plates. When the workers, who are hidden behind blank windows in the aforementioned image, later appear in the plates detailing the work carried on within the paper mill's walls, we see that, despite this factory's "modernity," the production techniques and working conditions varied little from those recorded in the earlier representations produced for the Académie. These were based on a study of an older establishment in the Auvergne and were drawn and engraved in the 1690s: since they are less well known, I have reproduced them here in preference to the *Encyclopédie* images with which they can be readily compared (plates 4.1 to 4.4). A number of studies have documented the prevailing working conditions in such institutions: for example, in the Montgolfier brothers' paper mill at Vidalon-le-Haut in the Rhone valley, the working day began at 4.00 A.M. and finished at 7.00 P.M., with thirteen actual work hours after breaks for meals were deducted. The women in this factory were also allowed a half hour to get their children up in the morning, and one hour in the day to feed them. At a very young age, the children were brought into the

factory to work alongside their mothers (Reynaud 1981, 144–47; Rosenband 2000, 93; see plate 4.2).

Guilbert draws attention to the large numbers of women and children in the manufactories of France in the latter part of the eighteenth century (1966, 35–43). In such establishments, employers were less restrained by trade guilds and their protectionist ethos. Both sets of images on papermaking show the clustering of women and children in many areas of the workshops (plates 4.1 to 4.4),[19] and Lalande confirms that they represented a significant proportion of the workforce in this industry (1762, 69), though the adult men (not featured here) retained the higher-status positions of making the molds and working at the vats (*Ency. Planches*, vol. 5: "Papetterie"). Likewise, in the manufactory where tin is made, we see significant numbers of women clustered as scourers (plate 4.15). In this operation, as in papermaking, tasks are broken down in a manner similar to the classic division of labor as described by Adam Smith, who probably used the *Encyclopédie* as the source for his famous description of pin making (1937: 5n6). In their study of the "small scale or unmechanized factory" in the American Northeast

from 1820 to 1850, Goldin and Sokoloff underlined how the use of simple tools, supervision, and a more disciplined work regime were reflected in the significantly higher proportion of female and child labor (1982). Our plates highlight, however, the extent to which many of the features Goldin and Sokoloff associate with the transitional period between artisanal production and fully fledged industrialization (with significant numbers of female and child workers) were already present in similar institutions at a much earlier period. For example, the text accompanying plate 4.4 points to the strict discipline imposed on the women workers.

In general, however, the texts that originally accompanied the images in this work showed little awareness of the social implications of these realities, highlighting gender difference only in terms of the labor costs—clearly identified as much less in the case of women, as well as children. The cheaper the labor and the more ready its supply, the better the economic outcome: in poor regions, women could be drafted to do skilled work for wages significantly below the rate afforded to men in more prestigious locations, where artisans' traditional rights could not be so easily bypassed. The text relating to the carpet makers of Aubusson (see plate 4.10) is an interesting case in point: it inadvertently confirms that in reality, many of the women carpet makers would have been the main breadwinners for their families (Duhamel Du Monceau 1766, 23), yet the low wages paid to such women reflected a general presumption that they were not autonomous individuals or heads of households (see Simonton 1998, 44–46). Likewise, in papermaking, as we shall see, women earned less than half the male wage and also got only half the food allowance.

The extent of child labor is one respect in which we can identify a difference in practice in the two different sets of images on papermaking from our collections: the *Encyclopédie* images (not reproduced here) show small boys, so young they must stand on wood blocks to reach the benches, cutting up the rags (*Ency. Planches*, vol. 5: "Papetterie, Pl. III"); this task is performed by adult women in the image from the earlier Académie collection. However, as the *Encyclopédie* images were probably based on practices in Montargis, and the earlier collection referred to an older manufactory in the Auvergne, it is impossible to be sure whether this reflects an evolution

in labor practices in the roughly sixty years intervening between the two "recordings" or simply a difference in local conditions relating, for example, to the age profile of the disposable labor.

Though the main thrust of the approach adopted by Diderot and his fellow *Encyclopédistes* was to denounce the guilds' ancient regulations and distinctions, which ensured a closed-shop ethos and protectionism, and to focus instead on the economic imperatives of a "free" market, the anonymous article "Manufacture" does admit that workers in the large manufactories suffered worse conditions than traditional guild workers. Whereas the journeyman in an artisan's workshop was treated as an equal by the master, asserts the writer (probably reflecting nostalgia for a golden age rather than contemporary reality: see Darnton 1985, 79–80), the worker in a centralized manufactory was treated "harshly and with contempt" by the foremen. How much more vulnerable were the women workers, who were located at the bottom of the scale in both of these contexts?

In the plates on paper- and soap making we see evidence of how women's role as load-bearers in the traditional economy carried over into these manufactories

(plates 4.4, 4.7). In glass manufacturing, likewise, women are shown undertaking heavy work, breaking up blocks of stone with a large mallet (plate 4.11) or pulverizing pieces of broken pottery for recycling (plate 4.12). Women's bodies were thus the site and source of energy production, as was also seen with regard to textiles in part 3 of this work. Vulnerable women, especially in poor regions where male employment was in short supply, had to accept dangerous working conditions that damaged their bodies and would inevitably result in their being unable to work at all: the revealing image of women in carpet making and its accompanying commentary allow us to see beyond the dominant optimistic rhetoric of our texts (plate 4.10). As Shahar has noted for an earlier period, it was occasionally argued that certain types of work were too dangerous for women, and for pregnant women in particular, but such arguments were made only in the context of attempts to exclude women from higher-status trades (1983, 199).

In this section, with a relatively small sample of images, there is less evidence of skilled work performed by women than in other sectors of the economy: this is undoubtedly related to the degree to which tasks in the larger establishments, whether paper-making or tinning, are broken down into discrete steps. These tasks demanded care and attention, but not the level of skill characteristic of the craft trades that dominated the French economy of this period. An exception is carpet-weaving, as is evident from the text that accompanied our plate 4.10.

Whether women benefited from the development of the factory system is a large and complex question. Berg has suggested that the highest-paid female workers of the eighteenth century in England were probably those girls and unmarried women who worked outside the home in early factories and large workshops (1994, 142–43), and the same may well have been true of women in some of the urban centers of France: this has already been shown in the present work with reference to hatmaking, where women could earn much more than the average female wage in other sectors. Such examples are counterbalanced, however, by examples of manufactories in rural areas, like Aubusson, where the wages were low. Pinchbeck's classic study, while showing the widespread exploitation of women and children in the early mills and factories in the period 1750–1850, also reveals the increased economic independence

"factory" wages afforded many young women (1969, 313–15). In the case of our collections, few conclusions can be drawn about the lives of the women reflected in the images; but there is little to suggest that they had much escape from sustained, exhausting, and low-paying labor, from tin making to paper and carpet manufacture. The sad condition of the silk workers, as has been described in part 3, was undoubtedly echoed in other trades, though our optimistic "technologists" chose not to foreground it in the images; the women who worked for fifteen or even eighteen hours a day, sleeping and eating within the confines of the great manufactories, led lives screened from the view of their contemporaries as well as from us and can have had few opportunities for distraction or relaxation. It is not surprising that the parents of young girls in rural environments regarded the possibility of their children going to work in these establishments as a last resort (Gullickson 1986, 137). When they worked at home, they had a domestic setting, however basic, and some social intercourse within and beyond their families.

Madeleine Guilbert has remarked that the early nineteenth-century moralists who catalogued conditions in contemporary factories rarely passed any judgment

concerning the effect of the "arduous, exhausting and dirty" tasks on the women involved, their attention being focused primarily on the problems of child labor. It was not until the second half of the nineteenth century that the working conditions of female factory workers in France began to attract serious attention (1966, 40).

::

The tasks assigned to women in papermaking are detailed in a series of images from the Académie's *Art de faire le papier*: they depict operations at an unidentified manufactory in the Auvergne first drawn in 1693 by the artist Pierre-Paul Sevin (Bibliothèque de l'Institut, ms. 2393; Pinault 2002, 156) and engraved by Simonneau in 1698. "The paper mills of the Auvergne are the most highly esteemed in the kingdom," wrote Savary des Bruslons (1742, 3: 26). The processes were essentially the same (with only minor technical variations) as those described in the *Encyclopédie*, which based its information on the Langlée manufactory, near Montargis, in the latter part of the following century. Most paper in this period was made from used textiles: the text recounts how women, called *pattières, chiffonnières,* or *drapelières* in different regions,

Pl. 4.1. Papermaking: rag shredding. Lalande, *Art de faire le papier*, Pl. I. [Des. Pierre-Paul Sevin, 1693], eng. Louis Simonneau, 1698.

traveled around the villages collecting rags for the local paper manufactories (Lalande 1762, 5–6). Plate 4.1 shows the *délisseuses*, or rag shredders, working in pairs. Each has a kind of apron, made of heavy cardboard and leather, on her knees, on which she works to open the seams and remove any dirt from the rags using a very sharp knife (illustrated at *C*). The rags are sorted according to quality and thrown into the containers with three sections positioned in front of each pair of women. The quality of the finished paper will reflect the texture of the rags. The rags are eventually dropped through the hole in the floor (center foreground) into the retting vats below, where the rotting process commences. The coarsest rags are thrown aside; they will be used for the roughest type of grey wrapping paper. The author comments that "as the job of the rag shredder demands concentration, judgment and precision, only persons of a mature age are given this position; it could not be entrusted to children" (Lalande, 8), the latter being the preferred cheap labor in this world of the early factories. The text gives very useful information on the women's pay: whereas the journeymen who worked dipping the molds at the vats were paid 120 *livres* per annum in wages, and 12 *sous* per day in food, the women rag shredders were paid 45 *livres* per annum in wages, and 6 *sous* per day in food (Lalande, 83). They were thus doubly disadvantaged: they had to sustain themselves by performing tiring tasks over the same lengthy day as the men, but

Fig. 1.

Partie des Etendoirs.

Pl. 4.2 and detail. Papermaking: drying room. Lalande. *Art de faire le papier*, Pl. XIII. [Des. Pierre-Paul Sevin, 1693], eng. Louis Simonneau, 1698.

with half the food value (and almost certainly less protein); and they were paid less than half the male wage. Many of them bore the additional burden of caring for children and performing basic household tasks; Lalande comments that in this type of manufactory, "the only days not worked are Sundays and the major Feast Days" (84). The corresponding *Encyclopédie* plate illustrates the same functions, with the women using a different type of hacking-blade (*Ency. Planches*, vol. 5: "Papetterie; Pl. I bis").

Plate 4.2 shows the drying room, where, after the paper has been sized, the woman on the right uses a peel to hang the sheet of wet paper on the drying cord. The text makes it clear, however, that the women would normally work in pairs, with one (*la jetteuse*) separating the wet sheet from the pile, sometimes by blowing on it, "with a skill that surprises those who witness it" (Lalande, 71). When the sheet has been half lifted from the pile, the second woman (*l'étendeuse*) slips the peel underneath and gently lifts the sheet up onto the drying

Pl. 4.3. Papermaking: drying room. *Ency. Planches*, vol. 5. "Papetterie; Pl. XII." S329.

cord: this action is more correctly illustrated in the *Encyclopédie* (plate 4.3). Great care must be taken to prevent the sheets from overlapping or sticking, which would destroy the quality of the paper. The woman on the left of plate 4.2 is removing the dry sheets, which are then stacked together (center). Since typically the whole family was housed within the factory complex itself, some of the women were allowed to bring their children into the workshops with them; very young children learned to help their mothers in their tasks until they were old enough to earn wages themselves, as we see in this instance (detail) where a little girl assists her mother in stacking paper (Reynaud 1981, 144–47; Rosenband 2000, 93). In the original drawing by the artist Sevin, this detail was not included: it was added by Simonneau, probably on the orders of the "technologists" with whom he was working, and presumably to reflect the practice in a factory known to them. The text mentions that work in the drying room is done as far as possible during the daylight hours, to avoid bringing in lights, which would create a fire hazard (Lalande, 72).

In another picture drawn in 1693 (plate 4.4), we see a woman in a paper factory transporting on her head a ream of newly dried sheets ready for separating and counting: in the original drawing (by Sevin, Bibliothèque de l'Institut, ms. 2393), two women are shown performing this function in different locations, and the burden is represented as considerably thicker and heavier than in the final plate. The engraver, on the other hand, has chosen to present the woman with the elegant deportment of a dancer, for aesthetic effect, and gives little indication of the physical effort such a heavy burden required. That women would continue to provide this load-bearing function—the energy of transport, which, as we saw, was also the work of women in the traditional economy—in

Pl. 4.4. Papermaking: glazing, sorting, counting sheets. Lalande. *Art de faire le papier*, Pl. XIV. [Des. Pierre-
Paul Sevin, 1693], eng. Louis Simonneau, 1698.

Pl. 4.5 and detail. Woman
porter in shipbuilder's
yard. *Ency. Planches*, vol.
7. "Marine: chantier de
construction." S134–35.

Pl. 4.6. Papermaking: little girl folding sheets. *Ency. Planches,* vol. 5. "Papetterie; Pl. XIII." S330.

the early manufactories and right across the economy, was so much taken for granted that we also find the designer casually adding just such a detail to a busy and highly impressive plate of a "modern" shipbuilder's yard (plate 4.5). In the image from the *Encyclopédie* we can just make out, in a shaded corner, the figure of a woman carrying a burden on her head. Appropriately, the woman is hidden in shadow, an apt metaphor for her place in the history of labor, where functions such as these went unrecorded in written texts.

The workers in the paper factory (plate 4.4) operate on both sides of long tables that are divided by a vertical plank down the middle, with the dual purpose, we are told, of avoiding confusion of the materials and "distraction of the female workers" (Lalande, 72). Some of the women are smoothing or glazing the paper on both sides using a specially shaped flint stone (illustrated separately as "1"): a woman could smooth six reams of paper a day in this way. The paper is next passed to the sorters, *les trieuses,* who must work close to the light to examine the paper for flaws, tufts, or dirt flecks, which they remove with a small sharp knife ("2"). They then grade the paper according to its degree of perfection or the flaws it contains; there were typically five grades. One worker could clear ten reams of paper in a day. Next in line are the counters (*compteuses*), who are always the most able workers and those with the best sight: they check the work of the sorters, then count the sheets into reams and assemble them in a particular order for pressing. "A good counter can furnish eighteen to twenty reams per day, if there is not too much to be redone after the sorters" (77). The corresponding *Encyclopédie* image additionally shows a "little girl" who folds the sheets (see *c* in plate 4.6). The candleholder attached to each partition (plate 4.4, mentioned in the text, 79) serves to remind us that the women typically worked late into the evening, winter and summer.

In one fascinating image from a large soap-making enterprise (plate 4.7a), three women carry the huge slabs of soap from the

Pl. 4.7a (and detail) and b. Soap
factory. MS Typ 432.1 (54).
Department of Printing and Graphic
Arts, Houghton Library, Harvard
College Library.

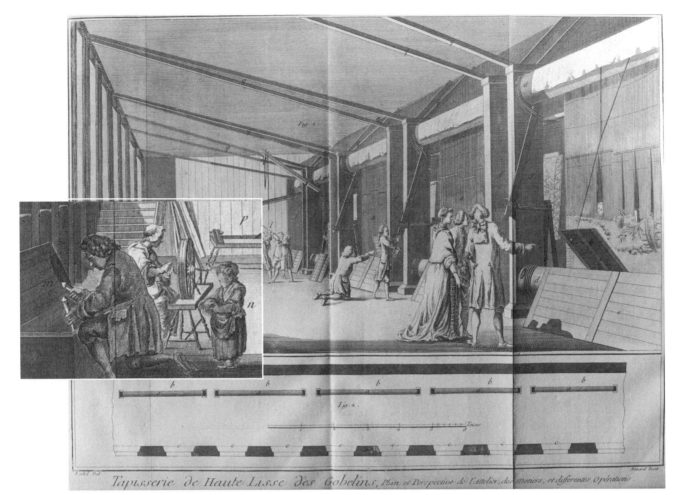

4.8 and detail. Les Gobelins: unwinding skeins of yarn. *Ency. Planches*, vol. 9.
"Tapisserie de haute lisse des Gobelins; Pl. I." S264-65.

workshop to the storehouse on their heads. The *Encyclopédie* article "Savon, Tables de" tells us that a typical slab weighed between 20 and 25 *livres*: the woman to the front of the image carries three slabs, unsurprising if we recall the kind of weight we have seen women porters carry in coalmining or fishing, or the women carrying reams of paper in plate 4.4. In this task, they are competing with men carrying ma-

terials, such as the pair with a bar across their shoulders, and with the packhorse. This is a complex and interesting engraving that both gives a sense of the movement, the hustle and bustle of a large workshop, and includes indicators of social stratification: in the middle of the picture, a group of elaborately dressed, affluent onlookers, presumably invited guests interested in seeing how the product is made, survey the

scene. The figure entering and gesturing to his companion (on the left) is probably the owner or director of the enterprise; he is well dressed and successful enough not to have to do any manual work himself. Above the heads of this microcosm of contemporary society is a quiet space where the jars of oil are stored and some weary workers lay out blankets to get a little rest, adding aesthetic balance to the picture.

Pl. 4.9. *La Savonnerie:* unwinding skein of wool. Duhamel, *Art de faire les tapis, façon de Turquie*, Pl. IV.

The very richness of this image must raise suspicions: it is clear that the aesthetic and ideological concerns of the creator(s) have had a strong impact on it. And in fact, we know a good deal about the evolution of this picture, because the original drawing of the workshop (designer unknown; plate 4.7b) is conserved in the papers that came from the estate of the author, Duhamel du Monceau (Houghton MS Typ 432.1[54]): it shows only the basic functional details of the manufacturing process. The resting workers, the visitors, and the porters, human and animal, are not present in the sketch. These were added later by the designer and engraver, Ransonette. Some additions were for aesthetic effect, like the draped blanket of the resting worker; the affluent visitors—who feature in a number of representations (see plate 4.8)—perhaps represent an attempt to valorize the world of production by reference to the consumer, or to proffer a paradigm of social cohesion. But what of the women carrying the slabs of soap? Is their value as social documentary evidence null and void? No, because these same archives show how the plates were developed through several iterations by consultation between expert and designer. Duhamel himself, the cautious academic scientist, oversaw the production of each plate, organizing and articulating the message, and it is very likely that either he himself, or his designer, had evidence of women performing this role. The Academician had acquired detailed descriptions of factories throughout France, from his home base in Denainvilliers to Marseille, and the women are, moreover, mentioned specifically in the plate legend (64). The plate I have reproduced here is an intermediate proof of the plate finally published as plate IV of *L'Art du savonnier*: the reference numbers and letters have been written in by hand, and shading has been added in grey wash. All the plates would have passed through such a proofing at least once before final approval.

The male workers in the prestigious royal manufactory of tapestries at Les Gobelins in Paris enjoyed the protection of special status, granted by royal decree. In plate 4.8 (from the *Encyclopédie*) the high status of the master craftsmen or journeymen is evoked by their bourgeois dress, with frock coats and wigs. As in plate 4.7, we see the affluent consumers, including a nobleman carrying his sword, and his sumptuously dressed female companion, inspecting work in progress. All are in sharp contrast to the

woman who is unwinding the skeins of yarn onto spindles, aided by her small child who is holding the next skein, and who probably spent the day by her side. She is tucked in the corner of the image, half hidden by the kneeling male worker, and her child's face is barely sketched in outline by the designer, Radel. In this model workshop the woman's work is still the least valued and can be easily occluded by the foregrounded male. In a very similar image from the Académie collection (plate 4.9), a woman in the royal manufactory where Turkish carpets were made, known as La Savonnerie, is likewise shown performing ancillary work, this time unwinding a skein of wool: these tasks were typical of the work women undertook throughout the world of textiles. A detail of a woman doing identical work is reproduced in the *Encyclopédie* ("Tapis de Turquie; Pl. V").

A small, modest detail in the *Encyclopédie* ("Tapis de Turquie; Pl. V"), also relating to the manufacture of Turkish carpets, is intriguing, but little information is offered to help decode it. It was, in fact, directly copied from an almost identical image in Duhamel's treatise for the Académie published some five years earlier (plate 4.10): no one on the *Encyclopédie* team sought

to elucidate the situation of the woman with the lamp. We learn from Duhamel that it depicts women workers at a Turkish carpet manufactory in Aubusson, which employed 250 women and girls: he had acquired his information directly from the royal inspector for Aubusson, M. Châteaufavier (1766, 1, 2, 20, 23). This factory had been set up in 1740 and sold carpets for very modest prices. We are assured that the women, who relied on this employment for their only income, had an "innate" aptitude for the work, showing an amazing dexterity and ease in performing their tasks from the age of nine; but such ability was not equivalent to "skill" and did not attract the benefits, in terms of money or status, associated with that elusive quality in the contemporary trade culture. The Aubusson women, Duhamel declares, "are willing to accept very modest wages [. . .] it would require triple the amount to employ men, and that would make these carpets too expensive." Many of these women may have been the main breadwinners for their families, but whatever the reality of their family circumstances, they were automatically classed by gender as cheap labor; it is clear from the text that their lower pay was also partly related to the poverty of the region.

Pl. 4.10. Making Turkish carpets. Duhamel, *Art de faire les tapis, façon de Turquie*, Pl. II.

With inferior pay came lesser status: when the factory was set up, the women in Aubusson used candles to light their work in winter, but "it was found to be more economical and more convenient to work with lamps." They subsequently wore metal plates tied to their chests holding a little lamp to light their work, which involved weaving the design onto the carpet, objectively the same task as that being carried out by the male weavers at the Savonnerie in plate 4.9. We can be sure that it was not the workers who found this arrangement "more convenient": the women would not have been able to direct the light, as the men at the royal manufactories did (using large candleholders with a movable arm: Duhamel 1766, 19). With such poor lighting, their eyesight must have been damaged by doing this work from a very young age; in addition, they clearly suffered from the fumes—from lamps burning some type of oil—going directly to their lungs, not to mention the risks of their clothes catching fire and serious burns resulting.

Several images recall the work of women in the great glass manufactories of France, the largest of which were located in the northwest (Normandy, Picardy), and in Lorraine in the northeast. Plate 4.11, never published, is an image prepared for the Académie series on the making of mirrors; overseen by Réaumur, the drawing was approved in 1712 and engraved in 1714 by Simonneau. A manuscript note indicates that this is the workshop where sandstone is prepared: the women use large mallets to gradually reduce the blocks of stone to sand. Other women use riddles to sift the sand, presumably into different degrees of fineness. This is an impressive example of the type of heavy physical work, like mining work, that became exclusively male gendered in the postrevolutionary period but, as this image shows, was once associated with women. Based on the mining reports of 1842, Pinchbeck de-

Pl. 4.11. Sandstone preparation. Institut ms. 1065bis, f. 158 ["Manufacture des glaces 3ᵉ"].
Art and eng. L. Simonneau, 1714.

Pl. 4.12. Breaking crucibles. *Ency. Planches*, vol. 10. "Verrerie en bois, petite verrerie à pivette; Pl. VII." S331.

scribed similar heavy work done by female limestone breakers in Britain, who broke from ten to fourteen tons of limestone per day (1966, 271). As in the case of the Aubusson carpets, it is likely that in the poorer regions, where these manufactories were located, female labor was relatively cheap and plentiful; two of the women in this image are barefoot, an indicator perhaps of their economic inability to acquire even a pair of wooden clogs to protect their feet, or alternatively, of their need for

Pl. XVI.

Fig. 1.

Fig. 2.

Fig. 3.

Radel Del.

Benard Fecit.

Pl. 4.13. Sorting broken glass. *Ency. Planches,* vol. 10. "Verrerie en bois, petite verrerie à pivette; Pl. XVI." S340.

stability to counterbalance themselves against the physical effort their task involved. The extent of this effort is further signalled by their clothing: the woman with

the raised mallet in particular seems to be wearing just a loose shift (with no corset or bodice) and a petticoat and apron. Images portraying women in such rela-

tive undress are rare (see Marly, 1990, 53).

Plate 4.12 from the *Ency-clopédie* shows how old crucibles for the melting of glass (*a*),

Pl. 4.14. Glass collector. *Ency. Planches*, vol. 10. "Verrerie en bois, grande verrerie à vitres, ou en plats; Pl. XVIII." S.371–72.

which burnt out in a short period of time, are broken up so that the pieces can then be recycled for the making of new furnaces and crucibles. The women sift the pieces, separating the pottery pieces—which will be added to a new mix of clay—from the bits of molten glass attaching to them, which will also be recycled (far right). They use hatchetlike tools to hammer and break down the pieces. There is no context provided for this beautifully drawn image, but it is clear from the women's postures, sitting or crouching on the floor, that this was physically demanding work.

In the center figure of plate 4.13, from the same series, we see a man and woman working together to pick over and sort scrap glass, or cullet, which will be mixed with frit to make new glass. They then carry the loaded basket to the washing area (top figure), where they shake the basket in a large barrel of water to wash it. The drum of water had to be brought from the well,

no doubt by the same workers. The images suggest this work is done outdoors; the woman's wooden clogs provide realistic detail, though the dress of her male companion appears far too elaborate for a worker involved in this type of menial and physically demanding work. This type of labor appears to be gender neutral and was probably given to the casual workers available (at low wages) at any given time.

In the magnificent engraving of a crown glass furnace room

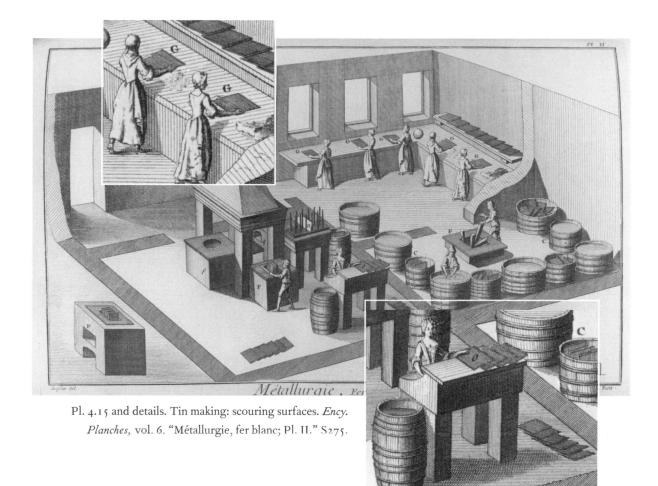

Pl. 4.15 and details. Tin making: scouring surfaces. *Ency.*
Planches, vol. 6. "Métallurgie, fer blanc; Pl. II." S275.

(plate 4.14), from a series of images justly regarded as among the
finest in the *Encyclopédie,* we
again see a woman (labeled "fig.
2") in the corner of the image,
separate from the high-status and
relatively well-paid glass workers.
Described as a glass collector (*ra-
masseuse de verre*), her job is to
clear the floor: she is dragging a
large piece of heavy glass, which
was poured as a test by the furnace master, to an area where it
would presumably be broken up
for recycling. The incline of her
body indicates the physical effort

involved in pulling the glass.

The making of tin took place
in relatively large establishments;
one crucible, we are told in the
text accompanying the *Encyclopédie* plates, would typically require one master, five journeymen, two *goujards* (a term
uniquely applied to general workers in this trade), and six
récureuses, women scourers or
polishers. Plate 4.15 shows us five
such women; they were employed
at various stages of the process,
before and after the sheets were
tinned, to clean and polish the

surfaces with bran (see detail).
One woman is illustrated placing
the metal sheets to drain (detail)
as they are removed from the crucible. The temperature in the
workrooms was maintained by
the furnaces (*F*), and they were
kept as airtight as possible—"bien
fermées"—to avoid the rusting of
the tin. The text makes it clear
that these were typically basement
chambers, probably little resem-
bling the well-lit, geometrically
proportioned workshops in this
interpretation by Diderot's designer. The conditions must have

been extremely difficult and unhealthy for the workers, especially during the warmer months. Pinchbeck has reported the high level of employment of women and girls in this manufacture in Britain, "both as assistants to different classes of workmen, and as rubbers, scourers and pickers in the finishing processes, some of which required a considerable amount of skill" (1969, 271).

5

Commercial Activity

HEREVER GOODS were sold to the public, women were to be found; this is one of the aspects of the economy where their work was most visible. We know that, among the poorer levels of society, women sold all types of goods in the streets of the towns and cities, from food to matchsticks. Hufton has remarked that on the lower end of the social scale, "women appear to have virtually monopolized the actual sale of objects made by their husbands" (1993, 32). Women also sold old clothes: in the 1760s Paris had 268 registered secondhand dealers, all of whom were married women or widows (Hufton, 33), although the *fripier*'s was in theory a male trade. In city and country markets, women sold all kinds of food. The fishwife or oyster seller was a common sight in city streets, and I have already mentioned how some of these women

can be seen in the popular *Cris de Paris* (Milliot 1995). They do not feature in our two collections, which focused on selling only as it related to the urban trades.

The world of industry and manufacture was not distinct from that of commerce in this period: the production of goods and their sale were frequently conducted by the same artisanal unit throughout the French corporate sector (Sewell 1980, 19–21). The function of women as traders and bookkeepers in their family businesses was a common phenomenon across all areas, to the extent that, taken for granted, it often remained unsung. In his groundbreaking study of the middle and lower bourgeoisie in France, Abensour indeed constantly underlined how husband and wife worked side by side as a unit; almost all the legal documents signed by merchants in the archives he consulted for Paris and the Ile de France, be they leases, contracts or receipts, were countersigned by wives (1923, 168). Absensour quotes Babeau's assertion in his *Bourgeois d'autre-fois* (1886) that in Orléans, the daughters and wives of merchants were everywhere to be found behind the counter, trading, doing accounts, writing; that in Rouen, the mothers and daughters looked after all the correspondence; and that in Bordeaux, mistresses in bookkeeping instructed the daughters of merchants (175). Women were thus frequently managers of many aspects of a production unit, at the interface between the workshop and the public. It is only in "alternative" sources, however, that we find details of their activities: police reports, where a dispute or brawl has occurred (Sargentson 1996, 136), or where a husband has been arrested and the wife takes over the running of the entire business (Sheridan 1992, 54–56); in rare diaries or journals; and in images. From the autobiography of a Parisian glazier, Jacques-Louis Ménétra, Daniel Roche concludes that "his wife, who throws her whole life and small capital into the future of her glazier, is a good manager essential to the success of the shop, for it is she who runs it" (1986, 73).

In his study of the luxury trades in Paris, Roche also notes the very high levels of literacy among the women active in artisanal commerce: 90–100 percent of the mistresses could sign their names, as could 75 percent of the humbler seamstresses and linen drapers (1989, 307). Maurice Garden has likewise demonstrated that girls raised in the city (in this case Lyon), and particularly those of the merchant class, had a much higher standard of literacy than was average for France, and this increased over the course of the century (1970, 352–53). Attendance at elementary school had been rising since the seventeenth century, but it was above all in the shop that young girls learned the basic skills of accounting, bookkeeping, and letter writing.

Wives and daughters thus made a major contribution to the family economy through their role in running shops; while typically not paid any wages, the capital their labor saved for the business was appreciable and would have kept a small firm afloat in times of recession, when paid workers or *servantes* might have to be let go. Hufton points out that, unlike girls from rural backgrounds, the daughters of small artisans and shop owners in the cities would not have amassed a dowry; but they had the huge

benefit of being fed and found in their own home, and they acquired a skill they could bring to a prospective marriage in lieu of a dowry (1975, 10). Widows had the right to continue their husband's trade within the guild system, and many would have tried to continue with the retail end of a business even if they had difficulty on the production side: maintaining the business represented their main hope of providing for their family and the crucial possibility of a son taking over the family business when he came of age. Many women succeeded in heading up large-scale enterprises, even in the male-dominated publishing trade (Sheridan 1992, 57–62). Some remarried, typically a man qualified in the relevant trade, though this was by no means as common as the myth of the "remarrying widow" once held it to be (Hufton 1984; Sheridan 2001, 202–4).

The small sample of images reproduced here of women working at the counter in a variety of trades points to a number of aspects of their role. While the interaction with the public was no doubt the most important, the plates also show the extent to which the mistress and her assistants performed a variety of other tasks while not so engaged. Many of these were finishing tasks and frequently involved needlework: in the hatter's shop the woman at the counter sews the lining, band, and brim (plate 5.3); the woman in the belt maker's *boutique* likewise has needle in hand (plate 5.4). And, not surprisingly, in the plates on the linen and fashion shops, we also see young women sewing, even though the trend was increasingly to relegate the actual production work away from the fashion counter. In the humble cork maker's establishment (plate 5.10), the wife sorts the corks while she waits for passing trade, while in the bakery, the assistant—possibly a daughter—makes breadcrumbs with stale bread (plate 5.8). The importance of keeping the books and records straight is highlighted in the same plate where the *boulangère* writes in her ledger, while the mistress of the cutlery shop must keep track of the pieces brought by clients for sharpening, as well as the items she sells (plate 5.7).

Nevertheless, the element of sociability at the interface between production and sales was of crucial importance, and it was here that the mistress's skills were most valuable; as Louis Sebastien Mercier has remarked, the wives of artisans were "the soul of a shop" (Amsterdam 1788, 9: 173, qtd. Sargentson 1996, 135). Prices were not fixed or marked on the goods in eighteenth-century retail outlets, other than for the most basic commodities such as bread; the mistress would haggle over the price with the client, this exchange being, no doubt, a valued part of the social experience. William Cole and Horace Walpole, on a visit to Paris in 1765, experienced the seduction of the mercer Mme Dulac: "the Mistress was as tempting as the Things she sold [. . .] so that it was no wonder that such a shop was thronged with customers, or that the Mistress of it might boldly set what price she thought proper upon her commodities [. . .] it was next to impossible to refuse her what she asked for them" (Cole 1931, 233–34, qtd. Sargentson 1996, 135). Everywhere in our images we see stools provided for the clients to sit at their ease, even in the humble tinsmith's shop, where mistress and client are, no doubt, discussing the quality and value of the piece.

It is in the fashion trades, however, that we see the most revealing details of the increasing emphasis on a consumer culture. By the second half of the eighteenth century, female businesswomen had become the dominant retail merchants for clothing, rising up "from within the cracks in the corporate system" (Jones 2004, 95). This promotion of women in the fashion trades of Paris, followed in other major cities, has been described by Daniel Roche; it was reflected, he suggests, in the way the workers began to imitate the style of their clients. They were led in this by the mistress linen drapers and seamstresses: one of the latter, Quentine Souply, on her marriage in 1749, had a wardrobe valued at 1,400 *livres,* including seven dresses, as many as an aristocratic woman in this period (Roche 1989, 306). Our images show the mistresses sumptuously dressed, as in the earlier image of the feather dresser, but also the young women—modestly paid seamstresses and shopgirls—fashionably attired with lace trims on their dresses and elaborate head coverings. It is clear that they too set great store on the acquisition of fine clothes. The girls working in linen-drapers' shops in the Palais Royal were known as *noguettes* and were celebrated in literary works from Rabelais to the Italian theater of Gherardi.[60] In the plate on the *marchande de mode* there is little to distinguish the social ranks, the workers from the clients, in a world transformed by commerce (plate 5.5).

This world of the fashion workers often gave rise to picturesque or sexualized representations of seductive young fashion workers sold by popular print shops, which are no doubt rather far removed from the daily reality. Nonetheless, Roche has underlined the degree to which these feminine spaces were increasingly marked by "the sociability of commerce" and did facilitate encounters between the sexes (1989, 305). That keen observer of urban life, Louis Sebastien Mercier, frequently evoked this aspect of Parisian life in his *Tableau de Paris*:

> Any stranger seeing a *Marchande de mode*'s shop for the first time will be struck by the thought of a *seraglio*. There are charming little countenances ranged side by side with ugly faces along the length of the counter; they are decorating those pompoms and gew-gaws which constantly change with fashion; we can ogle them in passing. These girls, needle in hand, are constantly glancing towards the street [. . .] As they pass in front of the shops, an *abbé*, a military man, a young senator will step inside to take a look at the *belles*. Their purchases are only a pretext. (Mercier 1788, 11: 110; Mercier 1783, 6: 311; qtd. Roche 1989, 304)

Jones has highlighted how moralistic observers and libertine writers alike perceived Paris to be awash with such *boutiques* (2004, 156) and equated them with harems and brothels. There was, indeed, a darker side to this story; the young, "seductive" women in the sewing and fashion trades were often easy prey for unscrupulous clients. Such was the case of a young lace mender who complained to the police that when she called at the home of the marquis de Pertuis, simply to collect some lacework, he tried to seduce and bully her; it was clear from her evidence that he had not expected resistance (Bibliothèque Nationale ms. fr. 11358, f. 482, qtd. Benabou 1987, 282). In reality, the precariousness of their employment, particularly when times were slow, very easily tipped the balance against the young women: many were forced to fall back on prostitution to survive (Roche 1989, 299). Benabou, in her study of young women arrested for prostitution in the 1760s, found that they came in large numbers from the *boutiques* of the linen drapers and the fashion merchants; many had started prostitution while still employed in their trade to top up their meager earnings (1987, 283).

Mercier, who commented so frequently on women in urban life, put his finger on one of the most significant aspects of their role in commerce: access to, and control of, money. Whether they are selling a sword, a rifle, a breastplate, or a clock, he remarks, weighing out a pound of macaroons or a pound of canon powder, "they work in conjunction with men, and are happy doing so, because they always handle a little money. This creates a perfect equality of roles, and the couple works all the better for it" (1788, 9: 173). These women, he suggests, were able to set aside a little money for their own purposes (176). On a grander scale, trade was one of the few ways in which a woman could acquire her own capital to establish a business. However, Jones suggests that the female commercial dominance of the fashion sector on the eve of the Revolution was to see a slow decline in the early years of the next century, when "new conceptions of proper womanhood slowly begin to relegate prominent female merchants to the back room, where they could stitch and sew but never command and control" (1996, 52–53).

Some of the plates featured here are among the finest and most detailed engravings in our collections, like the sumptuous images of the furrier's or *marchande de mode*'s establishments, or the double-sized image of the cutler's shop. Barthes has highlighted the significance of this rich imagery in his study of the plates of the *Encyclopédie*: "Aus-

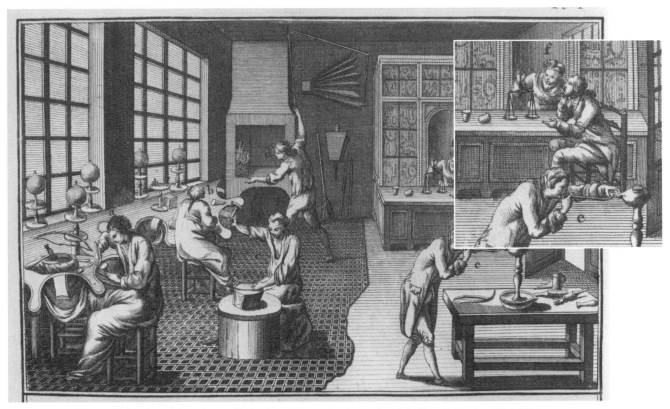

Pl. 5.1 and detail. Goldsmith-jeweller's shop. *Ency. Planches,* vol. 8. "Orfèvre bijoutier; Pl. I." S69.

terity in the act of creation, luxury in commerce, these are the twin orders of the encyclopædic object: the density of the image, its ornamental load always signifies that we are moving from production to consumption" (1964, 12). In this group of images we see women as the key economic agents offering fine lace goods, fur-lined pelisses, or game pies to catch the eye of the consumer.

::

Owing to the nature of the collections that are the subject of this study, the majority of the plates relating to buying and selling reflect the high-end craft trades. Generally, an artisan's workshop

and sales outlet occupied the same space, adjacent to the family residence, which facilitated the participation of the wife, daughters, or domestic servants. Plate 5.1 shows a goldsmith-jeweller's shop occupying an area opening directly onto the street. One worker, dressed in a frock coat (and so probably the master) is soldering a piece within this space, while at the back (in a space whose separation is signified by a different floor-covering) the workers in overalls create the gold and silver pieces (decorative boxes, cane handles, watchcases, and so on). "The Mistress" reigns at the counter, where she takes her

scales to weigh a piece in precious metal for a prospective client. This was one of the great luxury trades of Paris, and the wares are fittingly displayed in the large cabinet behind her.

The furrier's establishment (plate 5.2) is a splendid shop, separate, for obvious reasons, from the area where the skins are tanned and prepared, with the exception of one worker who is beating the skins, perhaps to show the quality of the goods to the aristocratic patrons. The sales are conducted by two women, who are showing muffs to the client: the huge selection on offer is obvious from the muff-boxes hang-

Pl. 5.2. Furrier's shop. *Ency. Planches,* vol. 4. "Fourreur, outils; Pl. V." S267.

ing from the ceiling and stored on the shelves. A fur-lined mantle or pelisse (*f*) has been hung at the side: perhaps the stylish lady, who is wearing just such a garment, had been interested in it, or the couple may have purchased some of the fur pieces in the box on the floor (*g*), which could be used to trim male as well as female garments. The level of attention and exchange between client and saleswoman is underlined by the furnishings, all designed to make the client more comfortable: a decorative stove, for heat (*h*), and nicely upholstered stools (*i*). The

skills of the retailer would have been of crucial importance to a business such as this. Like the preceding plate, this one is designed by Lucotte and is rich in ornamentation.

We have already seen some of the activities in a hatter's workshop (plate 2.34); in plate 5.3, we see the retail area. This is a simple establishment compared with the luxury shops just mentioned; hats were sold to a broad clientele across the social spectrum. On the left a worker paints a glue-based glazing finish onto the hats. The woman on the right, who tends

the sales counter, also does the important finishing work of sewing in the lining and band, attaching the brim where it is to be turned up, and adding braid or a plume where required, possibly in response to the individual client's wishes. Some details of this work are shown in the bottom section of the plate. A *cavalier,* carrying his sword, is trying on a hat in front of the mirror.

As in the hatter's establishment, the picture of a belt-maker's shop (plate 5.4) shows the woman who tends the counter while also employed in

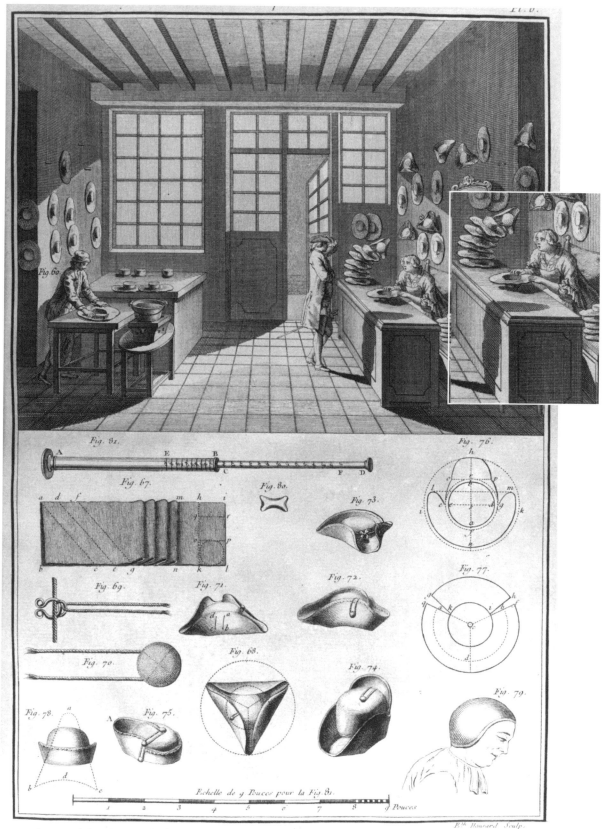

Pl. 5.3 and detail. Hatter's shop. Nollet, *L'Art de faire des chapeaux*, Pl. VI. Eng. Elisabeth Haussard.

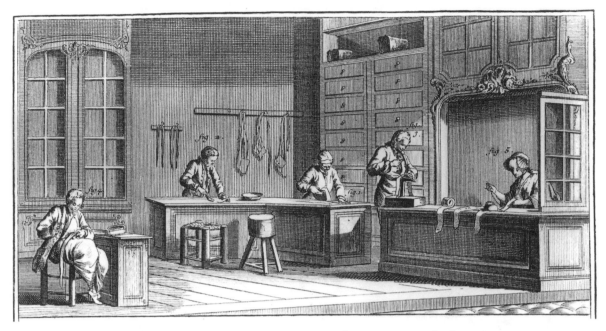

Pl. 5.4. Belt-maker's shop. *Ency. Planches*, vol. 2. "Ceinturier; Pl. I." S254.

sewing some of the products, which included sword belts and cross belts in a variety of materials, from velvet to leather. As belts were much less in vogue in the eighteenth than in the preceding centuries, this is a small *boutique* where all the work is undertaken in the same space. In the medieval period daughters of belt makers had access to apprenticeship (see Dixon 1895, 224), and the statutes for the Belt-makers' Guild issued in 1551 still gave the master the right to teach his trade to "*ses enfants,*" in addition to any apprentices (Savary 1762, 1: 718); it is likely that the practice of teaching daughters this trade continued into the eighteenth century, but without allowing them access to inde-

pendent rights as craftswomen in the later period, as has been discussed earlier.

The splendid vignette featuring the shop of a *marchande de mode* (plate 5.5), published in the *Suite du recueil de planches* in 1777, is a much revised version of its counterpart in the Académie collection (plate 2.27). The relationship between the two images is clearly established because the bottom section of this plate (not reproduced here) was directly copied from its predecessor: just one detail, of a "*coiffure*" or bonnet, was omitted, but this was transferred to the *Encyclopédie* plate "Lingere, Pl. I," also published in the *Suite* (but with no vignette). This alteration possibly reflected the opposition of the

Linen-drapers' Guild to incursions on their trade by these fashion shops of ambiguous status (see Coffin 1996, 27).

The changes reflected in the later *vignette* are also of significance: the shop featured here is much more elaborate and fashionable than the workspace portrayed in the earlier version. All the shopgirls, as well as the numerous clients, are decked out stylishly in the products of the trade, and the premises are richly furnished and decorated. This image reflects (and subsequently influenced) the efforts made by retailers to embellish their shops as part of a "marketing strategy," particularly in the period 1760–80: a document issued on behalf of the *Marchands Merciers* in 1761 highlighted the

Pl. 5.5 and detail. *Marchande de mode. Ency. Planches Suite.* "Marchande de modes." S188.

necessity to *"séduire par les apparences"* (Sargentson 1996, 113). The emphasis has shifted here to the commercial exchange, with five consumers at the very center of activity; just two young seamstresses are occupied with sewing in the background, and even one of these is engaging in conversation with a client (detail). The level of style reminds us that Paris was, already in this period, the international capital of fashion, and these *boutiques* were its most public face. A small number of *modistes* won international notoriety and were major creditors to the aristocracy: in 1785 the Queen, Marie-Antoinette, spent

250,000 *livres* (equivalent to as many days of labor) on her wardrobe, owing 90,000 and 25,000 *livres*, respectively, to two of the leading *marchandes*, Mlle Bertin and Mme Pompey (Roche 1989, 310).

Conspicuous consumption of fashion goods was reflected, on a different scale, down through the social levels, as is witnessed here by the workers. Daniel Roche has pointed out, with regard to this image, how such confusion between the social ranks challenged "physiocratic discourse" and "anti-egalitarian argument" (1989, 304). Denounced by moralists as dangerous to both

consumers and workers—Rose Bertin was the object of innumerable *libelles* in the Revolutionary period—these female-led establishments were gradually replaced in the following century by male-managed retail outlets, with women relegated to tailoring and sewing in the back rooms (Jones 1996, 25–48).

The plate from the Académie featuring a linen-draper's shop (plate 5.6) is rather similar to the previous plate in the modishness of both staff and clients, though there is a clear difference between mistress and shopgirls. The mistress *lingère* would undoubtedly have been a member of the Linen-

Pl. 5.6. Linen-draper's shop. Garsault. *L'Art de la lingère*, Pl. I. Des. Garsault, eng. Berthault.

drapers' Guild, one of the very few all-female guilds in France in this period (Coffin 1994); their sphere of activity is defined thus by Garsault, the author of the Académie's treatise: "The Linen drapers [. . .] not only have the right to sell all types of linen—whether cloth made of flax, hemp or cotton—and lace, but also to cut out, sew and finish all the linen garments which are made as basic necessities, to ensure cleanliness, or even as items of luxury. It is the Linen draper who covers man from the moment of his birth, throughout his life and even afterwards; it is she who embellishes tables, beds, altars etc." (Garsault 1771, 1). The author was closely advised in his descriptions of the trade by a Mlle Merlu, former head shop-assistant to Mme du Liège, one of the biggest linen drapers in Paris, with a shop in the rue Taranne. The mistress is richly dressed with a watch hanging at her waist; she carries a bolt of fabric to show to one of several clients. She is aided by three shop-girls: two of these are measuring the material, already chosen by the seated client, from which the garments will be made, while another cuts a piece of fabric to size. Along with the seamstresses, the linen drapers had to vigilantly protect the power and prerogatives conferred on them by guild status, which allowed them to train apprentices and thus pass on a skill with real market value to other women (Truant 1988). As Garsault points out, the number of accredited mistresses, together with the women they could house to work directly from their premises, would never have sufficed to supply the amount of fine linen required by the market; the mistresses could, therefore, authorize other women to sew linens. These "*ouvrières en linge*" were effectively outworkers, who had no right to trade in the goods themselves, on pain of having their wares seized by the guild. The mistresses jealously guarded their prerogatives by policing the cloth hall (*halle aux toiles*), where they alone had the right to trade in fabrics.

Diderot's own father was a cutler; the *Encyclopédie* published an image of a typical *boutique*, open to the street, with the mis-

Pl. XI.

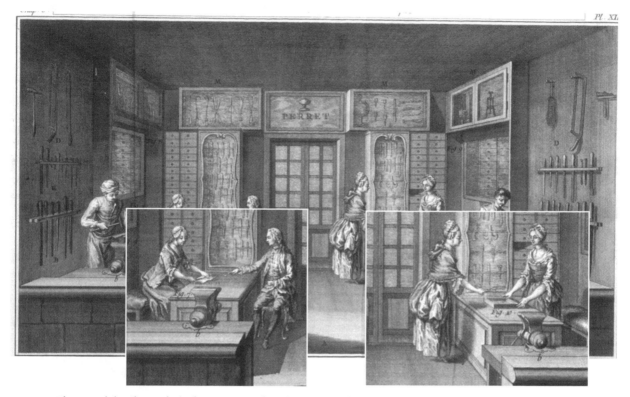

Pl. 5.7 and details. Cutler's shop. Perret, *L'Art du coutelier*, Pl. XII. A 10.10.15F (v. 12), Houghton Library, Harvard College Library. Des. Goussier, eng. Bénard.

tress behind the counter. The image reproduced here is the less well-known plate of a top-end shop—that of the cutler Perret, who wrote the description of the *Art du coutelier* for the Académie—with a magnificent display of the range of tools and utensils made by a master-merchant (plate 5.7). The text draws particular attention to the work of the mistress: "The Mistress must make sure that everything is in proper order, with fitting decorum; to that effect there must be glass-fronted cupboards around the shop, where dust and dampness cannot penetrate, so that the steel implements which

are exposed there do not rust [. . .]. The Mistress, who is at the counter, must be careful to wipe the instruments, with a fine, well-worn cloth, especially those which have been handled, so that rust does not attack them" (72). The strictures addressed to the mistress highlight the need for care in labeling the pieces that clients bring in for sharpening— scissors, razors, knives—to avoid confusion. The details show one saleswoman wrapping an object, perhaps a paper knife, for the male client who proffers a coin, while the female client looks at a pair of scissors from a collection in a box.

In contrast, the more humble premises of a baker are shown in the Académie treatise on that trade (plate 5.8). His product is a necessity of life, sold to rich and poor alike: both the client and the women serving are plainly dressed. The mistress is writing in a ledger, reminding us of one of the most important roles of women in such family businesses: managing and keeping the accounts. A local business such as this, like the high-end trades selling to the aristocracy, had to function on a credit basis; it was up to the mistress to judge when to send reminders for unpaid bills, or when to give a little leeway to a

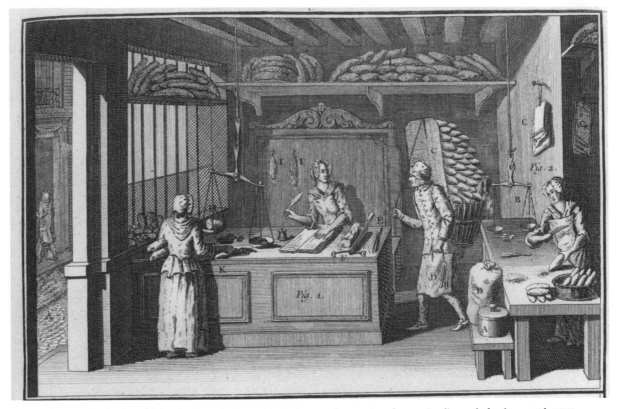

Pl. 5.8. Baker's shop. Malouin, *Description et détails des arts du meunier, du vermi-celier et du boulenger,* Pl. VIII.

neighbor in difficulties (Roche 1989, 307–8). To her right on the counter is the scales, all bread being sold by weight. The girl on the far right is making breadcrumbs, probably with bread that remained unsold from the previous bake. The assistant with the great *hotte* on his back is leaving to deliver bread in the town. Collins, in his study of tax records, noted that there were many female bakers and grain brokers, married women whose husbands carried on different trades (1989, 456).

The *pâtisserie* offered a variety of pastry goods, many only available to the higher social classes: in our image (plate 5.9) a well-dressed couple are buying a game pie—or perhaps arguing a point with the mistress, as the client appears to be pointing at the pie with her fan (detail). The rabbit, the hams, and game birds hanging from the ceiling indicate that, unlike in a modern *pâtisserie,* meat pies accounted for a considerable portion of the trade. In this case, the mistress's counter occupies a small area near the street entrance, with the oven and working spaces on view to the public.

The cork-maker's shop (plate 5.10) is a good example of a small family business, of which there were thousands in any large city. The man seated on the left side of the table is probably the master, with one worker assisting in cutting out the corks and rounding the tops. The mistress sorts the corks by size as she waits for passing trade. This was typical of the run-of-the mill Parisian trade shop, with no glazed window, just wooden shutters: the mistress wears a shawl to keep warm. The designer has sketched in what must have been, for him, a common sight: a man and woman pulling their cart through the streets. They may be returning from the *halles* or some other market, or simply transporting

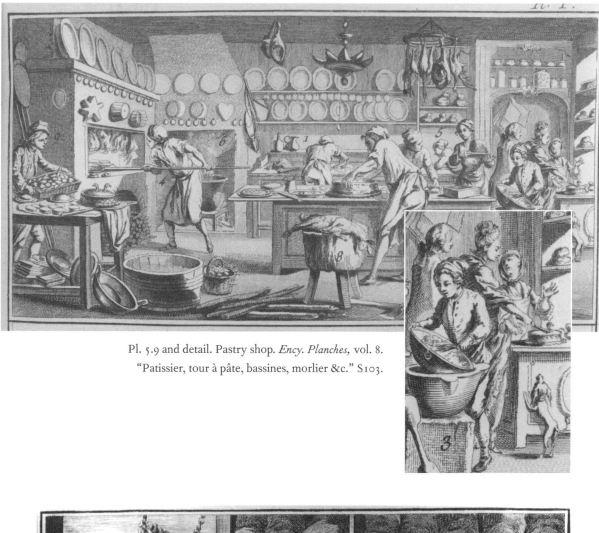

Pl. 5.9 and detail. Pastry shop. *Ency. Planches*, vol. 8.
"Patissier, tour à pâte, bassines, morlier &c." S103.

Pl. 5.10. Cork-maker's shop. *Ency. Planches*, vol. 2. "Bouchonnier." S.114.

Pl. 5.11. Tinsmith's shop. *Ency. Planches*, vol. 4. "Fer blantier; Pl. I." S116.

grass or hay for sale; too poor to have any beast to do the heavy drawing work, the wife accompanies the husband in their struggle for survival. This faceless couple remind us of the efforts to survive, at the most basic level of subsistence, that we witnessed in the plates from the traditional economy.

The tinsmith's shop (plate 5.11) is another such modest premises, selling kitchenware and vessels to those who could not afford silverware. The man in the center, presumably the master, is soldering a handle onto a coffee-pot. The wares are on display on the shelves behind the counter, and a client is examining a vase or jug. She is probably haggling the price with the mistress, as was customary. Shops such as these faced keen competition from the illegal *colporteurs*, who peddled cheap tinware items procured from the privileged Faubourgs around Paris, or workers in the trade who passed them on illegally (Fairchilds 1993, 237). The exchange between mistress and consumer was therefore of crucial importance in attracting and retaining loyal customers and represented an important element of urban sociability, as opposed to the quick (and often furtive) purchase in the street. Again, the designer has been tempted to enliven the urban streetscape, this time with a dog.

Conclusion

N THIS STUDY I asked how a particular corpus of images might speak, louder than words, about women workers in eighteenth-century France. The images I examined—in counterpoint with the texts relating to them—offer insights into the roles and tasks performed by women across the economy, and the context and conditions within which their work was undertaken. The period during which these images were created spanned from 1698 to 1788; occasionally, the juxtaposition of related images from the early and the later part of the century allowed me to note continuity or change in women's activities across a significant time period. For the most part, however, comparison of plates highlighted how little trade practices and gender relations actually evolved over the century, with no significant updating either in the technological processes or the gender-based division of roles (see Proust 1962, 164). There were undoubtedly labor shifts between one sector and another in eighteenth-century France, with more large-scale manufactories, for example, in the later period, but it is impossible to track such quantitative changes in the plates.

In certain of the examples from our collections, the image alone stands as a form of evidence of women's work activities, female-gendered tasks being taken for granted by the contemporary author and scarcely requiring mention: thus, women who did not figure in the text are pictured picking up curling tongs in a wig maker's establishment (plate 2.32), or sewing for a carriage maker (plate 2.35). Similarly, in our section on textiles, only an image from 1719 bears witness to the grueling work done by women as suppliers of energy for a yarn-twisting mill (plate 3.9). In other contexts, the image stood in contradiction to the written text: thus, for example, we spied a woman painting a frame in a framing workshop (plate 2.18), another turning the crank in a wax-blanching works (plate 2.43), and yet another finishing pewter vessels (plate 2.39): all were described in the accompanying texts as *ouvriers* in the masculine.

Women appeared across a range of small craft establishments, whether gilding a leather-bound book (interchangeably with the male workers in the shop, plate 2.20), or making the fans that supplied the luxury trade throughout Europe (plates 2.2 to 2.5). We have seen that in these and other trades (tailoring, plate 2.25, and bookbinding, plate 2.19, for example), the regulations of the dominant guilds, excluding women from workshop activities, appear to have been breached rather more than they were observed. The cumulative impact of the images highlights the extent to which women were drafted into family workshops, whether to do skilled work for which they had clearly been trained—as was the case of the feather dressers in plate 2.6, or the workers doing filigree and incrustation work on snuffboxes in plate 2.7—or to do ancillary work, such as working the bellows in a cutler's establishment (plate 2.47), warming the horn for bending into chess pieces (plate 2.38), or turning the crank to provide power in the manufacture of gold thread (plate 3.43). Their presence was particularly remarkable in trades with which historians have not traditionally

associated women, as in the plates on edge-tool making (plate 2.56) or the manufacture of catgut (plate 2.55). It has often been suggested that women were less likely to work with heavy or precision tools, particularly on metals, hard materials being culturally identified with men (see Coffin 1996, 40; Simonton 1998, 42); but our corpus offers examples of women in both of these contexts, such as the woman cross-hatching a metal plate (plate 2.14), or another using an engraving chisel for damascening steel (plate 2.13). Our evidence, albeit fragmentary, suggests that women's participation in artisan manufacturing activity in France was more extensive than the written record, to date, has indicated. In particular, the plates remind us of the extent to which workshops relied on the labor of female members of a master's extended family; their importance within a patriarchal guild economy has been underemphasized because it is so heavily occluded within official source documents. Clare Haru Crowston's study of the corporate identities of the Seamstresses and Tailors' Guilds in France casts an interesting light on this centrality of the family in the classic patriarchal model of the eighteenth-century guild (2000).

The commercial work of sell-

ing the products was closely allied with the craftwork itself, with workshop, sales counter, and family home frequently operating from the same premises; the master's wife and daughters made a major contribution to the family economy through their role in running the shops and keeping the accounts. This was one of the aspects of the economy where their work was most visible, if often unsung, and it was no great surprise to find women in those plates devoted to this element of the traditional artisanal economy, from the sumptuous *boutique* of the master cutler (plate 5.7), to the more modest premises of the cork maker (plate 5.10). In the large manufactories of the period, on the other hand, we might not have expected the strong presence of women, whether in the image depicting the tinning process (plate 4.15), or the poignant image from the Aubusson carpet manufactory (plate 4.10). The extent to which women and children were employed in such large-scale production across a range of areas in eighteenth-century France is undoubtedly, as I have already mentioned, a question deserving of more study.[61] Particularly interesting were the images from the great glass-making manufactories, where, in a plate dating from 1712, we saw women undertaking the physically demanding work of stone breaking (plate 4.11).

Such images have the power to disturb the modern reader in their depiction of women involved in tough physical labor requiring strength and stamina, precisely because the period of Enlightenment witnessed the beginnings of a fundamental transformation in ideas about gender and work that have shaped the way in which women's bodies are apprehended and represented in the modern period.[62] Already in 1762, the dualities that would come to dominate views on the gender division of labor were confidently trumpeted in Rousseau's influential *Emile*: nature dictated that men were strong and robust, women imaginative and "*sensible*" (1969). Voltaire, in his article "Femme (Physique et morale)" for *Questions sur l'Encyclopédie* (1768–77), asserted that the character of women was more gentle than that of men as a result of the fact that, being "more feeble of body," they were not suited to "the hard work of masonry, carpentry, metalwork or ploughing" but spent their time in more sedentary fashion, occupied with the "minor, lighter tasks" of housekeeping and childrearing. In compensation for their lack of strength, he suggested, women had greater dexterity, with more flexible fingers than men. Such

views rapidly became common currency among writers, although they were entirely alien to the lives and experience of contemporary laboring women; over and over again, Mercier, in his *Tableau de Paris*, asserted his convictions about the "natural" order of things: "it is grotesque to see [. . .] men pushing a needle, handling a shuttle, and usurping the sedentary life of women" (9: 178–79), notwithstanding the fact that tailoring and weaving had been male preserves for centuries. Conversely, he expressed his horror at the common sight of women pulling wagons or carrying heavy jugs of water: "A woman lugging jugs of water on the hard pavements of Paris! Nothing is more shocking" (10: 173, qtd. Jones 2004, 99). Judith Coffin has commented that "the spirit of self-evident rationality and naturalness with which Mercier presents his views illustrates the gulf that divided Enlightenment conceptions of the gender division of labor from corporate convictions about patriarchal authority" (1996, 41). Her research shows how, by 1776, women's guilds, such as those of the seamstresses and the linen drapers, were adopting elements of this "enlightened" discourse: to defend their position, they too argued that nature endowed men with "strength," giving women

"dexterity," fitting them for distinct and different occupations (2004, 81–88). Ironically, in making this distinction, they ensured that the quality of "dexterity," associated with the feminine, would become devalued.

Despite the stress on the use of technology in the overall corpus, the images presented here relating to the traditional economy mainly reflected a pre-Enlightenment society where it was taken for granted that women were responsible for much of the heavy work of transporting; and part 5, on manufactories, shows that in large-scale production units, the attribution of such work to women was not affected by the discourse of bourgeois print culture. The woman's body provided either the direct means of transport or the raw power to move the load from one location to the other. Although these images are, in their own way, highly stylized and barely indicate the effort and stress the work placed on the frame and muscles of the body, they offer an instructive contrast with the most common type of print showing women as load-carriers in the seventeenth and eighteenth centuries, the *Cris de Paris*, mentioned earlier. In these, the function of the woman in the image is frequently to act as the decorous (or decorative) object of a crude sexual joke, made explicit in the caption or verse beneath, with little signification in relation to the context of her work. [63] The focus of our prints is entirely different, with their unique emphasis on the body in relation to the object and the task. [64] In terms of art history, one of the few models for such images may be the work of Brueghel: Barnes describes a graphite sketch of market figures (in the National Gallery of Art, Washington D.C.) by David Teniers II (Antwerp 1610–90), based on works of Brueghel: the figures are studies of women carrying baskets of vegetables, jugs, and so forth on their heads and are highly evocative of the images permeating our corpus (see Barnes 1988, 35). Like our images, these sketches avoid the twin perils of the picturesque and the caricatural.

The conceptualization and portrayal of the laboring woman's body is undoubtedly a subject worthy of more attention than it has received; for example, in this period, it was deemed to be constitutionally different from that of her social superiors, those whom the *Encyclopédie* refers to as "persons of the female sex who have been brought up in a refined manner." Whereas the latter should avoid putting their hands or feet into cold water while menstruating, as such contact risks stopping their menstrual flow, it is to be noted that: "The women among the common people do their housework, wash their linen etc. during menstruation, and after childbirth, without adverse affect: but in this, as in all other aspects of lifestyle, one can draw no conclusion from their example for bodies which are not accustomed to these kind of hardships" ("Eau commune"). However, in an article elsewhere in the *Encyclopédie* addressing illnesses connected with menstruation, the chevalier de Jaucourt made the somewhat contradictory observation that "strong women, of a dry temperament, trained to heavy work, and accustomed to a hard life, not only have few periods, but can easily tolerate the suppression of menstruation" ("Règles, Maladies des"), and this notwithstanding the assertion a few paragraphs later that the suppression of menstruation is the cause of innumerable "*accidents.*" Londa Schiebinger has highlighted how, in debates about menstruation in this period, the heavier the flow, the higher one's place in nature was deemed to be; women of color, for example, like the laboring women, were considered to have a "less abundant" flow (1993, 91, and Fausto-Sterling 2000, 219). In the symbolic framework of Greek philosophical thinking relating to the human body and its humors, dryness was mainly linked to masculinity: "the woman is cold and wet, associated with water and negatively valued" (Héritier-Augé 1989, 288). De Jaucourt's phrase, emphasizing the "dry" temperament of laboring women, places such women in an ambiguous position on the side of masculinity in the prevailing gender ideology.

The body of the woman "accustomed to a hard life," such as we see in innumerable plates in our corpus, was apparently, then, deemed impervious to the effects or illnesses that would result from physical stress or contact with water in more delicate organisms. We will recall that in the plates on fisheries along the French coast, we saw bare-legged women carrying salted sardines into the cold Atlantic water to wash them (plate 1.43b), work demanding stamina and endurance, but the implications for their health attracted no comment from the writer of the text. Likewise, the 1719 engraving of the yarn-twisting machine (plate 3.9) afforded us a view of the kind of exhausting labor that, it was taken for granted, women would perform in textile mills and manufactories, their bodies being the producers of energy in this world of early mechanization. Referring to the *Encyclopédie,* Daniel Brewer has noted how the workers' bodies in plates such as this can be seen as an extension of the machine, which dwarfs them: "In this sense the machine is not a tool, but a mechanism for productively and efficiently transforming energy, the source of which in the majority of the encyclopædic plates is the human worker" (1993, 33). William Hamilton Sewell has further suggested that Diderot's plates "argue for a cultural construction of the capitalist mode of production well in advance of its practical realization" (1986, 279). Plates such as 3.9, dating from a half century earlier than the images discussed by Brewer and Sewell, add strength to their arguments: here, women, as the cheapest form of labor, are already the industrial workers of choice.

The 1714 image (plate 4.11) of women using large mallets to reduce blocks of sandstone to sand is a further impressive example of the type of heavy physical work that, like mining work, gradually became exclusively male-gendered in the post-Revolutionary period, but which, on the evidence of this image, was associated with women under the *ancien régime.* Occasional written reports from the eighteenth to the mid-nineteenth centuries substan-

tiate these glimpses of women's bodies as sites of intense physical effort, and even of extreme duress. I mentioned earlier the mining reports of 1842, which detailed how women worked almost naked or wearing men's trousers. William Hutton observed nailers in the Black Country (in the West Midlands of England) in 1741 and remarked: "In some of these shops I observed one or more females, stript of their upper garment . . . wielding the hammer with all the grace of the sex" (1817, 158; qtd. in Simonton 1998, 43); this suggests that they were working in a shift, without a bodice, rare for the period. Likewise, the punctilious inspector Louis Villermé, whose visits to manufactories in France from 1834 to 1837 informed his *Tableau de l'état physique et moral des ouvriers,* described a textile workshop making printed calico in the Upper Rhine area: "I saw female workers subjected to a temperature of 35° to 40°, that is to say a temperature which is sometimes equal to that of the body, and keeps them in a continual state of abundant perspiration. They are all barefoot, wearing only a shift and a very light petticoat" (1840, qtd. Guilbert 1966, 38). These nineteenth-century reactions reflect the growing moral concern, in this later period,

about working conditions, which were typically worse for women and children than for men: similar conditions had existed in the eighteenth century but attracted little comment. One exception is Louis-Sebastien Mercier, who, in the 1780s, captured some of the ambiguities in the contemporary culture when he expressed his sympathy for the women who carried the great *hottes* (such as we have seen illustrated) loaded with produce through the streets of Paris:

What is sad to see are those unfortunate women with heavy hods on their backs, faces red and eyes almost bloodshot, who are out before dawn in the muddy streets, or on pavements where ice crackles under the first footfall [. . .] We don't see the strain of their muscles as we do with men; it is more hidden; but we can sense it from their swollen neck, their laboured breathing, and compassion penetrates to the very bottom of your soul when you hear them swear in an altered, shrill voice as they make their exhausting way along [. . .] What a contrast! One woman struggles in a lather of sweat under a double load of pumpkins, crying *watch out, make way*! The other, in a lively equipage whose wheel brushes against the huge, bursting hod, is wasting away—rouge on her face and fan in her hand—from indolence. (1782–88, IV: 33–35, qtd. Albistur and Armogathe 1977, 181)

Such concern signalled a change in mentality whereby the second term of Mercier's contrast would influence the norm, and physical weakness and fragility would become inextricably associated with the female. By the middle of the nineteenth century, the ideas debated by Enlightenment writers concerning women's inferior strength, or their need for protection, were to coalesce with the major changes in industrial organization and lead to the exclusion of women from many of the roles, such as work in mining, they had previously filled.

Though we may lament the fate of many of the women in our images as victims of exploitation, working as many as fourteen hours a day, there are interesting questions to be addressed concerning their physical capacity for performing such work, as well as their own sense of their bodies as strong and powerful. We need to keep in mind how later cultural shifts affect the way in which we evaluate these images from a very different era. In the modern period, the relationship of the woman's body to movement, space, and the object was problematized most challengingly in Iris Marion Young's famous essay "Throwing Like a Girl." Taking Merleau-Ponty's reorientation of the very notion of subjectivity by locating it not in the mind or consciousness but in the body, she underlines how the possibilities open to an individual "depend on the mode and limits of the bodily 'I can'"; however, "Feminine bodily existence remains in immanence or, better, is overlaid with immanence, even as it moves toward the world in motions of grasping, manipulating, and so on" (1990, 148). She suggests that women's doubts about their body's capacity in modern Western society amount to a physical handicap, with far-reaching effects on all aspects of their existence, and are cultural and historical, not biological. It is clear from our images that in early modern society, women workers did not have such doubts about their body's capacity, and that their experience of their strength was very different from that mediated by modern culture.

The portrayal of women in these very physical roles nonetheless posed problems for the artists involved: it was a challenge for the artist to represent the women's bodies in cases where the physical nature of the tasks performed demanded that their working clothes break with polite notions of *bienséance* (decorum), which would have been applied in the depiction of leisured ladies. In the images on fishing just mentioned, women wore their skirts, or more likely just a shift, tucked up between their legs, exposing their lower limbs in a way extremely unusual in representations of women in this period. Women's legs were rarely shown in eighteenth-century images other than the pornographic (Harvey 2004), or those with erotic intent, including neoclassical representations of mythological figures—Boucher's images of Venus and Diana spring to mind. Anne Hollander (1975, 218–22) has remarked how refined legs appearing from under dishevelled skirts became a recurrent theme in the work of Jan Steen in the mid-seventeenth century: the latter's voyeuristic *Woman at Her Morning Toilet* (1663) is a good example. The same theme can be traced through the erotic genre scenes of Hogarth (1730s through 1750s), to Fragonard's *The Swing* (1767): eschewing realism, legs here show an idealized refinement.[65] All this was a far cry from the depiction of legs in our prints, for which the closest equivalent is perhaps to be found in classical art, where women's legs were shown only when involved in military engagements or hunting, while draped legs appeared everywhere else (for both sexes); thus, "the association was made between naked legs and strength" (Hollander 1978, 214). The naked legs depicted here signify the women's full physical engagement with their work tasks.

It was also extremely unusual for women in polite society to dress in anything that could be construed as male breeches or trousers. In the English context, Crown has pointed out that even at masquerades, when women were described as wearing male costume, this usually meant an adaptation of male garb, such as short skirts and exposed legs, whereas men often wore full female dress to masquerades (Crown, 2002, 126–29). Natalie Zemon Davis has also remarked how, in popular culture and festivities across many European cultures, male transvestism was more common than female transvestism (1987, 131–34); exceptions were actresses in "breeches performances" on the stage (see Wahrman 1998). In the Revolutionary period, some Jacobine women promenaded in Paris wearing pantaloons and red caps but quickly came under attack for allegedly trying to force other women "to wear a costume which they believe to be reserved to men" (Hunt 2000, 184). From the late eighteenth century onward, in both France and England, the wearing of breeches was presented as an attempt to arrogate male power, and as being dangerous and subversive, and this is reflected in images of this later period (Crown 2002, 129). But all of these contexts, which implied some form of display or performance, excluded the lowest social category of workers; how, then, could an artist react where the imperative was the very different one of representing the woman at work, as a subject in relation to the objects of production or transformation? I remarked on the unrealistic portrayal by the designer Catherine Haussard, in plate 1.52, of women climbing with skirts around their ankles; but the challenge was met in a more original manner by Angelique Moitte in plate 1.53, in which the women stringing sardines onto rods seemed to be wearing a type of pantaloons, with a good part of their legs bare above their wooden clogs. Here the designer clearly broke with the conventions of other genres of visual representation in the interest of providing a more faithful visual record of work practices. Likewise, in plate 1.30, we can just about see the trousers, which make the women almost indistinguishable from the men working alongside them. My certainty concerning the origin of these images adds greatly to their documentary value concerning the manner in which women dealt with the physical demands made upon them; they present a valuable opportunity for analyzing some of the ways in which women experienced their working bodies, as well as how they were perceived by others.

The plates revealed repeated evidence of skilled work—in the sense of complex, learned tasks— being performed by women. Many recent histories of women's work have examined the extent to which skill is a gendered concept, with shifting definitions serving to exclude women's tasks. Deborah Simonton suggests that, in the eighteenth century:

The notion of skill carried a sense of knowledge or discrimination, but described an ability to accomplish something, that is, a sense of not only *knowing* but being able to *do* something. While skill clearly referred to ability, it was not limited to a mechanical or technological sense as we know it today, and it paid heed to both experience and training as ways of knowing.

[. . .] Both French and English usage identify an important characteristic of skill, in that it is a linguistic device to claim and maintain control and exclusivity in the workplace.[. . .] Skill and status which boys could achieve through apprenticeship were simply not options for girls. While girls might have learned technical ability, they did not acquire the quality of "skill." (Simonton 1998, 76, 77, 81)[66]

While the texts accompanying our plates frequently referred to the need for experience on the part of the woman worker, and continually underlined the patience and care required in the performance of her tasks, they generally stopped short of epithets that might be taken as signifiers of "skill." I have noted the rare exceptions, such as the article on upholstery fringing (see plate 3.36), where Diderot used the word *habileté* in relation to the skill of the *guipeuses* (*Ency.* "Guiper"). From enamelling to damascening, from the decoration of snuffboxes to the embossing of rich brocades, we saw intricate, learned tasks performed by women. I have remarked on innumerable examples of the complex and delicate work they accomplished in textile manufacture, from the spinning of wool to the

reeling of silk warp. Hafter has highlighted how the statutes condemning female artisans' illegal work paid inadvertent tribute to their skill, as, for example, the ability of the silk winders to camouflage their theft of materials by producing a product that looked perfect (2001, 31).

Clearly, dexterity—which implies agility and control of the hands and fingers—was required, alongside training and experience, for all such tasks; but, as I have suggested, in the Enlightenment period this quality increasingly became associated with women, and was thus devalued, no longer regarded as a noteworthy component of "skill." In the case of the wig makers, for example, the text states that only women could weave the short and fine tufts of hair, because of "the delicacy and the agility of their hands," but despite the evident importance of this process, it was probably the lowest-paying job in the shop (when it was not done for free by members of the household), and it was typically the kind of work given to poor widows of masters. This sharpening of gender distinctions in the second half of the century further eroded the status of women workers, whose skills, as I noted in the introduction, were so often taken for granted by the patriarchal structures of fam-

ily and guild. Thus, we saw that as women progressively took over the work of sewing throughout the century, the Tailors' Guild defined it as "accessory," no longer a "skill" when not done by men. A similar distinction applied in the case of embroiderers, lace makers (who ranked among the lowest-paid workers), and the women making Turkish carpets: although they produced some of the most expensive and highly prized objects within the luxury economy, they never gained the status afforded to "skilled" workers. The exceptions were in the all-female trades of the linen draper and the seamstress, scantily represented in our corpus: mistresses in their own right, these women jealously guarded the considerable power and prerogatives conferred on them by guild status, which allowed them to train apprentices and thus pass on a marketable skill to other women. But even here, as Crowston has highlighted, a paradox operated whereby once women acquired a guild, "their example did much to crystallize existing notions of 'women's work,' contributing to a new articulation and rigidification of the traditional sexual division of labor" (2001, 185). With the feminization of the fashion trades, as Jones has shown, writers such as Louis-Sebastien Mercier and

Jean-Jacques Rousseau argued that sewing and clothing trades were not only naturally feminine, but that they were inappropriate for men, who became a common target for ridicule if they remained in such trades (2004, 98).

Another area in which the plates offered some interesting clarification was in the gender dimension of payment for work. In a few specific instances, we saw illustrated, side by side, almost identical tasks for which men and women were paid different rates, and even paid according to entirely different scales. In my discussion of the traditional economy (see part 1), we saw the herring-smoking unit (plate 1.52), where, although the work of the women illustrated in the bottom section was little different from that of the men shown in the upper section, they were paid less.[67] Likewise, in the hatting trade (plate 2.34), we saw that work on the most prestigious material (the beaver fur) was largely reserved for men, and that they were paid a set daily rate while the women were paid by the piece, although again, the actual nature of the task performed is very similar in terms of physical effort and skill. Such images graphically illustrate the degree to which payment for work was based on criteria extraneous to the actual task

itself; in the case of women, lower pay rates were based on the assumption that women were not heads of households and that adult males were responsible for providing the bulk of the family income. William Reddy has demonstrated how women's wages were largely dissociated from the market: their income did not increase even where demand for their labor was high, and this persisted right into the nineteenth century, when the market had supposedly been freed up (1984). In many instances, they were not paid directly at all but merely shared in the wage of a male family member.

Ironically, although one of the most skilled craft occupations in which women excelled was the art of engraving itself—a rare example of an area in which women could develop a respected career—no women were shown in the plates illustrating this trade in our collections:[68] these followed the tendency in most records to represent the outer, public face of a patriarchal workshop culture, leaving the women working away inside, hidden from view. This is a cautionary example of the extent to which women were undoubtedly omitted from images purporting to describe trades in which they did, in fact, play an important role. Happily, in this

instance, the engravings themselves stand as proof of the contribution of women as creators: at least twenty of our sample of plates from the *Descriptions* (almost a quarter), were engraved, and very probably designed, by women. None of the sample from the *Encyclopédie* carries a woman's signature, although we know that two or three women worked on the plates in that collection (Gardey 1964a, 38 and 40). These skilled women represent a triumph over a sort of double jeopardy. Situated halfway between the world of the artisan and the artist, with less prestige than painting and relatively low in the hierarchy of genres, engraving was less subject to the control and influence of the academic establishment, while it likewise escaped the regulation of a trade guild. Had it not done so, women would certainly have been excluded from apprenticeship and mastership (other than as widows), as they were in all other areas of the printing or book trades.[69] But it was, in fact, possible for young women to learn and practice engraving as a profession, as the tradition of many families in the trade was to train daughters alongside their brothers in their father's workshop; boys, and sometimes also girls, then finished their training in the workshop of a colleague (Dacier 1944, 77). This was the case for Marie-Jeanne Ozanne, who was employed as an engraver for the *Descriptions* (see plate 1.24): she was one of a family from Brest in which all four siblings acquired a reputation for engraving, especially marine and coastal scenes, as well as ship-design work. Both she and her sister Jeanne-Françoise were trained in the workshop of the renowned engraver Jacques Aliamet. She married another Paris-based engraver, Yves-Marie Le Gouaz, who collaborated on major projects with her family (see Michaud 1843, 31: 568–69; Nagler 1909, 12: 2–4).

Of particular note in our corpus are seven high-quality plates relating to fishing by Angelique Moitte, known for her landscape work (see for example plates 1.19, 1.43, and 1.44 from the *Descriptions;* she was the daughter of Pierre-Etienne Moitte, a member of the Académie, and Royal Engraver).[70] Her younger sister, Elisabeth-Mélanie, also showed great talent and engraved a number of works after Greuze. Catherine and Elisabeth Haussard between them engraved eleven of our plates from the *Descriptions*; they were the daughters of Jean Haussard, who worked on some of the early plates for the same collection (see, for example,

plates 2.10 and 2.11); they also contributed to other major projects, including several cartouches for the Robert de Vaugondy *Atlas Universel* in 1757. In our examples of their work, all the women seem to have fulfilled the dual function of artist and engraver and therefore would have had a significant degree of control over the illustrations: their plates are noteworthy both for the quality of the artistry and as reflections on the living and working conditions of their subjects.

The model represented by these women engravers, learning their trade within the family, may well have been far more extensive throughout the artisanal and proto-industrial sector than we know. In their case, they could legitimately sign and take credit for their work, and so have left their trace; but in many other trades, where guilds in theory excluded daughters, women nonetheless learned skills in a very similar manner. This was the case in printing, where daughters in small workshops learned to pull the press, particularly in regions where guild control was limited (see Sheridan 1992, 56–57). In the proto-industrial sphere, Gullickson (1990, 211) has drawn attention to the likelihood that the wives and daughters of weavers in the Caux district took turns at the

small looms weaving cotton or linen when the men were tired, although she could locate no written evidence to this effect. Vardi has found traces of some women and children of both sexes working the linen looms in Montigny, also in Northern France (Vardi 1993b, 132). Hafter has likewise suggested, in relation to the less privileged artisan families, that "in families on the margin, the need to earn overcame considerations of prescribed sex role behavior [. . .] it is not too far-fetched to imagine that necessity and habit tended to blur the partners' roles within working families" (1989, 421). However, we are unlikely to find any images reflecting such activity, which fell outside set patterns of thought and categories of work.

In commenting on the many images of disembodied hands in the *Encyclopédie,* Barthes suggested that these are signs of the human ability to dominate the object in this premodern world of craft, "the symbol of an artisanal world" (1964, 12). He did not remark that the hands illustrated, in the vast majority of cases, are male hands, even where the vignette shows only women workers: such was the case for the feather-dressers, for example, where the women in our vignette (plate 2.6) were shown working on the feathers with knives and scissors but the subsequent plate in the *Encyclopédie* showed male hands, clearly indicated by the male form of dress, cuffs at the wrist. I have, however, reproduced some rare examples of images of female hands (plates 3.28a and b); in a context where women were generally denied any recognition of "mastery" within the institutional framework of the *ancien régime*, they signify the female capacity to control matter and process. By their very rarity, they offer a reminder of the degree to which skilled craftswomen's abilities were occluded both by contemporary culture and by subsequent historiography.

I have noted the degree to which the social fabric of working women's lives in this period remains hidden; but in a number of workshop illustrations in the Académie's series, the designer has sketched a female figure passing by the doorway.[71] Was this just the artist's urge to fill an empty frame, or does it reflect her/his awareness of the presence, always close, of the female members of the master's family, coming and going throughout the day, helping out, shopping, preparing food, mingling with the life of the workshop? We remain largely in the dark as to what kind of social relationships the women who do feature in our images maintained with others within their working and living contexts. Whereas the guild organizations and journeymen's associations (*campagnonnages*) provided social outlets and relationships for men, and some documentation concerning them survives (see, for example Truant 1986), there were few equivalents for women. One interesting example where seamstresses in Caen did endeavor to exercise their rights to participate in a corporate public ritual (they were a subordinate group within the Tailors' Guild) is recounted by Crowston: the unmarried women's attempt to be pallbearers at a single colleague's burial was thwarted by male colleagues, who pushed them aside and subjected them to ridicule, thus giving rise to a police report where the events entered the record (2000, 358–61). Michael Sonenscher has wondered about the social bonds that might unite the substantial proportion of women working in an enterprise such as hatmaking but found little trace of their existence other than a cursory mention in one contemporary manuscript of a group of women hatmakers in Lyon banding together—"*une cabale terrible*"—to force a positive response to their demands (Sonenscher 1987, 147; 1989, 67).

William Reddy describes the disturbances at Rouen in April 1752, when a royal ordinance attempted to confine all trade in cotton fiber and yarn to the Cloth Hall, thus excluding large numbers of female cotton spinners from peddling on their own behalf; the resultant rioting by a large group of women forced the authorities to withdraw the ordinance. Reddy concludes, "These spinners were tied into a web of mutual social obligations, familial and otherwise, that determined their need to work in the first place and provided criteria by which to decide how much work and what kind of work they would do" (1984, 32–33), but such social networks remain largely unrecorded. James B. Collins has suggested that, in general, women in *ancien-régime* France were more disrespectful of authority than men and were "central figures in the constant animosity toward civil society that one sees in the taverns and streets of the working districts of Nantes" (1989, 469), a hypothesis that deserves more attention than it has received to date.

As for social entertainment, Truant thinks it likely that the merchant-mistress linen drapers celebrated publicly on the feast day of their patron saint, Veronica (1988, 135), and I have already mentioned the complaints recorded by Sonenscher concerning spinners in Reims "dancing and leaping about" on feast days. But this is thin fare, and it is likely that, given the domestic pressures on working women, social activities for any but single girls were minimal.

Childbirth was a regular occurrence for most married women working in trades or manufacture (Fairchilds 1984, 105), but in their circumstances, taking care of children was an enormous burden, and placing out infants for wet-nursing was frequently the only possibility left open to them. Very few of the women who worked on a loom in their husband's shop, or who stood at the counter in a baker's or butcher's business, could afford to be absent from their work to nurse an infant. Garden exposed the terrible statistics of infant mortality among those put out to wet-nurse in the Lyon area: families of merchants and masters suffered huge losses, but the lower socioeconomic groups, whose children were sent further away and to the poorest regions, almost certainly suffered most. In 1778 Antoine-François Prost de Royer described the "fathers in poverty and mothers in tears" ("*Pères pauvres et mères éplorées*"; qtd. Garden 1970, 137) who handed their children over to an often unscrupulous go-

between ("*entremetteuse*") promising to find a suitable nurse in the country. While statistics are difficult to establish, Garden concluded that the contemporary estimations, in the latter part of the century, surmising that two thirds of the children sent out to "mercenary" wet nurses died, were fairly close to the reality; the majority of these died in their first year (136–40). "On the image of a countryside furnishing manpower [to the city of Lyon] another superimposes itself: that of a countryside which devours children" (140; see also Sussman, 1982). Thus, despite a high birthrate, the majority of working families raised only a small number of live children, rarely more than four, while a lone surviving child was not unusual (Garden 1970, 151–56). The toll of frequent and often fruitless pregnancies on the woman worker is difficult to imagine; Garden remarked of the silk workers he studied that "the frequency of births eventually wears the mothers out, and the work on the looms further adds to their exhaustion." The death rate rose significantly for women between the ages of thirty and thirty-nine, after seven and more pregnancies (143). Such pressures were not alleviated but rather aggravated by rising food prices and population growth as

the century drew to its close. There was a world of difference between the experience of the working women such as featured in our plates and that of the "enlightened" aristocratic mothers who, like Mme Roland, had taken to extolling the pleasures of maternity (Fairchilds 1984, 100–103).

Very occasionally, however, the images do allow us to glimpse some of the familial and even emotional dimensions of our protagonists' lives not accessible from the texts. I have already mentioned the several images of women with young children holding their hand or skirt, or assisting them in little tasks in their workplace. Likewise, in the wigmaker's establishment, we saw a very young girl sitting at the wefting frame—probably the child or trainee of the woman sketched into the background (plate 2.32). Also noted was the originality of plate 2.12, where we saw women training very young girls in the art of making artificial flowers, while a young boy helped the men: these are, presumably, children of the master's extended family, sitting with their mothers, sharing their wage, and learning the trade. In Lucotte's charming image the older women turn solicitously to the young girls, apparently teaching them and encouraging their efforts. Admittedly, these are only brief glimpses suggesting the kind of intimate relationship that might have existed between the working mother and her young children, but they serve to remind us of the density of a life as it was lived, of the many dimensions that are now, for a large part, beyond our reach. Just as Snell has demonstrated—contrary to the assertions of earlier historians—the love and concern for family expressed in the letters of poor rural emigrants from England in the early part of the following century (1985, 10–11), our image of the flower makers evokes the care and affection that the working women of France undoubtedly experienced for their children. It casts some soft light into the often harsh and gray world occupied by the eighteenth-century woman worker, and reflected in the plates in this book.

Notes

1. The *Recueil de planches* (abbrev. *Ency. Planches*) of 11 volumes, together with the *Suite du recueil de planches* of 1777, contain some 2,784 plates; see Schwab 1984. I have also included two additional images from the later *Encyclopédie méthodique*, published by Panckouke in the 1780s (see plates 1.6 and 2.26). On the history of the *Encyclopédie* (abbrev. *Ency.*), see also Proust 1962; Lough 1971. One of the few articles to mention the portrayal of women in these plates is Malueg 1984.

2. This collection consisted of 113 separate *cahiers* that were bound in differing sets according to the purchaser's requirements; there are relatively few complete copies extant. The plates, in total approximately 1,850, were integrated into each separate volume. The most useful lists of the full collection, whose elements are frequently entered as stand-alone items in library catalogues, are Cole and Watts 1952, appendix A, 25–36; and Reno and Erb 1974, which amended some details of Cole and Watts.

3. These include the American Philosophical Society Library, Philadelphia; Bibliothèque de Institut de France, Paris; Bibliothèque de l'Arsenal, Paris; Bibliothèque Nationale, Paris; Houghton Library, Harvard University; Newberry Library, Chicago. See Jaoul and Pinault 1982 and 1986; also my list of plates regarding the images from these collections included in this work.

4. See, for example, Pinault 1992 and 2005; Watts 1958; and Cole and Watts 1952, 36–37.

5. In France there was a brief respite in February 1776, when Turgot abolished the guilds, giving the limited opportunities available to women as one of the reasons for his decision; after his downfall, the corporations of Paris were reinstated in August, albeit with some reforms (Musgrave 1997, 151).

6. See the list of plates in this volume.

7. See the Archives de l'Académie des Sciences, Paris, set of documents foliated consecutively from f. 149 to f. 160 and inserted at the back of vol. 13 of the Procès-verbaux de l'Académie, with the title "Description des Arts et Métiers. Des Séances de l'année 1695 jusqu'en 1696. Addition, jointe à ce volume de registres" [P-V]. Parts of this document are reproduced by Salomon-Bayet 1970, 245–50. Regarding Bignon and the Académie Royale des Sciences, see Sturdy 1995, 226.

8. See Houghton MS Typ 432.1 (1), f. 7, where Réaumur writes (in his notes for a preface to the *Descriptions*): "The description of the arts [crafts] was one of the first aims of the renewed academy [i.e. after 1699]. Prior to this Mr des billettes, et Mr Jaugeon formed a separate little academy etc. [*sic*]." Réaumur, a renowned scientist, would later become director of the Académie Royale des Sciences on eleven occasions.

9. See Guillerme and Sebestik 1968, 85, on the first appearance of the word *technology* in the modern sense in Phillips's *Dictionary* of 1706. Regarding the aims of the *Descriptions* project, see extracts from the *Histoire de l'Académie royale des sciences* (1699), quoted in Cole and Watts 1952, 6 and 7.

10. See, for example, the manuscript "Questions sur le batteur d'or" in Dossier biographique de Des Billettes, Archives de l'Académie des Sciences.

11. Réaumur, when writing for information about a sugar mill in Martinique some years later, specifies that the *Descriptions* include representations of "machines, tools, and even the postures of the workers" (Dossier biographique de Réaumur, Archives de l'Académie des Sciences).

12. In his discussion of the alternative institutional possibilities facing his group, Des Billettes had specifically considered the eventuality of becoming part of the Académie des Sciences but had suggested that in such an event he and his "technologist" collaborators should be placed in a separate "*dé-*

partement" (Note in Dossier biographique de Des Billettes, Archives de l'Académie des Sciences; qtd. in Salomon-Bayet 1970, 244). This did not happen. See Sheridan 2008 on this sequence of events.

13. See the manuscript "Description et perfection des arts et mestiers" (1704), ms. 2741, Bibliothèque de l'Institut de France, Paris.

14. On Fougeroux's extensive input, see Jaoul and Pinault 1986, 24–27.

15. See Proust 1962, 190–91. Some of the authors of the *Descriptions* were certainly guilty of excessive long-windedness, especially where the authors were being paid by volume of text, which encouraged inflation in the length. See letters from the publishers to the Académie published in Eriksen 1959, 162–63.

16. For the details of these events, see Huard 1952, 35–46; also Seguin 1964, 30–33. See my commentary on plate 3.40 in part 3 as an example of the way Diderot used the Académie's plates.

17. Initially (in 1745), there was to be just one volume of 120 plates (Proust 1962, 46) and four volumes of text. In relation to this study, it is significant that the seventeen volumes of text eventually published made only passing reference to working women; articles such as Desmahis's "*Femme, Morale*" refer exclusively to upper-class women who were accused of being vain and coquettish. The volumes of plates (with plate legends), however, focused on women in artisanal and peasant society. See Malueg 1984.

18. Proust 1962, 207, quotes Diderot's own remarks regretting the *Encyclopédie*'s failure in this respect; see also Proust 1957.

19. Houghton MS Typ 432.1 (1). All translations in this work are my own, unless otherwise specified.

20. The rivalry was more overt on the part of Diderot, who made vicious attacks on two of the Academicians central to the *Descriptions* project. Regarding his comments on Réaumur, see Proust 1962, 190–91. In describing a portrait of Duhamel by Moitte in his "Salon" of 1767, he wrote "This Duhamel invented an endless number of machines which have no purpose; wrote and translated an endless number of books on agriculture, with which no-one is now familiar; carried out experiments throughout his life from which we are still waiting to see any useful result. He's like a dog who follows on sight the game that dogs with a good nose have already raised, who abandons it to others, and who never catches it" (1875, 11: 366). With regard to Duhamel's writings on agriculture, and his work on the *Descriptions*, Diderot's comments were clearly intemperate and unjust.

21. Diderot and the publishers had decided to proceed with the publication of the plates with a separate royal *privilège*, the permission for the textual volumes having been withdrawn (see Proust 1962, 53–56.)

22. Ogilvie (2004, para 16) has emphasized that such all-female guilds were extremely rare in Europe, with only five recorded for German-speaking states, and none

for England. I discuss the Parisian all-female guilds in part 2.

23. This is all the more surprising in that he included an interesting section on the *Encyclopédie* in his study but did not remark on the plates showing women working (1986, 268–79).

24. *Ency. Planches,* "Pesches de Mer, plate III," reproduced with commentary by Jacques Proust 1985, plate 36. The information is correctly recorded in Duhamel 1769, "*Seconde section . . . Des filets; et des différentes façons de les employer,*" plate 30, and pp. 78–79 and 189. For a similar example, see my plate 4.10 and commentary.

25. There are, for example, a number of interesting plates (six or so) illustrating women involved in agricultural activities in the third edition of Louis Liger's *Nouvelle maison rustique,* published in Paris in 1721. These plates are similar in presentation to the plates on the traditional economy in this corpus and were possibly influenced by the work being carried out for the *Descriptions* since 1690, but they were an afterthought—no doubt to improve the attractiveness of the book originally published without these illustrations as *Œconomie générale de la campagne, ou Nouvelle maison rustique* in 1700—and were not integrated with the text. This limits the interpretive possibilities for the modern interlocutor.

26. See, for example, Cohen 2004. The influence of empiricism is reflected in Diderot's comments on Chardin in his "Salon" of 1765: "If it is true, as the philosophers say, that there is no reality other than

our sensory perceptions, that neither the emptiness of space nor even the solidity of volumes may count for anything in what we experience, then let these philosophers explain to me what difference they find between the Creator and you, when they stand four feet away from your paintings" (1875, 10: 299).

27. 1875, 10: 508; see Demetz 1963, 101. Seznec (1965) argues that despite his praise for Chardin and Greuze, and his leaning toward "realism" in his novels and plays, Diderot's comments tended rather to support the view promoted by the Académie Royale de Peinture et de Sculpture that historical, mythological, and religious scenes constitute the highest rank of painting. The Académie considered genre painting inferior even to portraiture (Walsh 1999, 93).

28. Luycken is included in the Chevalier de Jaucourt's list of outstanding engravers in the *Encyclopédie* article "Graveur."

29. The moralizing tone of such images evokes Hogarth's "Gin Lane" print (1751), where the point made is, precisely, that poor people are drinking instead of working.

30. See Walsh 1999, 92. Seguin 1964, 34, emphasizes that Diderot, following the lead of the Academicians, chose artisans rather than artists to work on the plates.

31. Over three-quarters of the plates of the *Encyclopédie* were designed by Goussier or Lucotte, with almost as many engraved by one craftsman, Robert Bénard (Schwab 1984, 457–64; Seguin 1964, 34). Goussier and Bénard were responsible for the great majority of the

plates in our *Encyclopédie* sample (designers and engravers can be identified by reference to the Schwab Inventory, the entry for each of which is noted in the captions to this work); this same pair also, in fact, did some work on the *Descriptions,* including some of the plates on silk manufacture reproduced here. The sample from the *Arts et métiers* is much more varied, with eleven different designers, along with many anonymous plates. On the designers who worked on this collection, see Pinault 2002, 154–64.

32. Some indications of the poor conditions in which apprentices and unqualified workers had to live can be found in Nicolas Contat's account of his apprenticeship in a printer's shop in Paris in the late 1730s: see Darnton 1985, 75–104.

33. See Jaugeon's preface, f. 7, ms. "Description et perfection des arts et mestiers" (1704), ms. 2741, Bibliothèque de l'Institut de France, Paris (see Sheridan 2008).

34. Milliot also points out that while, on the one hand, we can find echoes in the *Encyclopédie* (through the assimilation of the artisan and the mechanical) of a new dignity that associates the knowledge and skill of the worker with a scientific mode of functioning, on the other hand, this rationalist imperative tends to ignore actual practices and to displace, without really abolishing, the condescension of the elite vis-à-vis the working classes (1994, 26).

35. Barthes remarked, "There is not a single plate in the *Encyclopédie* which does not resonate way beyond

what it intended to show [. . .]. In a deeper part of ourselves, beyond the intellect, or at least on its hidden side, questions arise and overflow" (1964, 14).

36. Sewell remarked that he was taken by surprise in his study of engravings, having set out simply to identify some images that would embellish his book *Work and Revolution in France*, by the way in which the visual images refused simply to "illustrate" his points, remarking that "they had a dynamic and a language of their own that did not correspond in any direct way with the language or the dynamics of either intellectual discourse about labor or worker organizational practices" (1986, 259).

37. "The capacity to inform does not stop with what the image could say to the reader of the time: from this old picture the modern reader also receives information which the *Encyclopédiste* could not have foreseen" (Barthes 1964, 14).

38. From the *Children's Employment Commission (Mines): First Report*, Parliamentary Papers, 1842 (part xv: 31), qtd. Bradley 1989, 107.

39. "The woman porter shovels and carries coals in a wicker basket, / and she has a thankworthy task day and night. / No woman is tied down by greater work, / than the woman porter born in the district of Liège." My thanks to Fr. Senan Furlong OSB for this translation.

40. See Pinchbeck 1969, 255, on women's working hours in British mines; also see p. 185 above on the workdays in the Montgolfier paper mill.

41. There are two other related

manuscripts: Bibliothèque Nationale, Dépt. des Estampes, ms. Ke 83, and Bibliothèque Municipale de Bordeaux, ms. 562.

42. Letter 4 March 1769, addressed to Le Breton, qtd. by Pinault 1987, 343, from Diderot 1963, 9: 32.

43. On *Encyclopédie* plates illustrating children at work see Guyard, 1985.

44. There are, in fact, two versions of this plate: the other version, probably re-engraved for the Geneva edition, shows two children, emphasizing how the designer could make personal interventions in interpreting a model.

45. This article was by Le Romain; on the diversity of views on slavery expressed in the *Encyclopédie*, see Adams 2004.

46. See Benot 1981, 209; and Pomeau 1980, 45–46.

47. Hafter has remarked how, for many women, "even if guild statutes had not prevented their assimilation into a privileged professional association, their lack of money to pay the apprenticeship and entrance fees would have kept them out" (2001, 18).

48. Musgrave has shown how daughters in the textile and food-processing trades of eighteenth-century Nantes increasingly perceived themselves as inheriting economic rights to trade from their fathers, though the guilds did not formally recognize such rights (1997, 155; see also Guilbert 1966, 23).

49. See documents filed on behalf of the linen drapers' and the seamstresses' guilds: Bibliothèque

Nationale de France, Joly de Fleury, vol. 462, f. 117 (1776), and ff. 128–29: qtd. Coffin 1996, 32.

50. Qtd. by Kaplan 1988, 360, from document in Archives Nationales (Paris), F^{12} 781c.

51. Letter of July 10, 1719, Dossier biographique de Bignon, Archives de l'Académie des Sciences.

52. The drawing that corresponds to this engraving is in the Institut album (MS 1064, f. ci [A]; f. cii); (A) is the drawing for the other unpublished version, and (B) is the plate. Like many of the other unpublished plates, copies (some annotated by Réaumur) can also be found in the Bibliothèque de l'Arsenal, Gr. Fol. 435ter doss. 13, ff. 4–6; and in the Bibliothèque Nationale de France album, Rés. des Manuscrits, Ma Mat 39, f. 67.

53. Franklin notes twenty in 1725, and eight in 1779 (1884, "Brodeurs-Chasubliers, Découpeurs," 9).

54. The text describing this plate is in Mémoire no. 25, Houghton MS Typ 432.1 (3).

55. "Comment soulager la Fabrique," in Archives nationales, F12, 1441: qtd. Garden 1970, 53; see also Hafter 1979, 57.

56. Crowston's research identifying some fifteen towns where women were admitted to tailors' guilds (2000, 340) suggests that there is likely to be further evidence available relative to other guilds.

57. Sonenscher 1987, 67: from Archives Départementales, Marne, 18B 1349*, February 9, 1781. See also Ogilvie, who describes how unmarried women living independently

in eighteenth-century Württemberg were pejoratively referred to as *Eigenbrötlerinnen* ("own-breaders") and continually harassed by community councils (2004, para. 39).

58. The importance of the quality of the spinning to the manufacture of broadcloth was highlighted in the *Mémoire d'observations sur la fabrication des draps dans les manufactures d'Elbeuf et de Sedan* by Delo Desaunois, a trainee inspector at Sedan in 1756 (see Gayot 1995, 115–16).

59. See Guyard 1985 regarding children in the *Encyclopédie* plates.

60. See François Rabelais, *Pantgruel*, book 2, chap. 16, and *Arlequin lingère du Palais* in *Théâtre de Gherardi*, Amsterdam, 1717, i: 53, both qtd. in Franklin 1884, "Lingères," 10–11.

61. On the labor of children, see the *Encyclopédie* images on papermaking, which represent very young children standing on blocks to reach the benches in the paper mill at Montargis (*Ency. Planches*, vol. 1: "Papetterie, Pl. III.")

62. Regarding eighteenth-century definitions of gender, see, for example, Abensour 1923; Bradley, 1989; Spencer, 1984; Schiebinger 1989 and 2000.

63. Compare with Milliot, 1995;

see, for example, the image from 1746 (by Lagniet) of a milk seller with a large vessel on her head (187).

64. One interesting antecedent is a plate from Florini's 1702 *Œconomus prudens et legalis* (1191), which shows an unmarried woman carrying a great basket of bread on her back, presumably for delivery in the town (reproduced in Ogilvie 2004, para. 14).

65. See Anne Hollander, who remarks that Fragonard's portrayal of women's delicate ankles, rounded feet, and sophisticated shoes shows "some of the curved suggestiveness eventually to have such importance in the eroticism of feet and legs" (1978, 222).

66. Simonton highlights the example of the Wedgwood manufactories in Britain, where women were allotted delicate work such as transferring engravings onto porcelain but were not considered to be "skilled." Wedgwood's own comment on burnishers at the Chelsea manufactory illustrates the circular nature of the arguments concerning gender and trade skills: "I believe it is neither a secret or very curious art for Women only are employed in it" (Simonton 1998, 43).

67. "All these operations [per-

formed by women] are little different from those performed on the kippered herrings [by men]," wrote Duhamel (1769, part 2, vol. 2, sect. 3: 487; regarding payments, see 413–14).

68. See Jacques Jaugeon, "Description et perfection des arts et mestiers," 1704, in ms. 2741, Bibliothèque de l'Institut de France, and *Ency. Planches*, vol. 5: "Gravure."

69. See Sheridan 1992, 51–52, and 2003b, 165–67. In the mid-seventeenth century two proposals were made to impose regulation on the work of engravers, but the opposition of the majority of engravers carried the day (Courboin 1924, vii–ix).

70. He engraved the portrait of Duhamel du Monceau (possibly the one illustrated in a watercolor by Georges Malbeste, reproduced in Jaoul and Pinault 1986, 7), who was responsible for much of the work on our collection; the portrait was exhibited in the Salon of 1767 and praised by Diderot, though he castigated the unfortunate subject (1875, 11: 366). Regarding the Moitte family, see Michaud 1843, 28: 505, and Nagler 1909, 10: 419–20.

71. See, for example, Bibliothèque de l'Institut de France, ms. 1065, f. lxxi, and ms. 1065bis, f. 147.

Manuscript Sources

ARCHIVES DE
L'ACADÉMIE DES
SCIENCES, PARIS

Dossier biographique de Gilles Filleau Des Billettes

Dossier biographique de l'abbé Jean-Paul Bignon

Dossier biographique de René-Antoine Ferchault de Réaumur

Procès-verbaux de l'Académie royale des sciences: "Description des Arts et Métiers. Des Séances de l'année 1695 jusqu'en 1696. Addition, jointe à ce volume de registres."

BIBLIOTHÈQUE DE
L'ARSENAL, PARIS

Gr. Fol. 435 [Album: Descriptions des arts et métiers]

Gr. Fol. 435bis [Album: Descriptions des arts et métiers]

Gr. Fol. 435ter [Album: Descriptions des arts et métiers]

BIBLIOTHÈQUE DE
L'INSTITUT DE FRANCE,
PARIS

Ms. 1064 [Album: Descriptions des arts et métiers]

Ms. 1065 [Album: Descriptions des arts et métiers]

Ms. 1065bis [Album: Descriptions des arts et métiers]

Ms. 2393 "Description d'une des plus considérables papeteries d'Auvergne," [Pierre-Paul Sevin]

Ms. 2741, 424ff. "Description et Perfection Des Arts et Mestiers. Des Arts de Construire Les Caracteres. De Graver Les Poinçons de Lettres. De Fondre Les Lettres. D'Imprimer Les Lettres. et De Relier Les Livres. Tome Premier. Par Monsieur Jaugeon De L'Academie Royale Des Sciences. M. VCCIIII."

BIBLIOTHÈQUE
NATIONALE, PARIS

Dépt. des Estampes, Ms. Ke 82 "Recueil de différentes pêches."

Réserve des Manuscrits. Ma Mat 39. "Planches d'arts et de métiers."

HOUGHTON LIBRARY,
HARVARD UNIVERSITY,
CAMBRIDGE MASS.

MS Typ 432.1 (1) "Collections for the Descriptions . . . des arts et métiers."

Works Cited

Abensour, Léon. 1923. *La Femme et le féminisme avant la Révolution.* Paris: Ernest Leroux.

Adams, David. 2004. Slavery in the *Encyclopédie.* In *The enterprise of Enlightenment: a tribute to David Williams from his friends,* ed. Terry Pratt and David McCallam. Bern: Peter Lang.

Agricola, Georgius. 1950. *De re metallica.* Trans. Herbert Clark Hoover and Lou Henry Hoover. New York: Dover.

Albistur, Maïté, and Daniel Armogathe. 1977. *Histoire du féminisme français du moyen âge à nos jours.* Paris: Des Femmes.

Amman, Jost, and Hans Sachs. 1973. *The book of trades* [*Ständebuch*]. Introd. by Benjamin Rifkin. New York: Dover.

Balkestein, Marjan. 1995. The place of textile production in the hierarchy of trades and crafts: some print series from the Middle Ages, seventeenth and eighteenth centuries. In *Occupational titles and their classification: the case of the textile trade in past times,* ed. Herman Diederiks and Marjan Balkestein. Göttingen: Max-Planck-Institut für Geschichte.

Barnes, Donna R., ed. 1988. *People at work: seventeenth-century Dutch art.* New York: Hofstra University.

———. 1995. Jan Gillisz van Vliet: workers in the workplace. *Kroniek van het Rembrandthuis* 2: 1–17.

Barthes, Roland. 1964. Image, raison, déraison. In *L'Univers de l'Encyclopédie.* Paris: Libraires Associés.

———. 1993. *Œuvres complètes.* Paris: Seuil.

Benabou, Erica-Marie. 1987. *La Prostitution et la police des mœurs au XVIIIe siècle.* Paris: Perrin.

Benot, Yves. 1981. *Diderot, de l'athéisme à l'anticolonialisme.* Paris: Maspero.

Berg, Maxime. 1994. *The age of manufactures, 1700–1820.* London: Routledge.

Boxer, Marilyn J., and Jean H. Quataert, eds. 2000. *Connecting spheres: European women in a globalising world, 1500 to the present.* New York: Oxford University Press.

Bradley, Harriet. 1989. *Men's work, women's work.* Cambridge: Polity Press.

Brewer, Daniel. 1993. *The discourse of Enlightenment in eighteenth-century France.* Cambridge: Cambridge University Press.

Burton, Anthony. 1976. *The Miners.* London: André Deutsch.

Cayez, Pierre. 1978. *Métiers Jacquard et hauts fourneaux: aux origines de l'industrie lyonnaise*. Lyon: Presses Universitaires de Lyon.

Clark, Alice. 1992. *Working life of women in the seventeenth century*. Introd. by Amy Louise Erickson. London: Routledge.

Cochrane, Archibald, Earl of Dundonald. 1793. *Description of the estate and abbey of Culross*. Edinburgh: N.p.

Coffin, Judith. 1994. Gender and the guild order: the garment trades in eighteenth-century Paris. *Journal of Economic History* 54 (4): 768–93.

———. 1996. *The politics of women's work: the Paris garment trades, 1750–1915*. Princeton, N.J.: Princeton University Press.

Cohen, Sarah R. 2004. Chardin's fur: painting, materialism and the question of animal soul. *Eighteenth-century Studies* 38 (1): 39–61.

Cole, Arthur H., and George B. Watts. 1952. *The handicrafts of France as recorded in the* Descriptions des arts et métiers *(1761–1788)*. Boston: Baker Library.

Cole, William. 1931. *A journal of my journey to Paris in the year 1765*. Ed. Francis Griffin Stokes. London: Constable.

Collins, James B. 1989. The economic role of women in seventeenth-century France. *French Historical Studies* 16 (2): 436–70.

Courboin, François. 1924. *Histoire illustrée de la gravure en France*. Part 2. Paris: Le Garrec.

Crown, Patricia. 2002. Sporting with clothes; John Collet's satirical prints in the 1770s. *Eighteenth-century Life* 26 (1): 119–30.

Crowston, Clare Haru. 2000. Engendering the guilds: seamstresses, tailors, and the clash of corporate identities in Old Regime France. *French Historical Studies* 23 (Spring): 339–71.

———. 2001. *Fabricating women: the seamstresses of Old Regime France, 1675–1791*. Durham: Duke University Press.

Dacier, Émile. 1944. *La gravure française*. Paris: Larousse.

Dardel, Éric. 1941a. *État des pêches maritimes sur les côtes occidentales de la France au début du XVIIIe siècle d'après les procès-verbaux de visite de l'inspecteur des Pêches Le Masson du Parc (1723–1732)*. Paris: Presses Universitaires de France.

———. 1941b. *La Pêche harenguière en France. Étude d'histoire économique et sociale*. Paris: Presses Universitaires de France.

Darnton, Robert. 1979. *The business of Enlightenment: a publishing history of the* Encyclopédie, *1755–1800*. Cambridge, Mass.: Harvard University Press.

———. 1985. *The great cat massacre and other episodes in French cultural history*. New York: Vintage Books.

Davis, Natalie Zemon. 1986. Women in the crafts in sixteenth-century Lyon. In *Women and work in preindustrial Europe*, ed. Barbara A Hanawalt. Bloomington: Indiana University Press.

———. 1987. Women on top. In *Society and culture in early modern France*. Cambridge: Polity Press.

Demetz, Peter. 1963. Defenses of Dutch painting and the theory of realism. *Comparative Literature* 15 (2) Spring: 97–115.

Descriptions des arts et métiers, faites et approuvées par Messieurs de l'Académie royale des sciences avec figures. 1761–89. 76 vols. (See separate listings of volumes under authors' names).

Diderot, Denis. 1875–1877. *Œuvres complètes*. Ed. J. Assézat. Vols. 10 and 11. Paris: Garnier.

———. 1955–70. *Correspondance*. Ed. Georges Roth and Jean Varloot. 16 vols. Paris: Éd. de Minuit.

Dixon, Emily. 1895. Craftswomen in the *Livres des métiers*. *Economic Journal* 5 (18) June: 208–28.

Dubos, abbé Jean-Baptiste. 1733. *Réflexions critiques sur la poésie et la peinture*. Paris: P.-J. Mariette.

Dudin [?]. 1772. *L'Art du relieur doreur de livres*. [*Descriptions des arts et métiers*]. [Paris]: L. F. Delatour.

Duhamel Du Monceau, Henri-Louis. 1753–61. *Traité de la culture des terres suivant les principes de M. Tull*. Paris: H.-L. Guérin and L.-F. Delatour.

———. 1762a. *Art du cartier*. [*Descriptions des arts et métiers*]. N.p.

———. 1762b. *Eléments d'agriculture*. 2 vols. Paris: H.-L. Guérin and L.-F. Delatour.

———. 1764. *Art du chandelier*. [*Descriptions des arts et métiers*]. N.p.

———. 1765. *Art de la draperie, principalement pour ce qui regarde les draps fins*. [*Descriptions des arts et métiers*]. Paris: H.-L. Guérin and L.-F. Delatour.

———. 1766. *Art de faire les tapis, façon de Turquie, connus sous le nom de tapis de la savonnerie*. [*Descriptions des arts et métiers*]. [Paris]: L. F. Delatour.

———. 1769–[1782]. *Traité général des pesches, et histoire des poissons qu'elles fournissent, tant pour la subsistance des hommes, que pour plusieurs autres usages qui ont rapport aux arts et au commerce*. [Descriptions des arts et métiers]. Paris: Saillant, Nyon and Desaint.

———. 1773. *Art du potier de terre*. [*Descriptions des arts et métiers*]. [Paris]: L. F. Delatour.

———. 1774. *Art du savonnier*. [*Descriptions des arts et métiers*]. [Paris]: L. F. Delatour.

Encyclopédie, ou dictionnaire raisonné des sciences, des arts et des métiers, par une société de gens de lettres. 1751–65. Ed. Denis Diderot and Jean Le Rond d'Alembert. 17 vols. Paris: Libraires associés. (Abbreviation *Ency*.)

Encyclopédie méthodique. Manufactures, arts et métiers. 1782–91. Paris: Panckoucke; Liège: Plomteux.

Endrei, Walter. 1995. Jean Errard (1554–1610) and his book of machines: *Le Premier livre des instruments mathématiques méchaniques* of 1584. *History of Technology* 17: 179–90.

Eriksen, Svend. 1959. *En haandvaerkets bog fra det 18. aarhundrede: Descriptions des arts et métiers 1760–1788*. [Copenhagen]: N.p.

Fairchilds, Cissie. 1984. Women and family. In *French Women and the Age of Enlightenment*, ed. Samia I. Spencer. Bloomington: Indiana University Press.

———. 1993. The production and marketing of populuxe goods in eighteenth-century Paris. In *Consumption and the world of goods*, ed. John Brewer and Roy Porter. London: Routledge.

Farge, Arlette. 1977. Les Artisans malade de leur travail. *Annales E.S.C.* 5: 993–1006.

———. 1996. *Fragile lives: violence, power and solidarity in eighteenth-century Paris*. Cambridge: Polity Press.

Fausto-Sterling, Anne. 2000. Gender, race and nation: the comparative anatomy of "Hottentot" women in Europe, 1815–17. In *Feminism and the body*, ed. Londa Schiebinger. Oxford: Oxford University Press.

Fougeroux de Bondaroy, Auguste-Denis. 1771. *Observations faites par ordre du Roi sur les côtes de Normandie au sujet des effets pernicieux qui sont attribués dans le Pays de Caux à la fumée de varech lorsqu'on brûle cette plante pour la réduire en soude*. [Paris]: N.p.

———. 1772. *L'Art du coutelier en ouvrages communs*. [*Descriptions des arts et métiers*]. [Paris]: L. F. Delatour.

Franklin, Alfred. 1884. *Les Corporations ouvrières de Paris, du XIIe au XVIIIe siècle, histoire, statuts, armoiries, d'après des documents originaux ou inédits*. Paris: Firmin-Didot.

Garden, Maurice. 1970. *Lyon et les Lyonnais au XVIIIe siècle*. Paris: Flammarion.

Gardey, Françoise. 1964a. Notices des artistes dans l'*Encyclopédie*. In *L'Univers de l'*Encyclopédie. *135 planches de l'*Encyclopédie *de Diderot et d'Alembert*. Paris: Libraires Associés.

———. 1964b. Quelques planches des *Descriptions des arts et métiers* de l'Académie des Sciences, au cabinet des Estampes. *Nouvelles de l'Estampe* 3(6): 166–69.

Garsault, François-Alexandre-Pierre de. 1767. *Art du perruquier, contenant la façon de la barbe; la coupe des cheveux; la construction des perruques d'hommes et de femmes; le perruquier en vieux; et le baigneur-étuviste*. [*Descriptions des arts et métiers*]. N.p.

———. 1769. *Art du tailleur, contenant le tailleur d'habits d'hommes; les culottes de peau, le tailleur de corps de femme et enfants, la couturière, et la marchande de modes*. [*Descriptions des arts et métiers*]. [Paris]: L. F. Delatour.

———. 1771. *L'Art de la lingère*. [*Descriptions des arts et métiers*]. [Paris]: L. F. Delatour.

Gayne, Mary K. 2004. Illicit wig-making in eighteenth-century Paris. *Eighteenth-century Studies* 38 (1): 119–38.

Gayot, Gérard. 1995. Les Mots pour dire les gestes de la belle ouvrage dans la draperie française (XVIIème–XVIIIème). In *Occupational titles and their classification: the case of the textile trade in past times*, ed. Herman Diederiks and Marjan Balkestein. Göttingen: Max-Planck-Institut für Geschichte.

Gille, Bertrand. 1956. Machines. In *A history of technology*, ed. C. Singer et al. Vol. 2. Oxford: Clarendon Press.

Goldin, Claudia, and Sokoloff, Kenneth. 1982. Women, children and industrialisation in the early Republic. *Journal of Economic History* 42: 741c–74.

Goodman, Jordan. 1993. Cloth, gender and industrial organization: toward an anthropology of silk-workers in early modern Europe. In *La seta in Europa secx. XII–XX: atti della 24esima settimana di studi, Istituto Internazionale di Storia Economica "F. Datini," 4–9 May 1992*, ed. Simonetta Cavaciocchi. Florence: Le Monnier.

Goubert, Pierre. 1973. *The ancien regime, French society, 1600–1750*. Trans. Steve Cox. New York: Weidenfeld and Nicolson.

Guilbert, Madeleine. 1966. *Les Fonctions des femmes dans l'industrie*. Paris: Mouton.

Guillerme, Jacques, and Jan Sebestik. 1968. *Les Commencements de la technologie*. Paris: Thalès.

Gullickson, Gay. 1986. *Spinners and weavers of Auffay: rural industry and the sexual division of labor in a French village, 1750–1850*. Cambridge: Cambridge University Press.

———. 1990. Love and power in the proto-industrial family. In *Markets and manufacture in early industrial Europe*, ed. Maxime Berg. London: Routledge.

Guyard, Michel. 1985. La Représentation du travail des enfants dans les planches de l'*Encyclopédie* de Diderot. *Les Cahiers Haut-marnais* 163: 24–35.

Hafter, Daryl M. 1979. The "programmed" brocade loom and the decline of the drawgirl. In *Dynamos and virgins revisited. Women and technological change in history: an anthology*, ed. Martha Moore Trescott. Metuchen, N.J.: Scarecrow Press.

———. 1989. Gender formation from a working-class viewpoint: guildwomen in 18th-century Rouen. *Proceedings of the Annual Meeting of the Western Society for French History* 16: 415–22.

———. 1995. Women who wove in the eighteenth-century silk industry of Lyon. In *European women and preindustrial craft*, ed. Daryl Hafter. Bloomington: Indiana University Press.

———. 1997. Female masters in the ribbonmaking guild of eighteenth-century Rouen. *French Historical Studies* 20 (1): 1–14.

———. 2001. Women in the underground business of eighteenth-century Lyon. *Enterprise and Society* 2 (1): 11–40.

Hanawalt, Barbara A., ed. 1986. *Women and work in preindustrial Europe*. Bloomington: Indiana University Press.

Harvey, Karen. 2004. *Reading sex in the eighteenth century: bodies and gender in English erotic culture*. Cambridge: Cambridge University Press.

Héritier-Augé, Françoise. 1989. Older women, stout-hearted women, women of substance. In *Fragments for a history of the human body*, part 3, ed. Michel Freher. New York: Zone Books.

Hill, Bridget. 1984. *Eighteenth-century women: an anthology*. London: Allen and Unwin.

———. 1989. *Women and work in eighteenth-century England*. Oxford: B. Blackwell.

Hills, Richard L. 1993. From cocoon to cloth: the technology of silk production. In *La seta in Europa secx. XII-XX: atti della 24esima Settimana di Studi, Istituto Internazionale di Storia Economica "F. Datini," 4–9 May 1992*, ed. Simonetta Cavaciocchi. Florence: Le Monnier.

Holland, Henry. 1808. *General view of the agriculture of Cheshire*. London: Board of Agriculture.

Hollander, Anne. 1978. *Seeing through clothes*. New York: Viking Press.

Huard, Georges. 1952. Les Planches de l'*Encyclopédie* et celles de la *Description des Arts et métiers* de l'Académie des Sciences. In *L'Encyclopédie et le progrès des sciences et des techniques*, ed. Suzanne Delorme and René Taton. Paris: Presses Universitaires de France.

Hudson, Pat, and W. R. Lee. 1990. *Women's work and the family economy in historical perspective*. Manchester: Manchester University Press.

Hufton, Olwen. 1975. Women and the family economy in eighteenth-century France. *French Historical Studies* 9: 1–22.

———. 1984. Women without men: widows and spinsters in Britain and France in the eighteenth century. *Journal of Family History* 9 (Winter): 355–76.

———. 1993. Women, work and family. In vol. 3 of *A history of women in the west*, ed. Natalie Zemon Davis and Arlette Farge. Cambridge, Mass.: Harvard University Press, Belknap Press.

Humphries, Jane. 1984. Protective legislation, the capitalist state, and working class men: the case of the 1842 Mines Regulation Act. *Feminist Review* 7: 1–33.

Hunt, Lynn. 2000. Freedom of dress

in revolutionary France. In *Feminism and the body,* ed. Londa Schiebinger. Oxford: Oxford University Press.

Hutton, William. 1817. *History of Derby.* London: Nichols.

Jammes, André 1961. *La Réforme de la typographie royale sous Louis XIV: le Grandjean.* Paris: Paul Jammes.

Jaoul, Martine, and Madeleine Pinault. 1982. Sources inédites de la Houghton Library, Université de Harvard. *Ethnologie française* 12: 335–58.

———. 1986. Sources inédites provenant du château de Denainvilliers (2). *Ethnologie française* 16: 7–38.

John, Angela V. 1984. *By the sweat of their brow: women workers at Victorian coal mines.* London: Routledge and Kegan Paul.

Jones, Jennifer. 1996. *Coquettes* and *grisettes:* women buying and selling in ancien régime Paris. In *The sex of things: gender and consumption in historical perspective,* ed. Victoria de Grazia and Ellen Furlough. Berkeley: University of California Press.

———. 2004. *Sexing* La Mode*: gender, fashion and commercial culture in Old Regime France.* Oxford: Berg.

Kaplan, Steven L. 1981. The luxury guilds in Paris in the eighteenth century. *Francia* 9: 257–98.

———. 1988 . Les Corporations, les "faux ouvriers" et le Faubourg St. Antoine au XVIIIe siècle. *Annales E.S.C.* 43 (Mar.–Apr.): 353–78.

Koepp, Cynthia J. 1986. The alphabetical order in Diderot's *Encyclopédie.* In *Work in France: representations, meaning, organization, and practice,* ed. Steven L. Kaplan and Cynthia J. Koepp. Ithaca: Cornell University Press.

Lalande, Joseph Jérôme Le Français de. [c. 1762]. *Art de faire le papier.* [*Descriptions des arts et métiers*]. N.p.

Lespinasse, René de, ed. 1886–97. *Les Métiers et corporations de la ville de Paris.* 3 vols. Paris: Imprimerie Nationale.

Lough, John. 1971. *L'Encyclopédie.* London: Longman.

Malouin, Paul-Jacques. 1767. *Description et détails des arts du meunier, du vermicelier et du boulenger; avec une histoire abrégée de la boulangerie, et un dictionnaire de ces arts.* [*Descriptions des arts et métiers*]. N.p.

Malueg, Sara Ellen Procious. 1984. Women in the *Encyclopédie.* In *French women and the Age of Enlightenment,* ed. Samia I. Spencer. Bloomington: Indiana University Press.

Marly, Diana de. 1990. *Dress in North America.* New York: Holmes and Meier.

Mercier, Louis Sebastien. 1782–88. *Tableau de Paris.* Amsterdam: N.p.

Michaud, Louis Gabriel, ed. 1843. *Biographie universelle ancienne et moderne.* Paris: Leipzig.

Milliot, Vincent. 1994. Le Travail sans le geste. Les Représentations iconographiques des petits métiers parisiens (XVI–XVIIIe s.). *Revue d'histoire moderne et contemporaine* 41(1): 5–28.

———. 1995. *Les* Cris de Paris *ou le peuple travesti. Les Représentations des petits métiers parisiens (XVIe–XVIIIe siècles).* Paris: Publications de la Sorbonne.

Morand, Jean-François-Clément. 1768–79. *L'Art d'exploiter les mines de charbon de terre.* [*Descriptions des arts et métiers*]. N.p.

Musgrave, Elizabeth. 1997. Women and the craft guilds in eighteenth-century Nantes. In *The artisan and the European town,* ed. Geoffrey Crossick. Aldershot: Scolar Press.

Nagler, G. K., ed. 1909. *Neues allegemeines Künstler-Lexikon.* Linz.

Nochlin, Linda. 1971. *Realism.* Harmondsworth: Penguin.

———1999. *Representing women.* London: Thames and Hudson.

Nollet, Jean Antoine, abbé. 1765. *L'Art de faire des chapeaux.* [*Descriptions des arts et métiers*]. N.p.

Ogilvie, Sheilagh. 1990. Women and proto-industrialisation in a corporate society: Württemberg woollen weaving, 1590–1760. In *Women's work and the family economy in historical perspective,* ed. Pat Hudson and W. R. Lee. Manchester: Manchester University Press.

———. 2004. How does social capital affect women's guilds and communities in early modern Germany? *American Historical Review* 109 (2) April. http://www.historycooperative.org/journals/ahr/109.2/ogilvie.html (accessed March 22, 2007).

Paulet, J. 1773–78. *L'Art du fabriquant d'étoffes de soie.* [*Descriptions des arts et métiers*]. [Paris]: L. F. Delatour.

Paysages, paysans. *L'Art de la terre en

*Europe du moyen âge au XXe siè-
cle.* 1994. Dir. Emmanuel Le Roy
Ladurie. Paris: B.N.F./ R.M.N.

Perret, Jean-Jacques. 1771. *L'Art du
coutelier. Première partie.* [*Descriptions des arts et métiers*]. [Paris]: L.
F. Delatour.

Pinault Sørensen, Madeleine. 1987.
Diderot et les enquêtes de Le
Masson du Parc. In *La Mer au siè-
cle des encyclopédies. Actes recueil-
lis et présentés par Jean Balcou.*
Paris: Champion; Geneva:
Slatkine.

———. 1988. A propos des
planches de l'*Encyclopédie*. *Studies on Voltaire and the Eighteenth
Century* 254: 351–62.

———. 1992. La Métamorphoses
des planches de l'*Encyclopédie*:
quelques exemples. *Recherches sur
Diderot et sur l'Encyclopédie* 12:
98–112.

———. 2002. Les Dessinateurs de
l'Académie royale des sciences.
In *Règlement, usages et science
dans la France de l'absolutisme.
Actes du colloque international or-
ganisé par l'Académie des
sciences . . . 1999,* ed. Christiane
Demeulenaere-Douyère and Eric
Brian. Paris: Lavoisier.

———. 2005. Premiers regards sur les
planches de l'*Encyclopédie*
d'Yverdon: rapprochements et
différences avec l'*Encyclopédie* de
Paris. In *L'*Encyclopédie *d'Yverdon et sa résonance européenne,* ed.
Jean-Daniel Candaux et al.
Geneva: Slatkine.

Pinchbeck, Ivy. 1969. *Women workers
and the industrial revolution,
1750–1850.* London: Frank
Cass.

Pomeau, René, ed. 1980. *Candide ou
l'optimisme.* Oxford: Voltaire
Foundation.

Prost de Royer, Antoine-François.
1778. *Mémoire sur la conservation
des enfants.* Lyon: Aimé De-
laroche.

Proust, Jacques. 1957. La Documentation technique de Diderot dans
l'*Encyclopédie*. *Revue d'histoire lit-
téraire de la France* 57: 335–52.

———. 1962. *Diderot et l'*Encyclopédie. Paris: Colin (Reprint
Slatkine: Geneva, 1982).

———. 1973. L'Image du peuple au
travail dans les planches de l'*En-
cyclopédie*. In *Images du peuple au
XVIIIe siècle: colloque d'Aix-en-
Provence, 25 et 26 octobre 1969.*
Paris: Colin.

———. 1985. *Marges d'une utopie:
pour une lecture critique des
planches de l'*Encyclopédie. Co-
gnac: Le Temps qu'il fait.

Ramazzini, Bernardino. 1700. *De
morbis artificum diatrib.* Modena:
Capponi.

Raynal, Guillaume-Thomas. 1781.
*Histoire philosophique et politique
des établissemens et du commerce
des Européens dans les deux Indes.*
Geneva: J.-L. Pellet.

Réaumur, René-Antoine Ferchault
de. N.d. *Art de l'épinglier. Par M.
de Réaumur. Avec des additions de
M. Duhamel du Monceau, et des
remarques extraites des Mémoires
de M. Perronet, Inspecteur Général
des Ponts et Chaussées.* [*Descriptions des arts et métiers*]. N.p.

*Recueil de planches de l'*Encyclopédie,
par ordre de matières. 1782–91.
Paris: Panckouke; Liège: Plomteux.

*Recueil de planches sur les sciences, les
arts libéraux et les arts mécaniques,*
avec leur explication. 1762–72.
Ed. Denis Diderot. 11 vols. Paris:
Libraires associés. (Abbreviation
Ency. Planches)

Reddy, William R. 1984. *The rise of
market culture: the textile trade and
French society, 1750–1900.* London: Cambridge University
Press.

Reno, Jr., Edward A., and Betty H.
Erb. 1974. *The* Descriptions des
arts et métiers: *a reel index and
guide to the microform edition.*
New Haven: New Haven Re-
search Publications.

Reynaud, Marie-Hélène. 1981. *Les
Moulins à papier d'Annonay à l'ère
préindustrielle.* Annonay: Editions
du Vivarais.

Rifkin, Benjamin. 1973. Introd. to
The book of trades [*Ständebuch*],
by Jost Amman and Hans Sachs.
New York: Dove.

Roberts, Michael. 1979. "Sickles and
scythes: women's work and
men's work at harvest time." *History Workshop* 7: 3–28.

———. 1985. "Words they are
women, and deeds they are men":
images of work and gender in
early modern England. In *Women
and work in pre-industrial England,* ed. Lindsey Charles and
Lorna Duffin. London: Croom
Helm.

Roche, Daniel. 1986. Work, fellow-
ship and some economic realities
of eighteenth-century France. In
*Work in France: representations,
meaning, organization, and practice,* ed. Steven Laurence Kaplan
and Cynthia J. Koepp. Ithaca:
Cornell University Press.

———. 1989. *La Culture des apparences.* Paris: Fayard.

Roland de la Platière, [Jean-Marie]. 1780. *L'Art du fabricant d'étoffes en laines rases et seches, unies et croisées*. Paris: Moutard.

Rosenband, Leonard N. 2000. *Papermaking in eighteenth-century France: management, labor, and revolution at the Montgolfier Mill, 1761–1805*. Baltimore: Johns Hopkins University Press.

Rousseau, Jean-Jacques. 1969. *Émile. Œuvres complètes*, vol. 4. Paris: Gallimard (Pléiade).

Saint-Aubin, Charles Germain de. 1770. *L'Art du brodeur*. [*Descriptions des arts et métiers*]. [Paris]: L. F. Delatour.

Salomon-Bayet, Claire. 1970. Un Préambule théorique à une académie des arts. *Revue d'histoire des sciences et de leurs applications* 23: 229–50.

Salmon, [?]. 1788. *Art du potier d'étain*. [*Descriptions des arts et métiers*]. Paris: Moutard.

Sargentson, Carolyn. 1996. *Merchants and luxury markets: the Marchands Merciers of eighteenth-century Paris*. London: Victoria and Albert Museum.

Savary des Bruslons, Jacques. 1762. *Dictionnaire universel de commerce*. Geneva: Philibert.

Schiebinger, Londa. 1989. *The mind has no sex? Women in the origins of modern science*. Cambridge, Mass.: Harvard University Press.

———. 1993. *Nature's body: gender in the making of modern science*. Cambridge, Mass.: Harvard University Press.

———, ed. 2000. Feminism and the body. Oxford: Oxford University Press.

Schwab, Richard N. 1984. *Inventory of Diderot's Encyclopédie*. Vol. 7: *Inventory of the plates. Studies on Voltaire and the Eighteenth Century* 223. Oxford: Voltaire Foundation.

Segalen, Martine. 1983. *Love and power in the peasant family: rural France in the nineteenth century*. Oxford: Blackwell.

Seguin, Jean-Pierre. 1964. Courte histoire des planches de l'*Encyclopédie*. In *L'Univers de l'*Encyclopédie. *135 planches de l'*Encyclopédie *de Diderot et d'Alembert*. Paris: Libraires Associés.

Sewell, William Hamilton. 1980. *Work and revolution in France: the language of labor from the Old Regime to 1848*. Cambridge: Cambridge University Press.

———. 1986. Visions of labor: illustrations of the mechanical arts before, in, and after Diderot's *Encyclopédie*. In *Work in France: representations, meaning, organization, and practice*, ed. Steven Laurence Kaplan and Cynthia J. Koepp. Ithaca: Cornell University Press.

Seznec, Jean. 1965. Diderot and historical painting. In *Aspects of the eighteenth century*, ed. Earl R. Wasserman. Baltimore: Johns Hopkins University Press.

Shahar, Shulamith. 1983. The Fourth Estate: a history of women in the Middle Ages. London: Methuen.

Sheridan, Geraldine. 1992. Women in the book trade in eighteenth-century France. *British Journal for Eighteenth-century Studies* 15.1 (Spring): 51–69.

———. 2001. Women in the book trades: an untold story. In *Writing the history of women's writing: toward an international approach*, ed. Susan van Dijk, Lia van Gemert, and Sheila Ottway. Amsterdam: Royal Netherlands Academy of Arts and Sciences.

———. 2003a. Rationalist iconography and the representation of women's work in the *Encyclopédie*. *Diderot Studies* 29: 101–35.

———. 2003b. Views of women at work by the royal academicians: the collection *Descriptions des arts et métiers* (1761–89). *Studies in Eighteenth-century Culture* 32: 155–91.

———. 2007. Technological utopia in the plates of the *Encyclopédie*. In *Exploring the utopian impulse: essays on utopian thought and practice*, ed. Michael Griffin and Tom Moylan. Bern: Peter Lang.

———. 2008. Recording technology in France: the *Descriptions des arts*, methodological innovation and lost opportunities at the turn of the eighteenth century. *Cultural and Social History* 5: 329–54.

Simonton, Deborah. 1998. *A history of European women's work, 1700 to the present*. London: Routledge.

Smith, Adam. 1937. *The wealth of nations*, ed. Edwin Cannan. New York: Random House.

Snell, Keith D. M. 1985. *Annals of the labouring poor*. Cambridge: Cambridge University Press.

Solomon-Godeau, Abigail. 2001. Realism revisited. In *Self and history: a tribute to Linda Nochlin*, ed. Aruna D'Souza. London: Thames and Hudson.

Sonenscher Michael. 1983. Work and wages in Paris in the eighteenth century. In *Manufacture in town and country before the factory,* ed. Maxine Berg, Pat Hudson, and Michael Sonenscher. Cambridge: Cambridge University Press.

———. 1987. *The hatters of eighteenth-century France.* Berkeley: University of California Press.

———. 1989. *Work and wages: natural law, politics, and eighteenth-century French trades.* Cambridge: Cambridge University Press.

Samia I. Spencer, ed. 1984. *French women and the Age of Enlightenment.* Bloomington: Indiana University Press.

Stone-Ferrier, Linda. 1988. Origins and functions of seventeenth-century Dutch images of labor. In *People at work: seventeenth-century Dutch art,* ed. Donna R. Barnes. New York: Hofstra University.

Sturdy, David. 1995. *Science and social status. The members of the Académie des Sciences, 1666–1750.* Woodbridge: Boydell Press.

Suite du recueil de planches sur les sciences, les arts libéraux et les arts mécaniques, avec leur explication. 1777. Paris: Panckouke, Stoupe et Brunet; Amsterdam: Rey. (Abbreviation *Ency. Planches Suite*)

Sussman, George D. 1982. *Selling mother's milk: the wet-nursing business in France, 1715–1914.* Urbana: University of Illinois Press.

Sweets, John F. 1995. The lacemakers of Le Puy in the nineteenth century. In *European women and preindustrial craft,* ed. Daryl Hafter. Bloomington: Indiana University Press.

Thompson, Paul, Tony Wailey, and Trevor Lummis. 1983. *Living the fishing.* London: Routledge and Kegan Paul.

Tilly, Louise A., and Scott, Joan W. 1987. *Women, work and family.* New York: Methuen.

Truant, Cynthia. 1986. Journeymen and their rites in the Old Regime workplace. In *Work in France: representations, meaning, organization, and practice,* ed. Steven L. Kaplan and Cynthia J. Koepp. Ithaca: Cornell University Press.

———. 1988. The guildwomen of Paris: gender, power and sociability in the Old Regime. *Proceedings of the Annual Meeting of the Western Society for French History* 15: 130–38.

Vanja, Christina. 1993. Mining women in early modern European society. In *The workplace before the factory: artisans and proletarians, 1500–1800,* ed. Thomas Max Safley and Leonard N. Rosenband. Ithaca: Cornell University Press.

Vardi, Liana. 1993a. Construing the harvest: gleaners, farmers and officials in early modern France. *American Historical Review* 98 (December): 1424–47.

———. 1993b. *The land and the loom: peasants and profit in north-ern France, 1680–1800.* Durham: Duke University Press.

———. 1996. Imagining the harvest in early modern Europe. *American Historical Review* 101 (December): 1357–97.

Villermé, Louis-René. 1840. *Tableau de l'état physique et moral des ouvriers employés dans les manufactures de coton, de laine et de soie.* Paris: Renouard.

Voltaire, François-Marie Arouet de. 1768–77. *Collection complète des œuvres de M. de Voltaire,* Vol. 24. Geneva: [Cramer].

Wahrman, Dror. 1998. Percy's prologue: from gender play to gender panic in eighteenth-century England. *Past and Present* 159 (May): 113–60

Walsh. Linda. 1999. Charles Le Brun, "art dictator of France." In *Academies, museums and canons of art,* ed. Gill Perry and Colin Cunningham. New Haven: Yale University Press.

Watts, George B. 1958. The *Encyclopédie méthodique. PMLA* 73: 348–66.

Wiesner, Merry E. 2000. *Women and gender in early modern Europe.* Cambridge: Cambridge University Press.

Young, Iris Marion. 1990. *Throwing like a girl and other essays in feminist philosophy and social theory.* Bloomington: Indiana University Press.

Index

Page numbers in italics refer to illustrations.

Abbeville, 58
Abensour, Léon, 81, 203–204
abortion, 26
Académie Royale de Peinture et de Sculpture, 16, 233n27
Académie Royale des Sciences, 31, 66, 145, 150, 156, 162, 197
    Art de faire le papier, 187–192, *188–192*
    Descriptions des arts et métiers, 3–10, 15, 17, 21, 25, 27–29, 53, 81, 83, 85, 89, 93, 99, 101, 107, 112, 116–117, 119, 121, 131–132, 140–142, 150, 159, *176*, 179, 185–186, 194, 210–211, 213, 225–227, 232n8, 232n9, 232n11, 232n12, 232n15, 232n20, 233n25, 233n31
accounting, 204, 205. *See also* bookkeepers
Agricola, *De re metallica*, 5–6, 39, 124, 129
agriculture, 11, 21–24, 22–23, 29–35, *30*, *32*, 233n25
aides, 170
aiguillers, 131, 132, *134*, 135. *See also* Guild of Pin Makers
aissauges, 44
Alençon, 81
Aliamet, Jacques, 226
Amman, Jost, 13
Antony, 127, 129
apprenticeship, 76, 77, 80, 81, 89, 144, 145, 171, 210, 225–226, 233n32
aqueresses, 45
argenteurs, *98*
arracheuses, 119
arrondisseuses, 87
L'Art du filtier, 152, *154*
Art du savonnier, 196
artisanal trades, 75–140, 203–205, 207, 218, 226, 233n33. *See also* craftspeople; *specific trades*
Aubusson, 186, 187, 194, 194–195, 218
authority, 227
Auvergne, 185, 187
Aveline, Antoine, *111*

Babeau, Albert, *Bourgeouis d'autrefois*, 204
bait, gathering, 45, *47*, *48*, 48, 49, *50*
bakers. *See boulangères*
Barnes, Donna, 14, 220
barrow-women, *37*
Barthes, Roland, 4, 12, 15, 17, 19, 206–207, 226, 233–234n35
Bastille, 4
batteurs d'or, 76, 99, *100*, 100, 100, *100*. *See also* Guild of Gold Beaters
Bayeux, 44
Beaujolais, 143
belt-makers. *See ceinturiers*
Benabou, Erica-Marie, 82, 206
Bénard, Robert, *147*, *155*, *157*, 159, *159*, *160*, *162*, *163*, *164*, *167*, *169*, *213*, 233n31
Berg, Maxime, 183, 184, 187
Bernardin de Saint Pierre, Henri, 34

Berthault, Pierre Gabriel, *109*, *212*
Bertin, Rose, 211
berwetresses, 38
Bibliothèque Nationale, Paris, 45
Bignon, abbé Jean-Paul, 5, 6, 83
bimbelotiers, 83, *84*, 85, 135
binblottiers. See bimbelotiers
birth rates, 228
blanching workers. *See blanchisseurs de cire*
blanchisseurs de cire, 125, 127, *127*, 127, *127*, *128*, 129, 217, 219
bodies
    female, 219, 220–223
    working, 12
Bologna, 141, 172
bone, 218
bonnes à tout faire, 23
book binders. *See relieurs*
bookkeepers, 203, 205
Book of Hours, 10
book trades, 4
Bosse, Abraham, 14
botteresses, *38*, 39, *39*
Bouchardon, Edmé, *Vendeuse d'eau de vie*, 14
bouchonniers, 17, 205, 214, *215*, 216, 218
boulangères, 205, 213–214, *214*
Boulton, Matthew, 26
bouraques, 53
boutiques. See retail merchants
boutonniers-passementiers, 76, 112, 114, *114*, 114, *115*, 136–137, 175. *See also* Guild of Passementiers-Button Makers
Boutros, Nabil, *110*
boyaudiers, *139*
braid making. *See passementiers*
Bretez, Louis, *84*, *94*, *95*, *131*, 139, *140*, 150, 152, *152*, *154*
    "Les Blinblottiers Levé à Saumur", 83
Brewer, Daniel, 221
brocheuses, 101
brodeurs, 15, 76, 82, 83, 105, *106*, 107, *108*, 224. *See also* Guild of Embroiderers

Brueghel, Pieter, 10, 11, 220
Bugey, 143, 144
butter-making, 31, *32*, 33
button makers. *See boutonniers*
button mold making, *138*

Cabinet des Estampes (Bibliothèque Nationale), 9
Caen, 227
campagnonnages, 227
candle makers. *See chandelières*
Canton of Auffay, 142
capitation taxes, 82
caqueses, 66
caregivers, 9
carpet makers. *See tapissiers*
carpet manufactories, *193*, 194–195
carriage makers, 121, *121*
cartiers, 121, 122, *122*, 122, *123*
categories, 18–19
catgut making (for rackets and musical instruments), 137, 139
caudrettes, 51
Caux region of Normandy, 51, 142, 148, 226
Cayez, Pierre, 143
ceinturiers, 205, 208, 209, 210, *210*
Ceruti, Giacomo, 11
chambrelanes, 81, 83
chandelières, 127, 129, *130*, 184. *See also* Guild of Candle Makers
Chardin, Jean-Baptiste-Siméon, 12, 233n26, 233n27
    Ecureuse, 12
    Pourvoyeuse, 12
chasubliers, 105
Châteaufavier, Michel Laboreys de, 196
Chaufourier, Jean, *94*, *95*, 139, *140*, *152*
Chelsea manufactory, 235n66
chiffonnières, 187
children, 76, 185, 228–229
    child-bearing, 145, 228
    child labor, 185, 186, 187, 218, 235n61
    child-rearing, 17–18, 185, 219, 228

Children's Employment Commission on Mines for Great Britain, 25, 27
classical art, 222–223
clothing, 17, 27, 222–223
cloutiers d'épingles, 80, 132, *133*, 221
coal mining. *See* mining
Cochrane, Archibald, Earl of Dundonald, 26
cocoon unwinding, *156*
Coffin, Judith, 78, 181, 219
Colbert, Jean-Baptiste, 5, 183
Cole, William, 205
colleuses, 85
colliery women, 26. *See also* mining
Collins, James B., 29, 214, 227
colporteurs, 216
commercial activity, 203–216, 218
compensation, 107, 185–186, 187, 194–195, 206, 225
compteuses, 192
concubinage, 82
conspicuous consumption, 211
consumer culture, 203–216, 205–206
Contat, Nicolas, 233n32
cork makers. *See bouchonniers*
corporations, archives of, 3–4
cottage industry, 81, 142, 148
cotton industry, 34, *34*, 148
counters. *See compteuses*
coupeuses (in fan making), 87
coupeuses (in hat making), 119, *120*, 121, 135
Courbet, Gustave, *The Stone Breakers*, 12, 16
couturières, 79, 82, 109–110, *110*, 205, 211, 212, 219, 224. *See also* Guild of Seamstresses
craftspeople, 5, 13, 18, 194, 210. *See also* artisanal trades
craquelotières, 70
Cris de Paris, 14–15, 203, 219. *See also specific occupations*
Crown, Patricia, 223
Crowston, Clare Haru, 79, 109, 218, 224, 227, 234n56
crucible breaking, *198*, 199–200, 218–219
cutlers' shops, *213*, 218

daily life, depictions of, 10
dairymaids, 23–24, 31, *32*, 33
damasquineurs, 96, *97*, 218
Darnton, Robert, 17
daughters, 105, 107, 204, 210, 218, 226, 234n48
Daumier, Honoré, *The Laundress*, 17
Dauphiné, 117, 144
Davis, Natalie Zemon, 77, 83, 223
day laborers, 22
découpeurs, 103, *104*, 105
Defehrt, A.-J. (engraver), 85
Delaire, Alexandre, 131
délisseuses, 188, *188*
Denainvilliers, 194
dentellières, 15, 81, 111–112, *113*, 146, *178*, 179, 206, 224
Desaunois, Delo, 235n58
Des Billettes, Gilles Filleau, 5, 6, 16, 121, *161*, 232n12
dévideuses, 147, 155
dexterity, 219, 224
Diderot, Denis, 184, 233n27, 235n70. *See also Encyclopédie*; *Encyclopédie Planches*; *Encyclopédie Prospectus*
    Essai sur la peinture, 12
    on *habileté*, 224
    plagiarism by, 8
    "Salon", 12, 232n20, 233n26
    on slavery, 34–35
division of labor, 22, 77, 107, 185, 194–195, 217, 219, 221–222, 235n66
domestic servants, 9
dorelotiers, 146, 170–171
doreurs sur bois, 101, *101*, 217
doreurs sur métaux, 76. *See also* Guild of Metal Gilders
dowries, 23, 82, 144, 204. *See also* marriage
drapelières, 187
drawgirls, 143, 144, 145–146, 147, 172
Du Bos, abbé Jean-Baptiste, 11
Dudin, *L'Art du relieur doreur de livres*, *102*
Duhamel du Monceau, Henry-Louis, 6, 11, 21, 28, 30, *61*, 66, 121, 132,

141, 150, 232n20, 235n70
Art de faire les tapis, façon de Turquie, 194, 194–195, *195*
Art de la draperie, principalement pour ce qui regarde les draps fins, 150, *151*, *153*
Art d'exploiter les mines de charbon de terre, *122*
Art du cartier, 122
Art du chandelier, 129, *130*
Art du potier d'étain, *125*
Art du potier de terre, *124*, 124
Traité des pesches, 28, 42–44, 46–52, 51, 53, 54–57, 58, 58–59, 59–73, 70, 72
Dulac, Mme (mercer), 205
du Liège, Mme (linen-draper), 212
Dumenil, L. (designer), *97*, *115*
Dürer, Albrecht, 10
Dutch art, 10–12
Dutch genre paintings, 11–12, 15

edge-tool makers. *See taillandiers*
égratigneurs, 105
éjarreuses, 81, 121
émailleurs, 92, *92*, 93, *93*, 94, *95*
embroiderers. *See brodeurs*
empiricism, 12, 233n26
enamellers. *See émailleurs*
Encyclopédie, 3–10, 12, 15–17, 21, 24, 27–29, 31, 33–34, 39, 44, 67, 78, 83, 93, 95, 97, 101–103, 114, 122, 136, 142, 146, 185–187, 192, 206–207, 212–213, 220–221, 226–227, 232n20, 232n21, 233–234n35. *See also Encyclopédie Planches*; *Encyclopédie Prospectus*
    "Batteur", 99
    "Battre l'or", 99
    "Bimbloterie", 83, 85, 141
    "Blanchir", 127
    "Bouton, Moule de", 136–137
    "Boyaudier", *137*
    "Broderie", 107
    "Caractères d'imprimerie", 80
    "Chapeau", 119
    "Découpeur", 103, 105
    "Dentelle", 81, 111

    "Doreur sus bois", 100–101, *101*
    "Dragée", 85
    "Epingle", 131
    "Epinglier", 132
    "Fil", 148, 154
    "Guiper", *176*
    "Lainier", 154
    "Lisses, (Rub.)", 170
    "Manufacture", 183, 186
    "Plumassier", 89
    "Règles, Maladies des", 220
    "Salicots", 53
    "Savon, Tables de", 194
    "Soie", 156
    "Tapisserie de Gobelins", 184
    "Tireur d'or et d'argent", 179
Encyclopédie méthodique. See Panckouke, Charles-Joseph
Encyclopédie Planches, 78, 180, 233n31, 233n33
    "Agriculture, façon des foins, et moisson", 31, *32*
    "Agriculture, Labourage; Pl. I", 29–30, *30*
    "Aiguiller-bonnetier", *134*
    "Argenteur", *98*
    "Batteur d'or", 100, *100*
    "Blanchissage de cires", *127*
    "Bouchonnier", 214, *215*
    "Boutonnier, faiseur de moules", 137
    "Boutonnier passementier", *114*
    "Boyaudier", *139*
    "Brodeur", *106*, 107
    "Cartier", *123*
    "Ceinturier", 208, *210*
    "Cirier, en cire à cacheter", *128*
    "Cloutier d'epingles", *133*
    "Découpeur et gaufreur", *104*
    "Dentelle", *113*
    "Doreur sus bois", *101*, 101
    "Emailleur, a la lampe perles fausses", *92*, 93, *93*
    "Eventailliste, colage et preparation des papiers", *86*

"Eventailliste, monture des éventails", *89*

"Eventailliste, peinture des feuilles", *88*

"Ferblantier", 216, *216*

"Fil, roüet, dévidoirs", 148, *148, 149,* 150

"Fileur d'or", 180

"Fils et Laine, 2 bis, Moulin carré détail de ce moulin par coupes et plans", 154

"Fleuriste artificiel, plans d'emporte-pieces de feuilles de fleurs, 95, *96*

"Fonderie en caracteres", *136, 137*

"Fonte de la Dragée Moulée", *135*

"Fourreur, outils", 207–208, *208*

"Lingère", 210

"Marine: chantier de construction", 190, *191,* 192

"Métallurgie, fer blanc", *201*

"Metier à faire des bas", *161*

"OEconomie rustique, culture et arsonnage du coton", 34, *34*

"OEconomie rustique, culture et travail du chanvre", *33,* 33–34

"OEconomie rustique: Laiterie", 31, *32,* 33

"Orfèvre bijoutier", *207*

"Papetterie", 184, 185, 186, *190,* 190, *192*

"Passementerie", 173, 176, *177,* 177–178, *178*

"Patissier, tour à pâte, bassines, morlier &c", 214, *215*

"Perruquier barbier", 114, 117, *117*

"Pesches de mer", *43, 44, 45,* 72

"Piqueur et incrusteur de tabatiere, ouvrages et outils", 90, *91*

"Plumassier-panachier, différens ouvrages et outils", *90*

"Potier d'Etain Bimblotier", 85

"Relieur doreur", *103*

"Sellier-carossier, selles", *121*

"Soierie", 164

"Soierie, dévidage de la soie sur le tour d'Espagne, doublage et développement de l'escaladou", *158,* 159

"Soierie, fabrication des lisses et le lissoir en perspective", *170*

"Soierie, l'opération de relever", *166*

"Soierie, tirage de la soie et plan du tour de Piémont", 155, *156,* 156

"Tabletier Cornetier, Préparation de la Corne", *123*

"Tapis de Turquie", 194–195

"Tapisserie de haute lisse des Gobelins", 193, *194*

"Tapissier, intérieur d'une boutique et différens ouvrages", *116*

"Tireur d'or", 180

"Verrerie en bois, grande verrerie à vitres, ou en plats", *200,* 200–201

"Verrerie en bois, petite verrerie à pivette", *198, 199,* 200

Encyclopédie Planches Suite
"Marchande de Mode", 210, *211*

Encyclopédie Prospectus, 7–8

Encyclopédistes, 186

engravers, 9, 218, 225–226, 235n69

Enlightenment, 11, 219, 222, 224

entrepreneurs, 184

épingliers, 76, 80, 131, *131,* 131, 132, *133,* 221. See also *cloutiers d'épingles*; Guild of Pin Makers

essential goods, 124–140

étendeuses, 85, 87, 189

étiquettes, 45

"Eventailliste, colage et preparation des papiers", *86*

"Eventailliste, monture des éventails", *89*

"Eventailliste, peinture des feuilles", *88*

éventaillistes, 78, 82, 85, *86,* 87, *88,* 89, 218

exploitation, 222

Eygentliche Beschreibung aller Ständ auf Erden. See Ständebuch

fabricants, 144

Fairchilds, Cissie, 81, 82

Faiseur de moules de boutons, 138

family businesses, 75–78, 82, 145, 203–204, 213–214, 218, 226

family economy, 77

family wage, 27

fan makers. *See éventaillistes*

Farge, Arlette, 143

farmers, 22

farm servants, 23

fashion shops, 111, *111,* 205, 205–206, 211. See also *boutiques*; *marchandes de mode*

fashion trades, 205–206, 224–225

Faubourgs, 82–83, 137

Faubourg Saint-Antoine, 82–83

Faubourg Saint-Martin, 137

feather dressers. *See plumassiers-panachiers*

ferblantier, 216, *216*

fileuses, 142, 146, 147, *147,* 148, *149,* 150, *167,* 227, 235n58. See also Guild of Spinners; Guild of Spinners

fileuses d'or, 146, 179, *179, 180,* 180, *181,* 218

filles majeures, 79

fils de maîtres, 100

"Fils et Laine, 2 bis, Moulin carré détail de ce moulin par coupes et plans", 154

filtier, 148, *149, 154,* 220

finishers, 83

finishing tasks, 204–205

fishing, 21, 26–29, 42, 42–74, *43, 44,*

46, 47, 49, 50, 54–55, 60–67,
220, 222, 225
    fishing lines, 46
    fishing merchants, 29
    fishmongers, 72, 73, 74
    fish preparation, 64–65, 64–
        65, 66, 66, 67, 68–69, 70,
        70, 71, 72, 72, 225
    fishwives, 203
    harpoon fishing, 60
    in-shore fishing, 56, 57
    lance fishing, 49
    night fishing, 54
    shellfish fishing, 54
    shore fishing, 56, 57, 58, 59
    shrimp fishing, 51, 51, 52, 53,
        55
fleuristes, 95, 96, 228, 229
Florini, Francisci Philippi, 235n64
flower makers. *See fleuristes*
food preparation, 79–80, 125, 225,
    234n48. *See also* fishing
food selling, 203
Fossier (designer), 147
Fougeroux de Blaveau, Armand-
    Eustache-François, 152
Fougeroux de Bondaroy, Auguste-
    Denis, 6, 9, 51, 59, 66, 141, 152,
    171, 174
    *Art du coutellier en ouvrages
        communs*, 129, 130, 131
fourreurs, 119, 120, 207–208, 208
Fragonard, Jean-Honoré, 11, 235n65
    The Swing, 222
frame gilding. *See doreurs sur bois*
frangers, 146, 176, 224
Franklin, Alfred, 76, 105, 107, 112,
    234n53, 235, 241
    "Lingères", 79
frappeurs, 132
free love, 82
free market, 186
fresh-flower sellers, 79
fringe makers. *See frangers; guipeuses*
fripiers, 203
furriers. *See fourreurs*

Garden, Maurice, 82, 143, 144, 147,
    204, 228

Gardey, Françoise, 93
garment trades, 107. *See also specific
    trades*
Garsault, Maurice, 109
    Art de la lingère, 212
    Art du perruquier, 118
    Art du tailleur, 107, 109, 110,
        111
gaufreurs, 103
Gayne, Mary K., 117
gendered division of labor, 22, 77,
    107, 185, 194–195, 217, 219, 221–
    222, 235n66
gens de bras, 21
gens de métier, 21
Gherardi, Evaristo, 205
gilders. *See doreurs; doreurs sur bois;
    doreurs sur métaux*
glass manufacturing, 186, 197–201,
    198–201, 218–219
    crucible breaking, 198, 199–
        200
    glass collecting, 200, 200–201
    glass sorting, 199, 200
    sandstone preparation, 197–
        198
Gobelins manufactory, 150, 184, 196
Godet, Mme (fan painter), 82, 194
gold beaters. *See batteurs d'or*
Goldin, Claudia, 185
goldsmith-jewellers shops. *See or-
    fèvres bijoutiers*
Goodman, Jordan, 142
Gouaz, Yves Marie Le, 226
Goubert, Pierre, 21, 28
Goussier, Louis-Jacques, 8, 16, 29,
    85, 157, 159, 160, 162, 163, 164,
    213, 233n31
Grande Fabrique, 145. *See also* silk
    making
Greenlanders, 60
Greuze, Jean-Baptiste, 11, 12, 226,
    233n27
Guadeloupe, 34
Guilbert, Madeleine, 80, 185, 187
guild families, 4, 144–146
Guild of Candle Makers, 127
Guild of Embroiderers, 76, 105
Guild of Feather Dressers, 76

Guild of Gold Beaters, 76
Guild of Grocers, 125
Guild of Linen Drapers, 79, 210,
    211–212
Guild of Master Fan Makers (Even-
    taillistes), 85
Guild of Merchant Mercers, 81, 110
Guild of Metal Gilders, 81
Guild of Mirror-Lensmakers, 83
Guild of Passementiers, 112, 146
Guild of Passementiers-Button Mak-
    ers, 76, 112
Guild of Pin Makers, 76, 131, 131
Guild of Potters (clay), 76, 124
Guild of Potters (pewter), 124
Guild of Ribbon Makers, 76, 146
Guild of Seamstresses, 79, 105, 218
Guild of Spinners, 142
Guild of *Tabletiers-Peigniers*, 90
Guild of Tailors, 107, 218, 224, 227,
    234n56
Guild of Weavers, 145
Guild of Wool Carders, 76
guilds, 3, 27, 75, 78–79, 81, 82, 105,
    107, 110, 131, 144, 146, 184, 186,
    212, 226, 227, 231n5, 234n56. *See
    also specific guilds*
    all-female, 9, 78, 79, 109, 211–
        212, 219, 232–233n22
    food preparation, 79–80
    guild families, 4, 144–146
    guild regulations, 146, 186,
        210, 218, 226, 234n47
    guild rights, 4, 142, 144–145,
        146, 210, 224, 234n48
    guild system, 7, 184, 204, 218,
        224
guild system, gender equality and, 7,
    184, 204, 218, 224. *See also specific
    guilds*
Guillerme, Jacques, 232n9
guipeuses, 176, 224
Gullickson, Gay, 142, 148, 226

Hafter, Daryl, 4, 78, 146, 172, 224,
    226, 234n47
haggling, 205
Halles, 79
harvesting, 30, 32

hatmaking, 81, 117, 119, *120*, 121, 184. *See also coupeuses* (in hat making); *éjarreuses*

hatter's shops, 205, 208, *209*

Haussard, Catherine, 48, 51, *51*, *54*, *59*, 70, *70*, *71*, *73*, 223, 226

Haussard, Elisabeth, 47, 56, 61, 62, 63, 63, *63*, 152, *153*, 209, 226

Haussard, Jean-Baptiste, *94*, *95*, *97*, *115*, *138*, 150, *171*, *173–174*, 226

Haussard family, 136. *See also specific family members*

haymaking, 31, *32*

health problems, 80, 135–136. *See also* occupational hazards; working conditions

heddle making, 169–170, *169–170*

Helvétius, Claude Adrien, 34

hemp merchants, *33*, 33–34, 79

hod carriers. *See botteresses*

hods. *See hottes de quai*

Hogarth, William, 222, 233n29

Hollander, Anne, 222, 235n65

hooks, 45, *46*

horn, 218

horses, 22

Hôtel-Dieu, Lyon, 144, 146

hottes de quai, *38*, 39, *39*, *61*, 61

Houghton Library, Harvard University, 16

housekeeping, 219

Hudson, Pat, 19, 22

Hufton, Olwen, 22, 29, 77, 111, 112, 142, 147, 203, 204

Humphries, Jane, 25, 27

Hutton, William, 221

iconography, 10–11

ideology, 14

Ile de Ré, 49

illegal workers, 81, 117

illegitimacy, 82

industry, 203

infant mortality, 145, 228

inqueresses, 70

Isigny, Normandy, 58

Italian art, 11

Italy, 155

Jacobines, 223

Jansen, Antoni, 13

Jaoul, Martine, 9, 16

Jaucourt, chevalier de, 180, 220

Jaugeon, Jacques, 5, 6, 101

jetteuses, 189

jewellers. *See orfèvres bijoutiers*

John, Angela V., 25, 37

Jones, Jennifer, 206, 224–225

journalières, 23

journeyworkers, 77, 78, 144, 145, 147, 194, 227

Kaplan, Steven L., 81, 82–83

knickknack makers. *See bimbelotiers*

Koepp, Cynthia J., 17

labor, 14

lace makers. *See dentellières*

Lalande, Joseph Jérôme Le Français de, 185

Art de faire le papier, *188*

"Lames ou lisses à l'usage des tissutiers", *152*

Langlée paper manufactory, 184, 187

Languedoc, 58, 142

La Rochelle, 49

laundresses, 9

lead shot makers. *See shot makers*

leather-curriers, 80

Lee, W. R., 19, 22

Le Havre, 78

Le Mans, 79

Le Masson du Parc, François, 27, 28, 45, 49, *50*, 51, 53, 59

Le Nain brothers, 11

Lépicie, Nicolas-Bernard, 11

Lespinasse, René de, 29, 76, 89, 127

leveuses, 85

Liège, 24, 25, 26

lifting, heavy, 26

Liger, Louis, 233n25

limestone breakers, 198–199

lingères, 79, 81, 205, 206, 210, 211–212, *212*, 224, 227–228. *See also* Guild of Linen Drapers

literacy, 204

Loire, 49

Lorraine, 197

Louis XIV, 183

Lucas, Claude, *86*, *131*, 139, *140*, 152, *154*, *172*, *176*, *193*, *194*

Lucotte, Jacques-Raymond, 16, *207*, 208, 228, 233n31

Lummis, Trevor, 28

luxury trades, 78, 81, 83–124, 137, 204, 218, 224. *See also specific trades*

Luycken, Jan, *Het Menselyk Bedryf*, 13

Lyon, 4, 81, 82, 117, 143, 144, 145, 146, 147, 155, 172, 227, 228

Malbeste, Georges, 235n70

male workers, depictions of, 9

Malouin, Paul-Jacques, *Description et détails des arts dumeunier, du vericelier et du boulenger*, 125, *126*, *213–214*

managers, 204

Manchester, 24

manufacture dispersée, 183

manufacturing, 5, 18, 183–202, 203, 219

marchandes de mode, 17, 79, 110, *111*, 205–207, 210, *211*, 222

Marchands Merciers, 210–211

Marie-Antoinette, Queen, 211

"Marine: chantier de construction", 190, *191*, 192

marriage, 144–145, 204. *See also* dowries

Marseilles, 79, 117, 194

medieval art, 10

Ménétra, Jacques-Louis, 204

menstruation, 220

mercers, 81, 83, 110

merchants, 203–216

Mercier, Louis-Sebastien, 90, 205, 221–222, 224–225

Tableau de Paris, 206, 219

Merleau-Ponty, Maurice, 222

Merlu, Mlle (linen- draper), 212

metal gilders. *See doreurs sur métáux*

metallurgy, 187, 201–202, *201–202*, 218

metal workers, 96. *See also* metallurgy

"Métier à faire du gance", *172*
"Le metier de la tire", *171*
Metz, 74
Meunier, Constantin, 25
Millet, Jean-François, 24
    La Baratteuse, 31, 33
    L'Homme à la Houe, 12
Milliot, Vincent, 14, 233n33
Milsan, Charles, *60*, 67
mining, 7, 21, 22, 24–27, 35–41, *36–41*
miroitiers, 83, 99, *99*. See also Guild
    of Mirror-Lensmakers
mirror making. See *miroitiers*
miscarriage, 26
mistresses (fashion shops), 211–213, 224
modesty, 109
modistes. See marchandes de mode
Moitte, Angelique, *43, 44, 45, 46, 53, 55, 59, 61, 63, 64, 65, 69, 72, 73,* 223, 226, 232n20
Moitte, Elisabeth-Mélanie, 226
Moitte, Pierre-Etienne, 226, 235n70
Moitte family, 235n70. *See also spe-cific family members*
mold makers, 136
money, 206
monresses, 38
Montargis, 184, 186, 187, 235n61
monteuse, 87
Montgolfier paper mill, 185
Montigny, 142, 226
Morand, Jean-François, 7
    Art d'exploiter les mines de charbon de terre, 24–25, 26, 36–41, *37, 38, 39,* 39, *40, 41*
mortality rates, 228
Musgrave, Elizabeth, 234n48

nail makers. *See cloutiers d'épingles; épingliers*
Nantes, 57, 81, 234n48
nature, depictions of, 10–11
needle makers. *See aiguillers*
neoclassicism, 11
nets, *42,* 42, *43,* 44, 53, 55, 56
Newcastle, 24

Nîmes, 141, 156
Nochlin, Linda, 11–12
noguettes, 205
Nollet, abbé, 117
    L'Art de faire des chapeaux, 120, 208, *209*
Normandy, 66, 197

occupational hazards, 80, 85, 135–136, 144. *See also* health prob-lems; working conditions
"OEconomie rustique, culture et arsonnage du coton", 34, *34*
"OEconomie rustique, culture et travail du chanvre", *33,* 33–34
"OEconomie rustique: Laiterie", 31, *32,* 33
Ogilvie, Sheilagh, 142, 232–233n22
orfèvres bijoutiers, 207, *207*
Orléans, 204
Orléans, Louis, Duke of, 184
ornamental products, 83–124
Ottens, Joshua, 13–14
Ottens, Reiner, 13–14
ourdisseuses, 147, *147,* 150, 152, *152,* 152, *153,* 159, 160, 162, *162, 163,* 164–166, *164–166,* 167, 177–178, *178*
"Ouvrages des cartisanes, et les cordons à la jatte", *175*
ouvrières, 89, 99, 114, *116,* 127, 150, 170, 212
oyster sellers, 203
Ozanne, Jeanne-Françoise, 226
Ozanne, Marie-Jeanne, *50, 69,* 226

painting, versus printmaking, 12–13
Palais Royal, 205
Panckoucke, Charles-Joseph, 3
    Encyclopédie méthodique, 6, 10, 35, *35,* 79, 110, *110*
papermaking, 85, *86,* 87, 184, 185, 186, 187–192, *188–192,* 235n61
paper mills, 185
papetterie. See papermaking
paqueresses, 69
parcs, 58
Paris, 82, 117, 137, 146, 172, 196, 204, 205, 206, 211, 212

passementiers, 76, 103, 112, 114, *114, 115,* 136–137, 141, 145–146, *171,* 171–172, *172,* 173, 174–175, *175,* 176–178, *177, 178. See also* Guild of Passementiers
pastry shops, 214, *215*
pâtisseries. See pastry shops
patriarchy, 224
Patte, Pierre, 121, *122, 130,* 132, *133*
pattières, 187
Paulet, Jean, 141, 156
    L'Art du fabriquant d'étoffes de soie, 157, 159, 160, 162, 164, 164–165, *165, 166–169,* 166–170, *167*
Pays d'Ouche, 80
pearl making, 92, *92, 93,* 93, *94, 95*
peasants, 24
Pembrokeshire, 37
perforating. *See découpeurs*
Perret, Jean-Jacques, 129
    L'Art du coutelier, 213, *213*
Perronet, Jean-Rudolphe, 132
perruquiers, 114, 116, 117, *117,* 117, *118,* 217, 228.
Pertuis, marquis de, 206
"Pesches de mer", *43, 44, 45,* 72
philosophes, 11
physiocratic movement, 11
Picardy, 49, 148, 197
Pinault, Madeleine, 7, 9, 16, 27, 28
Pinchbeck, Ivy, 132, 187, 197–198, 202
pinking. *See découpeurs*
pin makers. *See aiguillers; épingliers;* Guild of Pin Makers
"Piqueur et incrusteur de tabatiere, ouvrages et outils", 90, *91*
playing card making. *See cartiers*
plowing, 29–30, *30*
plumassiers-panachiers, 76, 89, 90, *90,* 205, 226–227. *See also* Guild of Feather Dressers
Pompey, Mme (mercer), 211
Pontchartrain, Louis Phélypeaux, comte de Maurepas, 5
population growth, 228
porters, 190, *191,* 192, 194
potiers d'étain, 85, 124–125, *125,*

217–218. *See also* Guild of Potters
(pewter)

potiers de terre, 76, 80, 124, *124*, 124.
See also Guild of Potters (clay)

potters. *See potiers de terre; potiers
d'étain*

potters (clay). *See potiers de terre*

potters (pewter). *See potiers d'étain*

pregnancy, 26, 80, 144, 145, 228

Pringle, Arthur, 22

printing trade, 135–136

printmaking, 12–13, 225

print shops, 206

prostitution, 147, 206

protectionism, 186

Protestant ideology, 13

protoindustrial economy, 81, 142,
148, 184, 185, 226

Proust, Jacques, 6, 7, 16, 17, 184

Provence, 117

publishing, 4

pulling cords. *See* drawgirls

Questions sur l'Encyclopédie
(Voltaire), 219

quills, *169*, 169–170, 180

Quimper, 44

Rabelais, François, 205

Radel (architect and *ornemaniste*),
194

rag shredders. *See délisseuses*

rakoyeux, 38

Ramazzini, Bernadino, *De morbis
artificum diatriba*, 80

Ransonette, Pierre-Nicolas, 62, 66,
124, 194

Raynal, abbé Guillaume Thomas
François, *Histoire des deux Indes*,
34–35

realism, 11–12

reaping, 30

Réaumur, René-Antoine Ferchault
de, 5, 6, 8, 16, 81, 83, 94, 96, 99,
136, 139, 140, 171, 175–176, 197,
232n8, 232n11
Art de l'épinglier, *131*, 131,
132, *133*

Reddy, William, 148, 225, 227

reed making, 176–177, *177*

Reformation, 10

Reims, 147, 228

relieurs, 101–103, *102*, *103*, 218

remarriage, 204

remisseurs, 170

Renaissance, 10

repasseuses, 119

retail merchants, 203–216, 218. *See
also boutiques*

Revolutionary period, 12, 223

ribbon makers. *See rubanniers*

Rifkin, Benjamin, 13, 14

Roberts, Michael, 77

Roche, Daniel, 78, 204, 205, 206, 211

Rochefort, Pierre de Massart, dit de,
161

Roland de la Platière, Jean-Marie,
141
*Art du fabricant d'étoffes en
laines rases et seches*, 146,
147, 154, *155*

Roland de la Platière, Marie-Jeanne,
228

Rouen, 34, 78, 117, 142, 146, 148,
227

Rousseau, Jean-Jacques, 22, 225
Emile, 219

Royal Manufactories, 129, 184

Royal Society (London), 5

Royer, Antoine-François Prost de,
228

rubanniers, 76, 141, 146, 170–172,
171, *173–174*, 173–174. *See also*
Guild of Ribbon Makers

Sachs, Hans, 13

saddle makers, 121, *121*

Saint-Aubin, Charles Germain de,
Art du brodeur, *108*

Saint-Chamond, 172

Saint-Etienne en Forez, 129, 172

Saint-Eutrope, 124

Saint-Palais, 51

Salomon-Bayet, Claire, 6

sandstone preparation, 197–198

Santo Domingo, 34

Saumur, 83

Savary des Bruslons, Jacques, 76,

125, 127, 129, 183, 184, 187

La Savonnerie, 184, *194*, 195

savonnier, 196

Savoy, 143, 144

Saxony, 107

Schiebinger, Londa, 220

Schwab, Richard N., 4

science, 12, 16

scythes, 30

seamstresses. *See couturières*

Sebestik, Jan, 232n9

secondhand clothes traders, 9, 203

Sedan, 150

seeding machines, *30*, 30

Segalen, Martine, 22, 24, 30

selliers-carossiers, *121*

servantes, 143–144, 146–147, 204

Sevin, Pierre-Paul, 187, *188–192*,
190

Sevis, 148

Sewell, William Hamilton, 9, 14, 17,
221, 234n36

sewing, 107, 205, 217, 224. *See also
broucheuses; brodeurs; couturières;
garment trades; relieurs; tailleurs*

sexual harassment, 144

sexuality, 205–206, 219–220

Shahar, Shulamith, 24, 186

sharecroppers, 22

shopgirls, 205, 210, 211–212

shop owners, 204

shops, 203–216. *See also specific kinds
of shops*

shot makers, *135*, 135

shrimp fishing, *52*

Siberechts, Jan, 11

sickles, 30

silk making, 7, 141, 144–146, 150,
155–159, *156*, *158*, *159*, 159,
160, 161, *161*, *162*, 164–169,
164–169, 170, 172, 187, 228

silver plating, 96, 99

Simonneau, Louis, *99*, *102*, *179*, 180,
181, *188–192*, 190, 197, *198*

Simonton, Deborah, 80, 223–224,
235n66

skilled work, 111–112, 146, 148, 167,
218, 223–224, 225, 233n33,
235n66

slashing, 103

slavery, *34*, 34–35

slaves, 34, *34*

"small wheel" spinning technique, *147*, 147–148

Smith, Adam, *Wealth of Nations*, 131, 185

Snell, Keith D. M., 229

soapmaking, 186, 192, *193*, 194

sociability, 204, 205, 206

Sokoloff, Kenneth, 185

Sonenscher, Michael, 4, 18, 119, 147, 227, 228

sorters, 192

Soumille, abbé Bernard-Laurent, *30*

Souply, Quentine, 205

sowing, 29–30, *30*

spinners. *See fileuses*

Ständebuch, 13, 14

Steen, Jan, *Woman at Her Morning Toilet*, 222

stitchers. *See brocheuses*

stocking makers, *161*, 161–162

stone breaking, 218–219

Stone-Ferrier, Linda, 15

"Street Cries", 14–15

street sellers, 9

St. Tropez, 58

stud makers, 80

stylistic context, 10–18

subjectivity, 222

Suite du recueil de planches "Marchande de Mode", 210, *211*

supervision, 184, 185

tabletiers-cornetiers, 122, *123*. See also Guild of *Tabletiers-Peigniers*

taillandiers, 80, 139–140, *140*, 218

tailleurs, 107, 109, *109*, 109, 218, 224, 227, 234n56. *See also* Guild of Tailors

tailors. *See tailleurs*

tapissiers, 114, *116*, 186, *193*, 193, *193*, 193, *194*, 194–195, 218, 224

technology, 24, 30, *30*, 219, 232n9

Teniers II, David, 220

tentes, 58

textile trades, 7, 18, 111–112, 141–

181, *152*, 186, 217, 234n48. *See also specific textile trades*
   in France, 148
   traditional economy and, 142
   in urban centers, 143, 155

textile workshops, 152

Théâtres des machines, 6

Thompson, Paul, 28

thread reeling, *157*, *158*, *159*, 159, *160*, 161

tin makers. *See* metallurgy

tinsmiths' shops, 205, 216, *216*

tireurs d'or, 179–180, *179–180*, *181*

tissutiers, *152*, *176*

tissutiers-rubanniers, 146

tools, 185

tourbiers, *35*, 35

"Tour de Piémont", 155

Tours, 143

toy makers, 83, *84*

trade guilds. *See* guilds

traders, 203

trades, 18, 21. *See also specific trades*
   all-female, 224
   artisanal trades, 75–140
   laws regulating, 3–4
   luxury trades, 78
   urban, 203

traditional economy, 18, 21–74, 142, 186, 218, 233n25

transportation, 219

transvestism, 223

travail en chambre, 112

Tréport, 66

tresseuses (weaving hair), 116–117, *117*

trieuses (papermaking), 192

Troyes, 34

Truant, Cynthia, 78, 227–228

Truchet, Fr. Sebastien, 5

Tull, Jethro, 30

turf-cutting, *35*, 35

typecasters, 135–136, *136*, *137*

upholstery making, 114, *116*, *176*, 176

van den Velde, Willem, 15

van der Straet, Jan, 14

Van Gogh, Vincent, 25, 26

Vanja, Christina, 24, 35–36, 39

van Vliet, Joris, 13

Vardi, Liana, 11, 23, 30, 142, 226

Vaugondy, Robert de, *Atlas Universel*, 226

Vermeer, Johannes
   Lacemaker, 12
   Milkmaid, 12

vermicelières, 80, 125, *126*

vermicelli makers. *See vermicelières*

Veronica, Saint, 227–228

"Verrerie en bois, grande verrerie à vitres, ou en plats", 200, 200–201

"Verrerie en bois, petite verrerie à pivette", *198*, *199*, 200

Veys, 58

Vidalon-le-Haut, 185

Viger, Jean-François-Thomas-Thimoleon, 53

Villermé, Louis, 143
   Tableau de l'état physique et moral des ouvriers, 221

visual material, 4

Voltaire, 34
   "Femme (Physique et morale), 219
   Questions sur l'Encyclopédie, 219

Wailey, Tony, 28

Walpole, Horace, 205

warp reelers. *See ourdisseuses*

washerwomen, 9

Watt, James, 26

Watteau, Jean-Antoine, 11

wax making. *See blanchisseurs de cire*

weavers, 144–145, *149*, *172*, 226. *See also* spinners

Wedgwood manufactories, 235n66

West Indian colonies, *34*, 34

wet-nurses, 145, 228

widows, 3, 75–76, 78, 81–82, 101, 105, 145, 204

Wiesner, Merry, 156

wig makers. *See perruquiers*

windlass-women, *36*, 37, *37*

wives, 204, 218
women, ideological construction of,
22. *See also* women workers
women's work, 7
women workers, 25, 217. *See also specific occupations; specific trades*
bodies of, 220
child-rearing and, 17–18
depictions of, 10–15, 18–19,
205–206, 222, 226–227
exclusion from guilds, 127,
129
horses and, 22
in industrial work, 220–221
law regulating, 3–4

source documents about, 3–4
in the traditional economy,
21–74
unmarried, 82, 145–146, 147,
227
in urban centers, 206
woodcuts, 13, 38
wood gilders, 100–101
wool manufacture
wool carders, 76. *See also* Guild of
Wool Carders
wool industry, 142, 143, 147–148.
See also spinners
wool thread reeling, *155*
wool winding, *149, 150*

working conditions, 80, 82, 85,
143–144, 154–156, 181, 184–
187, 219, 221–222, 233n32
work practices, codification of, 5
work regimes, 184, 185
work regulations, 3–4, 75
workshops, 6, 16–17, 75, 77–79, 81,
85, 92–93, 95, 129, 147, 218, 225–
226, 228. *See also specific workshops*

yarn making. *See filtier*
Young, Arthur, *Six weeks tour*, 132
Young, Iris Marion, 222